Alice in Action

Computing Through Animation

Joel Adams

Calvin College

COURSE TECHNOLOGY
CENGAGE Learning

Alice in Action: Computing Through Animation
Joel Adams

Senior Product Manager: Alyssa Pratt

Production Editor: GEX Publishing Services

Marketing Manager: Penelope Crosby

Editorial Assistant: Erin Kennedy

Print Buyer: Julio Esperas

Art Director: Bruce Bond

Cover Designer: Suzanne Heiser

Compositor: GEX Publishing Services

For product information and technology assistance, contact us at
Cengage Learning Customer & Sales Support, 1-800-354-9706

For permission to use material from this text or product, submit all requests online at **cengage.com/permissions**

Further permissions questions can be emailed to
permissionrequest@cengage.com

ISBN-13: 978-1-4188-3771-6

ISBN-10: 1-4188-3771-7

Course Technology
25 Thomson Place
Boston, Massachusetts 02210
USA

Cengage Learning is a leading provider of customized learning solutions with office locations around the globe, including Singapore, the United Kingdom, Australia, Mexico, Brazil, and Japan. Locate your local office at:
international.cengage.com/region

Cengage Learning products are represented in Canada by Nelson Education, Ltd.

For your lifelong learning solutions, visit **course.cengage.com**

Purchase any of our products at your local college store or at our preferred online store **www.ichapters.com**

Printed in China by China Translation & Printing Services Limited
4 5 6 7 8 9 10 09

Contents

Chapter 1   Getting Started with Alice   1

1.1   Getting and Running Alice   2
    1.1.1   Downloading Alice   2
    1.1.2   Installing Alice   2
    1.1.3   Running Alice   2

1.2   The Alice Tutorials   2

1.3   Program Design   4
    1.3.1   User Stories   4
    1.3.2   Storyboard-Sketches   5
    1.3.3   Transition Diagrams   7

1.4   Program Implementation in Alice   7
    1.4.1   Program Style   10
    1.4.2   Adding Objects to Alice   11
    1.4.3   Accessing Object Subparts   13
    1.4.4   Sending Messages   14
    1.4.5   Testing and Debugging   15
    1.4.6   Coding the Other Actions   16
    1.4.7   Statements   17
    1.4.8   The Final Action   18
    1.4.9   Final Testing   19
    1.4.10   The Software Engineering Process   20

1.5   Alice's Details Area   20
    1.5.1   The *properties* Pane   21
    1.5.2   The *methods* Pane   23
    1.5.3   The *functions* Pane   25

1.6   Alice Tip: Positioning Objects Using Quad View   26

1.7   Chapter Summary   28
    1.7.1   Key Terms   28
           Programming Projects   28

Chapter 2   Methods   31

2.1   World Methods for Scenes and Shots   32
    2.1.1   Methods For Scenes   32
    2.1.2   Methods For Shots   36

2.2   Object Methods for Object Behaviors   38
    2.2.1   Example 1: Telling a Dragon to Flap Its Wings   38
    2.2.2   Example 2: Telling a Toy Soldier to March   42

2.3   Alice Tip: Reusing Your Work   45
    2.3.1   Using the Clipboard   45
    2.3.2   Reusing an Object in a Different World   46

2.4   Alice Tip: Using Dummies   50
    2.4.1   Dummies   50
    2.4.2   Using `setPointOfView()` to Control the Camera   54

2.5   Thinking in 3D   57
    2.5.1   An Object's Position   57
    2.5.2   An Object's Orientation   59
    2.5.3   Point of View   62

2.6   Chapter Summary   62
    2.6.1   Key Terms   63
    Programming Projects   63

Chapter 3   Variables and Functions   65

3.1   Method Variables   66
    3.1.1   Example 1: Storing a Computed Value   66
    3.1.2   Example 2: Storing a User-Entered Value   74

3.2   Parameters   80
    3.2.1   Example 1: Old MacDonald Had a Farm   81
    3.2.2   Example 2: Jumping Fish!   84

3.3   Property Variables   88

3.4   Alice Tip: Using the Vehicle Property   91

3.5   Functions   94
    3.5.1   Example: Retrieving an Attribute from an Object   94
    3.5.2   Functions with Parameters   98

3.6   Chapter Summary   101
    3.6.1   Key Terms   101
    Programming Projects   102

Chapter 4   Flow Control   105

4.1   The **Boolean** Type   106
    4.1.1   **Boolean** Functions   107
    4.1.2   **Boolean** Variables   108
    4.1.3   Relational Operators   108
    4.1.4   **Boolean** Operators   109

4.2   The **if** Statement   110
    4.2.1   Introducing Selective Flow Control   110
    4.2.2   **if** Statement Mechanics   112
    4.2.3   Building **if** Statement Conditions   113
    4.2.4   The **wait()** Statement   115
    4.2.5   Validating Parameter Values   116

4.3   The **for** Statement   119
    4.3.1   Introducing Repetition   119
    4.3.2   Mechanics of the **for** Statement   121
    4.3.3   Nested Loops   123

4.4   The **while** Statement   125
    4.4.1   Introducing the **while** Statement   125
    4.4.2   **while** Statement Mechanics   129
    4.4.3   Comparing the **for** and **while** Statements   129
    4.4.4   A Second Example   130

4.5   Flow-Control in Functions   132
    4.5.1   Spirals and the Fibonacci Function   132
    4.5.2   The Fibonacci Function   134

4.6   Chapter Summary   137
    4.6.1   Key Terms   138
        Programming Projects   138

Chapter 5   Lists and Arrays   141

5.1   The List Structure   143
    5.1.1   List Example 1: Flight of the Bumble Bees   143
    5.1.2   List Operations   148
    5.1.3   List Example 2: Buying Tickets   152

5.2   The Array Structure   155
    5.2.1   Array Example 1: The Ants Go Marching   155
    5.2.2   Array Operations   159
    5.2.3   Array Example 2: Random Access   161

5.3   Alice Tip: Using the **partNamed()** Function   165

5.4   Chapter Summary   172
    5.4.1   Key Terms   172
        Programming Projects   172

Chapter 6   Events   175

6.1   Handling Mouse Clicks: The Magical Doors   177
    6.1.1   The Right Door   178
    6.1.2   The Left Door   179
    6.1.3   The Right Door Revisited   180
    6.1.4   Event Handling Is Simultaneous   182
    6.1.5   Categorizing Events   183

6.2   Handling Key Presses: A Helicopter Flight Simulator   183
    6.2.1   The Problem   184
    6.2.2   Design   184
    6.2.3   Programming in Alice   184

6.3   Alice Tip: Using 3D Text   192
    6.3.1   Repositioning Text that Is Off-Camera   194
    6.3.2   Adding a Background   194
    6.3.3   Making Text Appear or Disappear   196

6.4   Alice Tip: Scene Transitional Effects for the Camera   198
    6.4.1   Setup for Special Effects   199
    6.4.2   The Fade Effect   200
    6.4.3   The Barndoor Edge Wipe Effect   202
    6.4.4   The Box Iris Wipe Effect   203
    6.4.5   Reusing Transition Effects   205

6.5   Chapter Summary   206
    6.5.1   Key Terms   206
        Programming Projects   206

Appendix A   Alice Standard Methods and Functions   209

A.1   Alice Standard Methods   209
A.2   Alice Standard Object Functions   211
A.3   Alice World Functions   213

Appendix B   Recursion   217

B.1   Tail Recursion   219
B.2   General Recursion   222
B.3   Recursion and Design   227
    B.3.1   The Trivial Case   229
    B.3.2   The Nontrivial Cases   229
    B.3.3   Solving the Problem   229
B.4   A Final Recursive Method   231
    B.4.1   The Trivial Case   234
    B.4.2   The Nontrivial Cases   235

Index   239

Preface

I wrote this book to remedy some of the problems in today's introductory computer programming (CS1) courses. To put it politely, most CS1 books are less than engaging, and simply fail to capture the imaginations of most of today's students. No matter how often I say it, many of my students never bother to "read the book." Now, these students aren't blameless, but it isn't entirely their fault. Many CS1 books present computer programming in a dry, abstract, mind-numbing way that's great if you're trying to fall asleep, but not so good if you want to learn.

This is a tragedy, because writing software is one of the best opportunities to exercise creativity in today's world. Traditional engineers and scientists are limited in what they can do by the physical laws that govern our world. But if a software engineer can imagine something, he or she can usually make it happen in the virtual world of the computer. In its 2006 "Best Jobs in America" study, *Money Magazine* listed software engineer #1 on its list of best jobs, because of its *creativity*, pay, and prestige. According to the U.S. Bureau of Labor Statistics, software engineering is also expected to be one of the fastest-growing job markets in the next decade.

This growing demand for software engineers poses a problem, because ever since the dot-com bust in 2001-2, fewer and fewer students have been enrolling in CS1 courses. Of those who do enroll, many drop out, at least in part because the subject matter fails to engage them. CS1 courses are the starting point for software engineers; every student who drops out of CS1 is one less prospective software engineer. Those of us who are CS1 instructors need to do everything we can to (1) attract students to CS1, and (2) retain as many of those students as possible. I wrote this book to try to help attract students to and retain students in CS1.

The Advantages of Alice

At the 2003 ACM SIGCSE conference, I saw Carnegie Mellon's Randy Pausch demonstrate 3D animation software he called Alice. Using Alice, he built a sophisticated 3D animation (like *Shrek* or *Toy Story*, but much simpler) in just a few minutes. To do so, he used the traditional computer programming tools: variables, if statements, loops, subprograms, and so on. But his Alice software offered some startling advantages over traditional programming, including the following:

- *The allure of 3D graphics.* It is difficult to overstate the visual appeal of 3D animations, especially to today's visually-oriented students. When your program works, you feel euphoric! But even when you make a mistake (a logic error), the results are often comical, producing laughter instead of frustration.

- *The Alice IDE*. Alice includes a drag-and-drop integrated development environment (IDE) that eliminates syntax errors. This IDE eliminates all of the missing semicolons, curly braces, quotation marks, misspelled keywords or identifiers, and other syntax problems that bedevil CS1 students.

- *Object-based programming*. Alice includes a huge library of off-the-shelf 3D objects — ranging from astronauts to ants, cowboys to castles, fairies to farms, mummies to motorboats, ponds to pagodas, robots to rowboats, skyscrapers to space shuttles, turtles to T-rexes, wizards to waterfalls, and zombies to Zambonis — each of which can be animated through a variety of predefined methods. Alice makes it easy to build 3D worlds from these objects. Those objects can then be animated using object-based programming.

By using 3D animation to motivate students, eliminating syntax errors, and turning logic errors into comedy, Alice transforms the CS1 experience from frustration to joy. In short, Alice makes it *fun* to learn object-based programming!

As I watched Professor Pausch's demonstration, it became apparent to me that Alice could solve many of the problems afflicting CS1 courses. If instructors would use Alice to initially *introduce* each programming topic, Alice's engaging environment would help motivate students to master that topic. Then, with that mastery to build upon, the instructor could *review* that topic in a traditional programming language like Java or C++, reinforcing its importance.

Imaginary Worlds

In the summer of 2003, I decided to put some of these ideas to the test, by offering a summer "computer camp" in which we would use Alice to teach some middle school students how to program. Our pilot group of 6th, 7th, and 8th graders learned object-based programming, and had a lot of fun doing so!

Our 2003 results were very encouraging, so in the summer of 2004, we began offering *The Imaginary Worlds Camps*, with 28 middle school boys and 25 middle school girls signing up. The results were amazing. Alice captured their imaginations and wouldn't let them go. Some students wanted to stay at the end of the day to keep working on their programs — we had to force them to leave! Others wanted to skip the snack break. (My college students have never passed up food to keep working on a project.) At the end of the camp, the feedback was loud and uniformly positive: these students had loved learning how to program with Alice.

The *Imaginary Worlds Camps* gave me the chance to experiment with Alice, trying out different examples, and honing them to teach a concept in the simplest way possible. Many of those examples have made their way into this book, and I owe a debt of gratitude to all of the young boys and girls whose creativity, energy, and enthusiasm made these camps so much fun.

Why This Book?

Despite what I said at the beginning of this Preface, many instructors are content with the textbooks they use in their CS1 courses. In order for such instructors to use Alice, someone needed to write a *concise* Alice book to supplement their CS1 texts. I decided to write a "short and sweet" book, that would present just what you need to know to use Alice well, and skip over its more specialized features.

I spent the Fall 2004 semester on sabbatical at Carnegie Mellon. Each week, I spent three days writing parts of this book and three days working as a member of the Alice team, helping them find errors in Alice. Working with these people was invaluable, as they helped me better understand Alice's strengths and weaknesses. This in turn helped me decide which Alice features to include in the book, and which features to exclude.

Pedagogical Features

To help students master the concepts of object-based programming, this book uses a number of pedagogical features, including the following:

- *Movie Metaphors.* Movies are pervasive in our culture. Since Alice programs are similar to movies, this book uses the language of movies to introduce software design. Using this approach, the book builds a conceptual bridge from a student's existing knowledge of movies to the new ideas of software design.

- *Detailed Diagrams.* This book contains approximately 75 color screen captures. Many of these demonstrate the exact drag-and-drop steps needed to use Alice effectively.

- *Engaging Examples.* Using Alice's rich library of 3D objects, this book includes examples that keep students captivated, such as:

  - a dragon flapping its wings

  - a scarecrow singing "Old MacDonald Had a Farm"

  - a fish jumping out of the water

  - three trolls facing off against a wizard

  - a girl walking in a spiral to follow a treasure map

  - and many more!

- *Integrated Software Design.* Beginning in Chapter 1 and continuing throughout, this book emphasizes software design. Each chapter shows how that chapter's concepts fit into the overall software design methodology. Students following this methodology can never say, "I don't know where to start."

- *Alice Tips.* Most chapters include one or more special "Alice Tip" sections that cover critical details students need to know to use Alice effectively.

- *Chapter Summaries.* The final section of each chapter includes a bulleted list of the key concepts covered in that chapter, plus a separate list of that chapter's key vocabulary terms.

- *Programming Projects.* Each chapter concludes with 10-12 programming projects, of varying levels of difficulty.

Using This Book

This book is intended as a supplement for CS1 courses, but it can be used in any course where an instructor wishes to teach the ideas of object-based programming. The book covers these ideas in six chapters, arranged as follows:

1. Getting started: using objects and methods

2. Building methods: using abstraction to hide details

3. Variables, parameters, and functions: computing and storing data for later use

4. Control structures: controlling flow via **if**, **while**, and **for** statements

5. Data structures: using and processing arrays and lists

6. Events: handling mouse and keyboard input

These six chapters can be used in a variety of ways, including:

- *The Spiral Approach*: Spend 4-6 weeks introducing all of the programming concepts using Alice (the first spiral). Then spend the remainder of the semester revisiting those same concepts in Java or a different language (the second spiral). In this approach, the programming concepts are covered in two distinct "batches": an Alice batch, followed by a Java batch.

- *The Interleaved Approach*: For each concept (for example, parameters), introduce that concept using Alice. After the students have had hands-on experience with that concept in Alice, immediately revisit that same concept in Java or a different language. In this approach, the programming concepts are covered sequentially, with the Alice and Java coverage interleaved.

If an instructor does not normally cover event-driven programming, Chapter 6 may be omitted, or deferred until the end of the course. However, most students find this material to be *very* engaging, because it allows them to start building games! If an instructor wishes to do so, events may be introduced at any point after Chapter 3.

As students work through the examples in this book, they should make sure to save their Alice worlds regularly. We will begin some worlds in one chapter and add to those same worlds in a later chapter, so students should save at the end of each example. Each world should be saved with a unique, descriptive name, so that it can be easily identified later.

Appendices and Cover Material

The appendices provide resources and material supplementing what is covered in the chapters. Appendix A presents an exhaustive list of Alice's standard methods and functions, including detailed behavioral descriptions. Appendix B provides a "mini-chapter" on recursion, with examples that help students visualize recursion.

The inside covers contain two useful Alice "Quick Reference" pages. Inside the front cover is a complete list of the standard methods and functions that can be applied to an Alice object. Inside the back cover is a complete list of the standard functions that can be applied to an Alice world. Unlike the lists in Appendix A, these "Quick References" display each method, function, and parameter exactly as they appear in Alice. By presenting all of these methods and functions together, a student can see all of the methods and functions at once, and quickly locate a particular method or function.

Web Materials

Copies of the example programs from this book are available online, at

- the Student Downloads section of the Course Technology Web site (**www.course.com**)
- the author's Alice Web site (**http://alice.calvin.edu**)

A feedback link and errata list are also available at the author's Web site. If you find a mistake, or want to point out a feature that works especially well, please use that feedback link. Such feedback will help me improve future editions of the book.

The Alice 2.0 software can be freely downloaded from **http://alice.org**.

Acknowledgments

A book cannot be developed without the support of many people. My heartfelt thanks go to *Randy Pausch* of Carnegie Mellon for creating Alice, and pursuing his vision to its fruition. I would also like to thank the Alice team: *Dennis Cosgrove, Dave Culyba, Mike Darga, Caitlin Kelleher,* and *Gabe Yu.* Each person patiently answered my questions and made me feel welcome at Carnegie Mellon.

The following people served as reviewers, whose careful reading of early drafts and constructive criticism helped make this book what it is. My thanks to: *Gian Mario Besana*, DePaul University; *Barbara Boucher Owens*, Southwestern University; *Nan Schaller*, Rochester Institute of Technology; *Mark Shwayder*, University of Montana; and *Leila Wallace*, Geneva College.

A number of people at Course Technology also played important roles. My thanks to *Alyssa Pratt*, Senior Product Manager, and *Mary Franz*, Senior Acquisitions Editor, for helping me produce the book, as well as *Peter Stefanis* and *Chris Scriver*, who checked and rechecked each chapter and program for quality assurance. I am especially grateful to *John Bosco*, of Green Pen Quality Assurance, who helped me polish the manuscript. This book would not be what it is without the careful attention to detail of all of these people.

I would also like to thank the staff at GEX Publishing Services, especially *Gina Dishman*, who smoothly guided the production process.

A special "thank you" goes to numerous *Imaginary Worlds Camps* students, who inspired some of the examples in this book; and the *Department of Computer Science* at *Calvin College*, whose support made it possible.

I also wish to thank my wife *Barbara*, and my sons *Roy* and *Ian*, for their patience, understanding, and support over many months of writing. Their love and encouragement sustained me through the process.

Last in order but first in importance, I wish to thank *God*, the original creative Person. I believe that the joy we experience in being creative stems from our bearing His image. To Him be the glory.

-Joel C. Adams

For Barbara, Roy, and Ian:
May your lives always be full of wonder.

Chapter 1
Getting Started With Alice

*T*he computer programmer ... is a creator of universes for which he [or she] alone is the lawgiver ... universes of virtually unlimited complexity can be created in the form of computer programs. Moreover ... systems so formulated and elaborated act out their programmed scripts. They compliantly obey their laws and vividly exhibit their obedient behavior. No playwright, no stage director, no emperor, however powerful, has ever exercised such absolute authority to arrange a stage or a field of battle and to command such unswervingly dutiful actors or troops.

JOSEPH WEIZENBAUM

*I*f you don't know where you're going, you're liable to wind up somewhere else.

YOGI BERRA

*L*ouis, I think this is the beginning of a beautiful friendship.
RICK (HUMPHREY BOGART) TO CAPTAIN RENAULT (CLAUDE RAINS), IN *CASABLANCA*

Objectives

Upon completion of this chapter, you will be able to:

❏ Design a simple Alice program

❏ Build a simple Alice program

❏ Animate Alice objects by sending them messages

❏ Use the Alice **doInOrder** and **doTogether** controls

❏ Change an object's properties from within a program

❏ Use Alice's **quad view** to position objects near one another

1

Welcome to the fun and exciting world of computer programming! In this chapter, we are going to build our first computer program using **Alice**, a free software tool for creating virtual worlds.

1.1   Getting and Running Alice

1.1.1   Downloading Alice

Alice can be freely downloaded from the Alice website at **http://alice.org**. For the Windows version, clicking the download link begins the transfer of a compressed archive file named **Alice.zip** to your computer. (For MacOS, the file is named **Alice.dmg**.) Save this file to your computer's desktop.

1.1.2   Installing Alice

Alice does not have a special installer like other programs you might have used. When the download has finished, double-click the **Alice.zip** (or **Alice.dmg**) file to open the archive file. Your computer will open a window containing a folder named **Alice**. Drag that **Alice** folder from the window onto your computer's desktop.

If you'd rather not have the **Alice** folder on your desktop, open a window to the folder in which you wish to store **Alice** (for example, **C:\Program Files**). Then drag the **Alice** folder from your desktop into that window.

Once the **Alice** folder is where you want it, open the **Alice** folder, and locate the file named **Alice.exe** (or just **Alice** in MacOS). In Windows, right-click the file, and from the menu that appears, choose **Create Shortcut** to create a shortcut (alias) to **Alice.exe**. (MacOS users, select the file and choose **File->Make Alias**.) Drag the resulting shortcut to your desktop and rename it **Alice**, so that you can launch Alice conveniently.

1.1.3   Running Alice

To start Alice, just double-click the **Alice** icon on your desktop. Congratulations!

1.2   The Alice Tutorials

As shown in Figure 1-1, when you start Alice for the first time, Alice gives you the option of working through a set of interactive tutorials. These excellent tutorials cover the basics of using Alice while giving you hands-on practice working in the Alice environment. Because they are such effective learning tools, we are going to let these tutorials teach you the basics of Alice. This chapter will concentrate on aspects of Alice *not* covered in the tutorials.

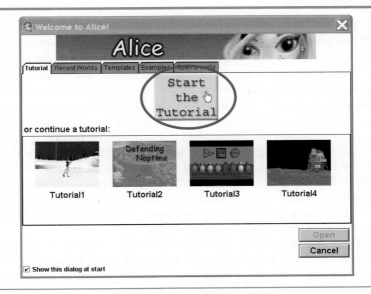

FIGURE 1-1   The Alice Tutorial window

(If this window does not appear, you can make it appear by clicking on Alice's **Help** menu and then selecting the **Tutorial** choice.) To activate the tutorials, click the **Start the Tutorial** button, and then work your way through the four tutorials. Remember, the point of these tutorials is to learn how to use Alice, not to see how fast you can finish them. Read carefully, taking special note of *what* you are doing at each step, *how* you are doing it, and *why* you are doing it. Close Alice when you are finished with the tutorials.

The rest of this chapter assumes you have completed the tutorials, so if you have not yet done so, you should *complete the tutorials now, before proceeding further*. If for some reason you cannot complete the tutorials right away, feel free to keep reading, but I strongly encourage you to complete the tutorials as soon as possible, and then *re-read this chapter*.

Developing programs to solve problems is a complex process that is both an art and a science. It is an art in that it requires a good deal of imagination, creativity, and ingenuity. But it is also a science in that it uses certain techniques and methodologies. In this chapter, we're going to work through the *thought process* that goes into creating computer software.

If you can manage it, the very best way to read this book is at a computer, doing each step or action as we describe it. By doing so, you will be engaging in *active learning*, which is a much better way to learn than by trying to absorb the ideas through passive reading.

1.3   Program Design

Now that you have finished the tutorials, we are ready to build our first computer program and put into practice several of the skills you learned in the tutorials. Programming in Alice is similar to *filmmaking*, so let's begin with how a film is put together.

When filmmakers begin a film project, they do not begin filming right away. Instead, they begin by *writing*. Sometimes they start with a short prose version of the film called a **treatment**; eventually they write out the film's dialog in a **screenplay**, but they always begin by *writing*, to define the basic structure of the *story* their film is telling.

A screenplay is usually organized as a series of **scenes**. A scene is one piece of the story the film is telling, usually set in the same location. A scene is usually made up of multiple **shots**. A shot is a piece of the story that is told with the **camera** in the same position. Each change of the camera's **viewpoint** in a scene requires a different shot. For example, if a scene has two characters talking in a restaurant, followed by a closeup of one of the character's faces, the viewpoint showing the two characters is one shot; the viewpoint of the closeup is a different shot.

Once the screen play is complete, the filmmaker develops **storyboards**, which are drawings that show the position and motion of each character in a shot. Each storyboard provides a sort of blueprint for a shot, indicating where the actors stand, where the camera should be placed with respect to them, and so on. (You may have seen storyboards on the extras that come with the DVD version of a film.)

Creating an Alice program is much like creating a film, and modern computer software projects are often managed in a way that is quite similar to film projects.

1.3.1   User Stories

A modern software designer begins by writing a prose description of what the software is to do, from the perspective of a person using the software. This is called a **user story**. For example, here is a user story for the first program we are going to build:

> When the program begins, Alice and the White Rabbit are facing each other, Alice on the left and the White Rabbit on the right. Alice turns her head and then greets us. The White Rabbit also turns and greets us. Alice and the White Rabbit introduce themselves. Simultaneously, Alice and the White Rabbit say "Welcome to our world."

A user story provides several important pieces of information, including:

- A basic description of what happens when the user runs the program
- The *nouns* in the story (for example, Alice, the White Rabbit) correspond to the **objects** we need to place in the Alice world. Objects include the characters in the story — background items like plants, buildings, or vehicles, and so on.
- The *verbs* in the story (for example, turns, says) correspond to the *actions* we want the objects to perform in the story.
- The chronological *flow* of actions in the story tells us what has to happen *first*, what happens *next*, what happens *after that*, and so on. The *flow* thus describes the *sequence of actions* that take place in the story.

By providing the objects, behaviors, sequence of actions, and description of what the program will do, a user story provides an important first step in the software design process, upon which the other steps are based. The user story is to a good software product as the screenplay is to a good film.

It is often useful to write out the flow of the story as a numbered sequence of objects and actions. For example, we can write out the flow in the user story as shown in Figure 1-2:

Scene: Alice is on the left, the White Rabbit is on the right.

1. Alice turns her head toward the user.
2. Alice greets the user.
3. The White Rabbit turns to face the user.
4. The White Rabbit greets the user.
5. Alice introduces herself.
6. The White Rabbit introduces himself.
7. Simultaneously, Alice and the White Rabbit say "Welcome to our world".

FIGURE 1-2   First program flow (algorithm)

A **flow** is thus a series of steps that precisely specify (in order) the behavior of each object in the story. In programming terminology, a flow — a sequence of steps that solve a problem — is called an **algorithm**.

1.3.2   Storyboard-Sketches

When they have a completed screenplay, filmmakers often hire an artist to sketch each shot in the film. For each different shot in each scene, the artist creates a drawing (in consultation with the filmmaker) of that shot, with arrows to show movements of the characters or camera within the shot. These drawings are called **storyboards**. When completed, the collection of storyboards provides a graphical version of the story that the filmmaker can use to help the actors visualize what is going to happen in the shot, before filming begins.

To illustrate, Figure 1-3 shows a pair of storyboards for a scene we will develop in Section 2.4.1. The first storyboard frames the scene, showing three trolls menacing a wizard, with the wizard's castle in the background. In the second storyboard, we zoom in on the wizard to get a better view of his reaction. The progression of storyboards thus serves as a kind of cartoon version of the story, which the filmmaker uses to decide how the film will look, before the actual filming begins. By first trying out his or her ideas on paper, a filmmaker can identify and discard bad ideas early in the process, before time, effort, and money are wasted filming (or in our case, programming) them.

Scene 2 Shot 1   Scene 2 Shot 2

FIGURE 1-3   A storyboard and corresponding scene

In a similar fashion, the designers of modern computer software draw sketches of what the screen will look like as their software runs, showing any changes that occur. Just as each distinct shot in a film scene requires its own storyboard, each distinct screen in a computer application requires a different sketch, so we will call these **storyboard-sketches**. Since our first program has just one scene, it has just one storyboard-sketch, as shown in Figure 1-4.

FIGURE 1-4   Storyboard-sketches

In Alice programming, the storyboard-sketches provide important information for the programmer about each object visible on the screen, including:

- Its **position** (where it is with respect to the other objects)
- Its **pose** (what are the positions of its limbs, if it has any)
- Its **orientation** (what direction it is facing)

Storyboard-sketches also indicate where Alice's **camera** object should be positioned, whether it is stationary or moving during the shot, and so on.

1.3.3   Transition Diagrams

When a program has multiple scenes, it has multiple storyboards. When all the storyboard-sketches are completed, they are linked together in a **transition diagram** that shows any special events that are required to make the transition from one sketch to the next. In a movie, there are no special events, so the transition diagram is a simple linear sequence, as shown in Figure 1-5.

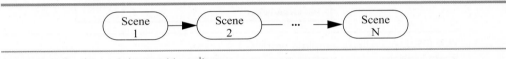

FIGURE 1-5   A movie's transition diagram

1.4   Program Implementation In Alice

With a user story, storyboard-sketches, and transition diagram in hand, the program's **design** is done, and we are ready to build it in Alice. We begin by starting Alice. Alice displays a **Welcome to Alice** window that allows us to choose a **Template** (background and sky) for the world, as shown in Figure 1-6.

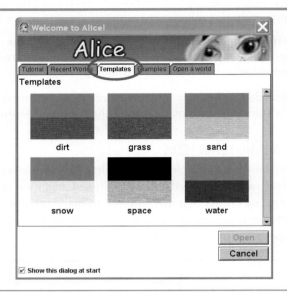

FIGURE 1-6   Alice's template worlds

(You can also get this window to appear by clicking Alice's **File** menu, and then choosing **New World**.) Double-click the template you want to use (we will choose the **grass** template here), and Alice will create a pristine[1] three-dimensional world for you, using that template, as shown in Figure 1-7. (Your screen may look slightly different.) For consistency with the tutorials, we have added the names for the various areas in Alice to Figure 1-7.

---

1.   Here and elsewhere, we will use the word *pristine* to describe an Alice world in its beginning state — before any objects have been added to it.

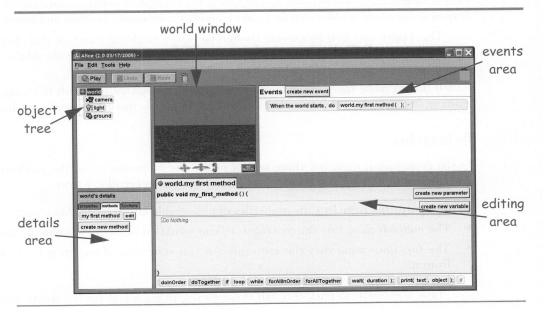

FIGURE 1-7   A pristine Alice world

Menus

At the top of the Alice window are four menus:

- **File** lets you load and save your Alice programs/worlds (and other things).
- **Edit** lets you change your preferences.
- **Tools** lets you examine your world's statistics, error console, and so on.
- **Help** lets you access the Alice tutorials, some example worlds, and so on.

Buttons

Below Alice's menus are three buttons:

- **Play** runs the program associated with the current world.
- **Undo** undoes your most recent action (this is very handy!).
- **Redo** redoes the most recently undone action.

If you are like me, you will find yourself using the **Play** button frequently (every time you want to run your program); the **Undo** buton when using trial-and-error to find just the right effect, and the **Redo** button very rarely.

The Object Tree

The *object tree* is where the objects in your world are listed. Even in a pristine world, the *object tree* contains several objects, namely the **camera**, the **light**, and the **ground**. Like other objects in Alice, the **camera** can be moved within the world. Its position determines what is seen in the *world window*. As you saw in the tutorials, the blue arrow-controls at the bottom of the *world window* can be used to modify the **camera**'s position and orientation.

The **light** can also be moved, though we won't be doing much of that. If you are working on a shot and find that you need more light, you can change the **light**'s position, orientation, color, and brightness.

It doesn't make much sense to move the ground, though we may wish to change it (for example, from grass to snow, or sand, or ...). We'll see how to do this in Section 2.3 in Chapter 2.

The Details Area

In the *details area*, there are three *tabbed panes*: the *properties* pane, the *methods* pane, and the *functions* pane. For whatever object is selected in the *object tree*:

- The *properties* pane lists the properties or changeable attributes of that object;
- The *methods* pane lists the messages we can send that object to animate it; and
- The *functions* pane lists the messages we can send that object to get information from it.

Take a moment to click through these panes, to get a feel for the things they contain. We'll present an overview of them in Section 1.5.

The Editing Area

The *editing area* is where we will edit or build the program that controls the animation. As can be seen in Figure 1-7, the *editing area* of a pristine world contains a method named **World.my first method** that is empty, meaning it contains no *statements*. Very shortly, we will see how to build our first program by adding statements to this method.

At the bottom of the *editing area* are *controls* (**doInOrder**, **doTogether**, **if**, **loop**, and so on) that can be used to build Alice statements. We will introduce these controls one by one, as we need them, throughout the next few chapters.

The Events Area

The *events area* is where we can tell Alice what to do when special actions called **events** occur. A pristine world contains just one event, as can be seen in Figure 1-7. This event tells Alice to send the **my first method** message to the **World** object when the world starts (that is, when the user clicks the **Play** button). Clicking the **Play** button thus causes **my first method** to **run**, meaning any statements within it are performed. Programmers often use the phrases ***run*** a **program** and ***execute*** a **program** interchangeably.

1.4.1   Program Style

Before we begin programming, you may want to alter the *style* in which Alice displays the program. Click the **Edit** menu, followed by the **Preferences** choice, and Alice will display the *Preferences* window shown in Figure 1-8.

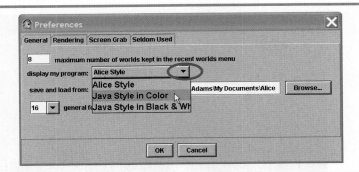

FIGURE 1-8   Using Java style

Since Java is a popular programming language, we will be displaying our programs using Alice's *Java style in Color*. By doing so, Alice will provide us with an introduction to the Java we will learn later in the course. If you want your programs to look consistent with those in the text, please make this change on your copy of Alice. You will then need to restart Alice for the changes to take effect.

1.4.2   Adding Objects to Alice

Once we have a pristine world, the next step is to populate it with objects using the skills you learned in the Alice tutorials. By clicking the **ADD OBJECTS** button below the *world window*, locating **Class AliceLiddell** and **Class WhiteRabbit** in the Alice Gallery (under **People** and **Animals**, respectively), adding them to the world, and repositioning and rotating them, we can build the scene from our first storyboard-sketch, as shown in Figure 1-9.

FIGURE 1-9   Alice Liddell and the White Rabbit

The items in the Alice Gallery are not objects but are like blueprints that Alice uses to build objects. Such blueprints are called **classes**. Whenever we drag a class from the Gallery into the *world window*, Alice uses the class to build an object for the world.

For example, when we drag the **AliceLiddell** and **WhiteRabbit** classes to the world, Alice adds two new objects to the world, and lists them in the *object tree*: **aliceLiddell** and **whiteRabbit**. If we were to drag **Class WhiteRabbit** into the world again, Alice would again use the class to create an object for the world, but this object would be named **whiteRabbit2**. Feel free to try this; you can always delete **whiteRabbit2** (or any object in the *object tree*), either by dragging it to the **Trash**, or by right-clicking it and selecting **delete** from the menu that appears.

The key idea is that each object is made from a class. Even though the world might contain ten **whiteRabbit** objects, there would still be just one **WhiteRabbit** class from which all of the **whiteRabbit** objects were made.

To distinguish objects from classes, Alice follows this convention: each word in the name of a *class* is capitalized (for example, **AliceLiddell**, **WhiteRabbit**); but for an *object*, each word in the name *except the first* is capitalized (for example, **aliceLiddell**, **whiteRabbit**).

If you don't like the name Alice gives an object, you can always rename it by (1) right-clicking the object's name in the *object tree*, and (2) choosing **rename** from the menu that appears, and (3) typing your new name for the object. Alice will then update all statements that refer to the object to use the new name.

With the objects **aliceLiddel** and **whiteRabbit** in place, we are almost ready to begin programming! In Alice, programming is accomplished mainly in the *object tree* (to select the object being animated), the *details area* (the **properties** or characteristics of an object are listed under the *properties* tab, and the **messages** we can send an object are listed under the *methods* and *functions* tabs), and the *editing area* (to add statements to the program that animate the selected object).

1.4.3 Accessing Object Subparts

In the user story, the first action is that Alice should seem to see us (the user) and turn her head toward us. To make this happen, we will use skills from the Alice tutorials.

If we click on **aliceLiddell** in the *object tree*, then we select all of **aliceLiddell**. However, the user story says that Alice is to turn her head, so we just want to select that part of her. To do so, we click the **+** sign next to **aliceLiddell** in the *object tree* to view her subparts, and then do the same on her **neck**, exposing her **head**, which we then select as shown in Figure 1-10.

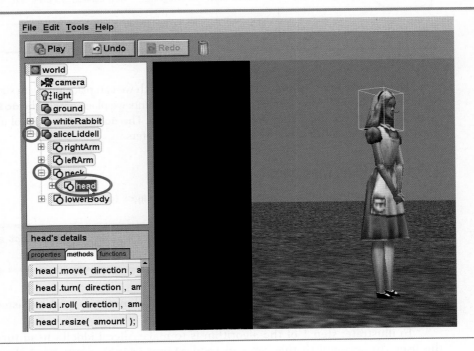

FIGURE 1-10   Accessing an object's subparts

As can be seen in Figure 1-10, when we click on an object in the *object tree* (for example, Alice Liddell's **head**), Alice draws a box around that object in the *world window*, to highlight it and show its boundaries. This box is called an object's **bounding box**, and every Alice object has one.

Selecting an object's subpart in the *object tree* also changes the *details area* to indicate the *properties*, *methods*, and *functions* for that subpart.

Since the steps in a flow or algorithm need to be performed in a specified order, we begin programming by dragging a **doInOrder** control from the bottom of the *editing area*, as shown in Figure 1-11.

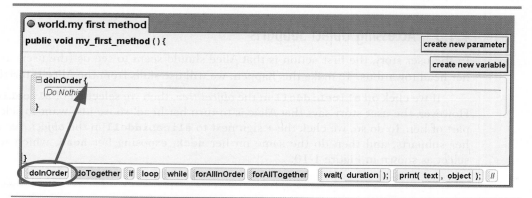

FIGURE 1-11   Dragging the **doInOrder** control

The **doInOrder** control is a structure within which we can place program statements (see Section 1.4.7 below). As its name suggests, any statements we place within the **doInOrder** will be performed in the order they appear, top-to-bottom. The **doInOrder** control also has additional convenient features that we will see in later chapters.

1.4.4 Sending Messages

Alice programming consists largely of sending messages to objects.

> You can get an object to perform a desired behavior by sending the object a **message** that asks the object to produce that behavior.

In Alice, behavior-producing messages are called **methods**, and are listed under the *methods pane* of the *details area*.

To illustrate, step 1 of the algorithm is to make Alice Liddell's head turn to look at the user. To accomplish this, we can send **aliceLiddell.neck.head** the **pointAt()** message, and specify the **camera** as the thing her head is to face. (Similarly, to make the White Rabbit say "Hello", we can send **whiteRabbit** the **say()** message, and specify **Hello** as the thing we want him to say.) With Alice Liddell's **head** selected in the *object tree*, we scan through the methods in the *details area* until we see **pointAt()**. We then click on **pointAt()**, drag it into the *editing area*, and drop it.

As we drag a method, Alice surrounds it with a red border so long as the mouse is in a place where dropping it has no benefit. When the mouse moves into an area where we can drop the method beneficially, Alice changes the method's border's color from red to green. Alice consistently uses the color red to warn you that you *should not* do something (for example, drop the method), and uses the color green to indicate when you *may* do something.

The **pointAt()** message requires that we specify a **target** — the thing at which we want Alice Liddell's head to point. When you drop the **pointAt()** method in the *editing area*, Alice displays a menu of the objects in your world, from which you can choose the **target**, as shown in Figure 1-12.

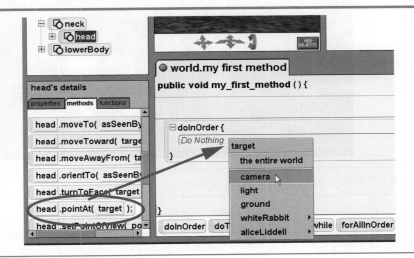

FIGURE 1-12   Dragging the **pointAt()** message

When we select the **camera**, Alice redraws the *editing area* as shown in Figure 1-13.

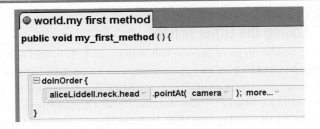

FIGURE 1-13   Our first message

1.4.5   Testing and Debugging

If we now click the **Play** button, you will see **aliceLiddell**'s head turn and seem to look at you (the user)! Figure 1-14 shows the end result.

FIGURE 1-14   Alice Liddell looks at the user

(If you are not at a computer doing this interactively, compare Figure 1-14 to Figure 1-9 to see the effect of sending Alice's **head** the **pointAt(camera)** message.)

By clicking the **Play** button, we are **testing** the program, to see if it produces the desired result. If the program does something other than what we wanted, then it contains an **error** or **bug**. Finding and fixing the error is called **debugging** the program. If you have followed the steps carefully so far, your program should have no bugs, so let's continue. (If your program does have a bug, compare your editing area against that shown in Figure 1-13 to see where you went wrong.)

1.4.6   Coding the Other Actions

We can use similar steps to accomplish actions 2, 3, 4, 5, and 6 of the algorithm in Figure 1-2 by sending **pointAt()** or **say()** messages to **aliceLiddell** or the **whiteRabbit**. When we send an object the **say()** message, Alice displays a menu from which we can select what we want the object to say. To customize the greetings, select the **other...** menu-choice; then in the dialog box that appears, type what you want the object to say. After a few minutes of clicking, dragging, and dropping, we can have the partial program shown in Figure 1-15.

```
● world.my first method
public void my_first_method ( ) {


   ⊟ doInOrder {
        aliceLiddell.neck.head ▽  .pointAt( camera ▽ );  more... ▽
        aliceLiddell ▽  .say( Oh, hello there! ▽ );  duration = 2 seconds ▽  fontSize = 30 ▽  more... ▽
        whiteRabbit ▽  .pointAt( camera ▽ );  more... ▽
        whiteRabbit ▽  .say( Uhm, yes.  Hello there! ▽ );  duration = 2 seconds ▽  fontSize = 30 ▽  more... ▽
        aliceLiddell ▽  .say( My name is Alice Liddell. ▽ );  duration = 2 seconds ▽  fontSize = 30 ▽  more... ▽
        whiteRabbit ▽  .say( And I am the White Rabbit. ▽ );  duration = 2 seconds ▽  fontSize = 30 ▽  more... ▽

   }
```

FIGURE 1-15   A partial program

By clicking on the **more...** to the right of a message in the *editing area*, we can customize various attributes of that message. For example, in Figure 1-15, we have increased the **duration** attribute of each **say()** message (depending on the length of what is being said), to give the user sufficient time to read.

> For **say()** messages, set the duration to 2–3 seconds per line of text being displayed, to give the user time to read what is being said.

You can also adjust the **fontSize** (and other attributes) to specify the appearance of a **say()** message's letters. We will always use a **fontSize** of at least **30**, to ensure that the letters display well on high-resolution computer screens (see Figure 1-15).

1.4.7   Statements

Most of the lines in the program have the same basic structure:

```
object.message(value); more...
```

In programming terminology, such a line is sometimes called a **statement**. A computer program consists of a collection of statements, the combination of which produce some desirable behavior. The basic structure shown above is quite common, and is what we will use most often.

The **doInOrder** control is also a statement; however it is a statement that controls *how other statements are performed* (that is, one at a time, top-to-bottom).

1.4.8   The Final Action

We are nearly done! All that is left is the final step in the algorithm, in which Alice Liddell and the White Rabbit say "Welcome to our world" simultaneously. It should be evident that we can accomplish this in part by sending **say()** messages to **aliceLiddell** and the **whiteRabbit**. For both objects, the value accompanying the **say()** message should be the same value: **Welcome to our world**.

As we have seen, the **doInOrder** control performs the first statement within it, then the next statement, then the next statement, and so on. This is sometimes called **sequential execution**, meaning the statements are performed in order or *in sequence*. Sequential execution means that if we were to send **aliceLiddell** the **say()** message, and then send **whiteRabbit** the **say()** message, the message to the White Rabbit would not be performed until after the message to Alice Liddell had been completed.

To achieve the effect specified in the user story, we must send **say()** messages to **aliceLiddell** and the **whiteRabbit** *simultaneously*. We can accomplish this using the **doTogether** control, located at the bottom of the *editing area*. To use this control, we click on **doTogether**, drag it upwards into the *editing area*, and drop it when the green bar appears below the last statement in the program, producing the program shown in Figure 1-16.

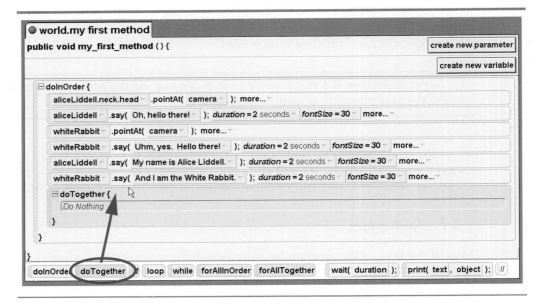

FIGURE 1-16   Dragging the **doTogether** control

The **doTogether** control is another Alice statement. Like the **doInOrder**, it has a form different from the **object.message()** structure we saw previously. When the program performs a **doTogether** statement, all statements within it are performed simultaneously, so it should provide the behavior we need to finish the program.

Using the same skills we used earlier, we can send **say()** messages to **aliceLiddell** and to the **whiteRabbit**. However, now we drop these messages inside the **doTogether** statement, yielding the final program, shown in Figure 1-17.

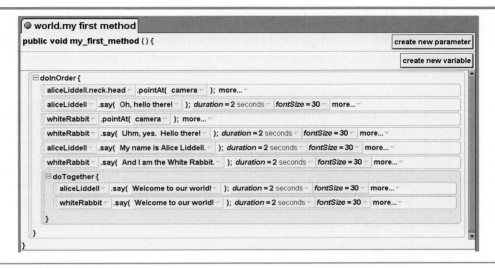

FIGURE 1-17 Our first program

1.4.9 Final Testing

When we run the program, the final scene appears as shown in Figure 1-18.

FIGURE 1-18 Alice Liddell and the White Rabbit speaking together

We saw earlier that the Alice **doInOrder** statement performs the statements within it *sequentially*. By contrast, the **doTogether** statement performs the statements it contains *simultaneously* or *concurrently*.

1.4.10 The Software Engineering Process

The approach we just used to create our first program is an example of a methodical, disciplined way that computer software can be created. The process consists of the following steps:

---

1. Write the *user story*. Identify the nouns and verbs within it. Organize the nouns and verbs into a *flow* or *algorithm*.

2. Draw the *storyboard-sketches*, one per distinct shot in your program, and create a *transition diagram* that relates them to each other. If you have some users available, have them review your sketches for feedback, and take seriously any improvements they suggest. Update your user story and algorithm, if necessary.

3. For each noun in your algorithm: add an *object* to your Alice world.

4. For each verb in your algorithm:

   a. Find a *message* that performs that verb's action, and send it to the verb's object. (If the object has no message that provides that verb's action, we'll see how to build our own methods in Chapter 2.)

   b. Test the message sent in Step 4a, to check that it produces the desired action. If not, either alter how the message is being sent (with its **more...** attributes), or find a different message (and if you cannot find one, build your own).

Steps 1 and 2 of this process are called **software design**. Steps 3 and 4 — in which we build the program and then verify that it does what it is supposed to do — are called **software implementation and testing**. Together, software design, implementation, and testing are important parts of **software engineering** — a methodical way to build computer programs.

We will use this same basic process to create most of the programs in this book. You should go through each of these steps for each program you write, because the result will be better-crafted programs.

1.5   Alice's Details Area

As mentioned earlier, Alice's *details area* provides three tabbed panes. Whenever an object is selected in the *object tree*, these three panes list the properties or characteristics of that object, the methods for that object, and the functions, or questions that we can ask that object. In this section, we provide an overview of this *details area*.

1.5.1 The *properties* Pane

To see the properties of an object, first click on that object in the *object tree*, and then click the *properties* tab in the *details area*, as shown in Figure 1-19.

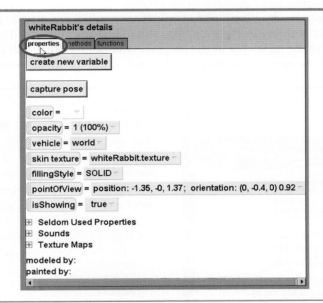

FIGURE 1-19 The *properties* pane

Here, we can see an object's properties, including its color, opacity, vehicle, skin texture, fill style, point of view (position + orientation), and whether or not it is showing.

The values of an object's properties determine the object's appearance and behavior when you run your program. Feel free to experiment with these settings, to see what they do. (You can always use Alice's **Undo** button if you make a mistake.) For example, if the White Rabbit's ghost were an object in the story, we might add a **whiteRabbit** to the world, and change its opacity to 30%, so that 70% of the light in the world passes through him. The result would be a ghostly translucent **whiteRabbit** in the program.

Changing A Property From Within A Program

When you set an object's property to a value within the *properties* pane, that property has that value when your program begins running, and will keep that value unless your program causes it to change. For example, suppose that we wanted the White Rabbit to magically disappear after he and Alice have greeted us, and Alice to then say, "Now where did he go this time?" We can easily elicit the required behavior from **aliceLiddel** by sending her a **say()** message; but how do we get the **whiteRabbit** to disappear before she says it?

There are actually two ways to accomplish this special effect. If we desire the White Rabbit to disappear instantly, we can do this by setting his **isShowing** property to **false** at the right place in the program. If we want him to disappear slowly (say, over the course of a few seconds), we can do this by setting his **opacity** property to **0** at the right place in the program, and then modifying the statement's **duration** attribute to the required length of time. Either approach requires that we learn how to set one of the **whiteRabbit**'s properties, so we will use the latter approach, and leave the use of the first approach as an exercise.

To set an object's property to a different value at a specific point in the program, we click that property in the *properties* pane, drag it into the *editing area* until a green bar appears at the right spot in the program, and drop it. Alice will then display a drop-down menu of the options for the property's new value, as can be seen in Figure 1-20.

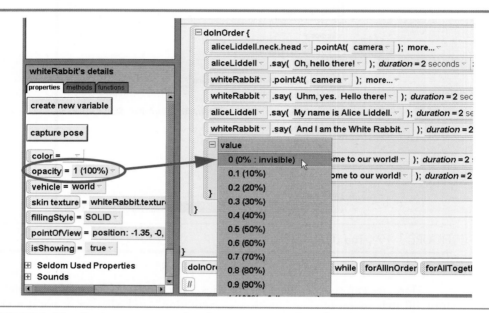

FIGURE 1-20   Setting a property by dragging it into the editing area

When we select a value from that menu, Alice inserts a new statement into the *editing area*. This statement sends a special **set()** message to the **whiteRabbit**, telling it to set its **opacity** property to the value we selected from the menu. By default, the **duration** of this **set()** message is one second, so to make the White Rabbit disappear more slowly, we set it to two seconds, yielding the statement shown in Figure 1-21.

```
┌─────────────────────────────────────────────────────────────────────────────────┐
│ ⊟ doTogether {                                                                     │
│    aliceLiddell ▽ .say( Welcome to our world! ▽ ); duration = 2 seconds ▽ fontSize = 30 ▽ more... ▽ │
│    whiteRabbit ▽ .say( Welcome to our world! ▽ ); duration = 2 seconds ▽ fontSize = 30 ▽ more... ▽ │
│ }                                                                                  │
│    whiteRabbit ▽ .set( opacity , 0 (0%) ▽ ); duration = 2 seconds ▽ more... ▽      │
│ }                                                                                  │
└─────────────────────────────────────────────────────────────────────────────────┘
```

FIGURE 1-21   The special set() message Alice generates to set a property

Adding the statement to make Alice say "Now where did he go this time?" is straightforward, and is left as an exercise.

1.5.2   The *methods* Pane

Click the *methods* tab of the *details area* and you will see the behavior-generating messages that you can send to the object selected in the *object tree*. Figure 1-22 shows some of the behavior-generating messages that are common to all Alice objects; a complete list is given in Appendix A.

FIGURE 1-22   The *methods* pane

These messages provide a rich set of operations that, together with the **doTogether** and **doInOrder** controls, let us build complex animations. Since we can send these messages to any Alice object, they allow us to build worlds containing talking animals, dancing trees, singing buildings, and just about anything else we can imagine!

The **resize()** message is especially fun, as it lets you make an object change size (for example, **resize(2)** to grow twice as big, or **resize(0.5)** to shrink to half size) as your program runs. The **resize()** message's **more...** menu includes a **dimension** choice that you can use to change an object's *width* (**LEFT_TO_RIGHT**), *height* (**TOP_TO_BOTTOM**), or *depth* (**FRONT_TO_BACK**), letting you create some interesting visual effects as your program runs.

In addition to these basic messages, some Alice objects respond to additional (non-basic) messages. For example, in the **People** folder of the Alice Gallery are tools called the **heBuilder** and **sheBuilder** that allow you to build custom male and female characters for your world. Each "person" built using one of these tools will respond to the additional messages. Figure 1-23 shows a person built using the **heBuilder**, whom we have renamed **bob**, and the non-basic messages that can be sent to such a person.

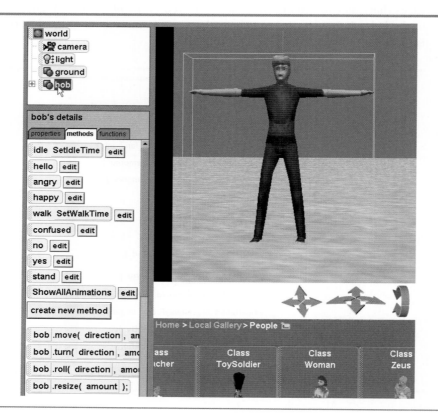

FIGURE 1-23   Non-basic methods

Other Alice classes (for example, **Frog**, **Monkey**, **Penquin**) provide different non-basic methods. To discover them, just add an object to your world and see what methods appear in the *details area*.

1.5.3   The *functions* Pane

If we click the *functions* tab in the *details area* as shown in Figure 1-24, we will see the list of functions or question messages that we can send to the object selected in the *object tree*.

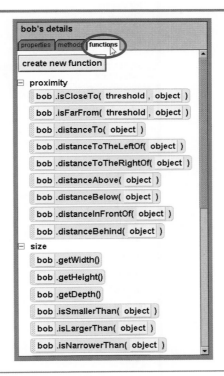

FIGURE 1-24   The *functions* pane

Functions are messages that we can send to an object to retrieve information from it. Where the *methods* tab provides standard behavior-generating messages, the *functions* tab provides a set of standard messages that we can send to an object to "ask it a question." The standard Alice functions let us ask an object about its:

- **proximity** to another object (that is, how close or how far the other object is)
- **size** (its *height*, *width*, or *depth*, and how these compare to another object)
- **spatial relation** to another object (*position* or *orientation* with respect to the other object)
- **point of view** (*position* and *orientation* within the world)
- **subparts**

Many of these standard functions refer to an object's bounding box (or one of its edges) that we saw in Section 1.4.3.

Alice also provides a different group of function messages we can send to the world. That is, if we select the **world** object and then the *functions* tab, Alice displays a group of world functions, some of which are shown in Figure 1-25.

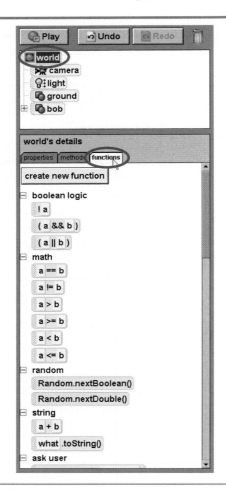

FIGURE 1-25   The *world functions* pane

We will see how to use these different kinds of messages in the coming chapters.

1.6   Alice Tip: Positioning Objects Using Quad View

In the Alice tutorials, we saw how the **ADD OBJECTS** button in the *world window* lets us navigate the Alice Gallery, locate classes, and use them to add objects to the world.

By default, **ADD OBJECTS** displays just the *world window*. However, trying to position two objects in close proximity to one another (for example, trying to position a person on the back of a horse) can be difficult using this single window, since it offers just one view. For such situations, Alice has the **quad view** that provides the *world window*, plus views from the top, right, and front of the scene. To use it, click the **quad view** radio button near the top of the window, as shown in Figure 1-26.

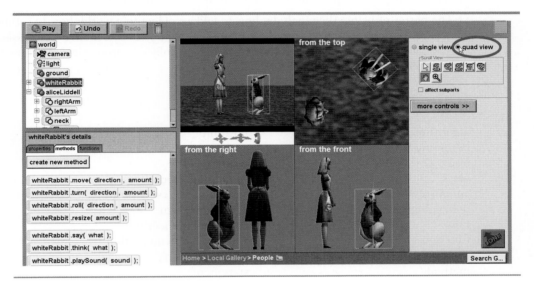

FIGURE 1-26   The quad view

As can be seen above, the quad view provides two additional controls:

- a "hand" control that lets you (within any of the views) drag the mouse to move the camera left, right, up, or down to view a different part of the scene
- a "magnifying glass" control that lets you drag the mouse *down* to zoom the camera *in* on some detail of the scene, or drag *up* to zoom the camera *out* to see more of the scene

These additional controls are very useful when you shift to the quad view and the characters you wanted to see are nowhere to be seen. When this happens, just click the magnifying glass and then drag *up* within the view to zoom out until the characters become visible (probably very small), switch to the hand control and move the camera until the characters are centered, then switch back to the magnifying glass and drag *down* within the view to zoom back in.

1.7   Chapter Summary

❑ The *user story* describes the behavior of a computer program.

❑ *Storyboard-sketches* indicate the appearance of each of the program's scenes.

❑ *Transition diagrams* relate the storyboard-sketches to one another.

❑ A *flow* or *algorithm* provides a concise summary of the user story.

❑ The basics of using Alice include: how to add an object to a world; how to set its initial position, orientation, and pose; how to animate an object by sending it a message; how to select an object's subparts; how to change an object's properties; and how to send multiple messages simultaneously.

1.7.1   Key Terms

algorithm	position
bounding box	pose
bug	property
class	sequential execution
concurrent execution	simultaneous execution
debugging	software design
flow	software engineering
function	software implementation
message	software testing
method	statement
object	storyboard-sketches
orientation	user story
point of view	

Programming Projects

1.1 Modify the world we created in Section 1.4 so that, after Alice and the White Rabbit introduce themselves, Alice tells the user she and the White Rabbit would like to sing a duet, after which they sing a simple song, such as *Mary Had A Little Lamb*. Have Alice and the White Rabbit sing alternate lines of the song.

Mary had a little lamb, little lamb, little lamb. Mary had a little lamb it's fleece was white as snow.	And everywhere that Mary went, Mary went, Mary went. And everywhere that Mary went the lamb was sure to go.
It followed her to school one day, school one day, school one day. It followed her to school one day which was against the rules.	It made the children laugh and play, laugh and play, laugh and play. It made the children laugh and play to see a lamb at school.

1.2 Finish the world we modified in Section 1.5.1, so that the movie ends with **aliceLiddell** saying, *Now where did he go this time?* Modify the world so that the **whiteRabbit** disappears instantly. Modify the world to make a **pop** sound when the **whiteRabbit** disappears.

1.3 If your computer has a microphone, modify the world we created in Section 1.4, using **doTogether** controls and **playSound()** messages to record voices for Alice and the White Rabbit, so that the user can hear what each character says instead of having to read it. Alter your voice for each character.

1.4 Using any two characters from the Alice Gallery, design and build a world in which one tells the other a knock-knock joke. (If you don't know any knock-knock jokes, see **www.knock-knock-joke.com**). Make your story end with both characters laughing.

1.5 Using the **heBuilder** or **sheBuilder** (under **People** in the **Local Gallery**), build a superhero named **Resizer**, who can alter his or her size at will. Build a world in which **Resizer** demonstrates his or her powers to the user by growing and shrinking. Make sure that **Resizer** tells the user what he or she is going to do before doing it.

1.6 Build a world containing one of the hopping animals (for example, a bunny or a frog). Write a program that makes the animal hop once, as realistically as possible (that is, legs extending and retracting, head bobbing, and so on). Bonus: Send your animal **playSound()** messages, so that the predefined sound **thud1** is played as it leaves the ground, **whoosh2** is played while it is in the air, and **thud2** is played when it lands.

1.7 Using the **heBuilder** or **sheBuilder** (under **People** in the **Local Gallery**), build a person. Place the person in a world containing a building. Using the **walk()**, **move()**, and **turn()** messages, write a program that makes him or her walk around the building.

1.8 Using the **heBuilder** or **sheBuilder** (under **People** in the **Local Gallery**), build a person. Then build a world containing your person and one of the items from the **Sports** section of the Gallery (for example, a baseball or a basketball). Write a program in which your person uses the item for that sport (for example, pitches the baseball or dribbles the basketball).

1.9 Choose one of your favorite movie scenes that contains just two or three characters. Use Alice to create an animated version of that scene, substituting characters from the Alice Gallery for the characters in the movie.

1.10 Write an original short story (10-20 seconds long), and use Alice to create an animated version of it. Your story should have at least two characters, and each character should perform at least five actions that combine to make an interesting story.

1.11 *Mules* is a silly (and confusing!) song with the lyrics shown below (sung to the tune of *Auld Lang Syne*). Build a world containing a horse (the closest thing in the Alice Gallery to a mule) and a person. Build a program that animates the person and horse appropriately while the person "sings" the lyrics to the song. For example, the person should point to the different legs (front or back) as he or she sings about them, move to the back of the horse when the song calls for it, get kicked as the sixth line is sung, and so on.

On mules we find two legs behind,	When we're behind the two behind,
and two we find before.	we find what these be for —
We stand behind before we find,	so stand before the two behind,
what the two behind be for!	behind the two before!

Chapter 2
Methods

Great things can be reduced to small things, and small things can be reduced to nothing.

CHINESE PROVERB

Weeks of programming can save you hours of planning.

ANONYMOUS

When do you show the consequences? On TV, that mouse pulled out that cat's lungs and played them like a bagpipe, but in the next scene, the cat was breathing comfortably.

MARGE SIMPSON (JULIE KAVNER), IN "ITCHY AND SCRATCHY LAND," THE SIMPSONS

Objectives

Upon completion of this chapter, you will be able to:

❑ Build world-level methods to help organize a story into scenes and shots

❑ Build class-level methods to elicit desirable behaviors from objects

❑ Reuse a class-level method in multiple worlds

❑ Use dummies to reposition the camera for different shots within a scene

❑ Understand how an object's *position*, *orientation*, and *point of view* are determined

In the last chapter, we saw how to design and build computer programs. We also saw how Alice lets us build programs consisting of *statements*, in which we often send *messages* to *objects*. Finally, we saw that Alice provides us with a rich set of predefined messages that let us create programs to generate fun and interesting animations.

Alice's predefined messages provide an excellent set of *basic operations* for animation. However, for most Alice objects, these basic operations are *all* that are predefined. (The people we can create using the **heBuilder** and **sheBuilder** tools are unusual in providing methods beyond the basic ones.) The result is that for many of the behaviors we might want Alice objects to exhibit, there are no predefined methods to elicit those behaviors. For example, a horse should be able to walk, trot, and gallop, but there are no predefined **Horse** methods for these behaviors. A dragon or pterodactyl should at least be able to flap its wings (if not fly), but the **Dragon** and **Pterodactyl** classes do not provide methods for such behavior. A wizard should be able to cast a spell, but the **Wizard** class does not contain a **castSpell** message.

When an Alice class does not provide a method for a behavior we need, Alice lets us create a new method to provide the behavior. Once we have created the method, we can send the corresponding message to the object to elicit the behavior.

There are actually two quite different reasons for building your own methods. The first reason is to divide your story into manageable pieces to help keep it more organized. The second reason is to provide an object with a behavior it should have, but does not. In this chapter, we will examine both approaches. As we shall see, the motivation, thought process, and circumstances are quite different for these two different approaches.

2.1   World Methods for Scenes and Shots

As we mentioned in Chapter 1, films (and by extension, animations) are often broken down into **scenes**, with each scene making up one piece of the story. Scenes can be further broken down into **shots**, with each shot consisting of a set and whatever characters are in the shot, filmed from a particular camera position. When a film crew has finished one shot, they begin work on the next one. When all the shots for a particular scene are finished, the shots are combined to form the scene and that scene is done. Work then begins on the next scene.

Scenes and shots thus provide a logical and convenient way to break a big film project down into smaller, more manageable pieces. We can use the same approach in Alice. By organizing your user story into a series of scenes, and organizing each complex scene into a series of shots, you can work through the story shot by shot and scene by scene, without being overwhelmed by the size of the project. This approach — in which you solve a "big" problem by (1) breaking it into "small" problems, (2) solving each "small" problem, and (3) combining the "small" problem solutions into a solution to the "big" problem — is called **divide and conquer**.

2.1.1   Methods For Scenes

To illustrate how this approach can be used in Alice, suppose that we have a user story consisting of three scenes. When we first start Alice (even before we have added any objects to the world), we can organize our Alice program to reflect the scene structure of our user story. To create a method for our first scene, we first select **world** in the *object tree*, make certain that the *methods* tab is selected in the *details area*, and then click the **create new method** button there, as shown in Figure 2-1.

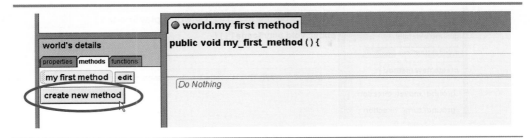

FIGURE 2-1   The **create new method** button

Clicking this box pops up a small **New Method** dialog box into which we can type the name we wish to give the new method. A method name should usually be (1) a *verb* or *verb phrase*, and (2) descriptive of what it does. Since we are creating a method to play the first scene, we will choose the name **playScene1**.

> Method names should begin with a lowercase letter and contain no spaces. If a name consists of multiple words, capitalize the first letter of each word after the first.

When we click the **New Method** dialog box's **OK** button, Alice does two things:

1. Alice creates a new pane in the *editing area*, labeled **world.playScene1**, containing an empty method definition for the **playScene1()** method.

2. Alice updates the *details area*, adding **playScene1** to the world's list of methods.

If you compare Figure 2-2 (below) to Figure 2-1, you will see both of these changes.

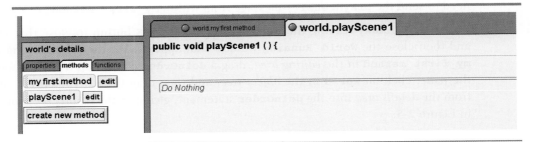

FIGURE 2-2   A new **playScene1()** method

One way to check that the method is working is to send a **say()** message to the world's **ground** object in **playScene1()**, as shown in Figure 2-3.[1]

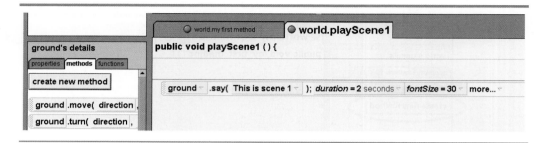

FIGURE 2-3   A simple method test

However, when we click Alice's **Play** button, the warning dialog box in Figure 2-4 appears.

FIGURE 2-4   The "Method Not Called" warning

Alice is warning us that although we have *defined* a new method, there are no statements in the program that send the corresponding message. The problem is that **my_first_method()** is empty, and since that is where the program begins running, we need to send the **playScene1()** message from within **my_first_method()**.

After carefully reading the warning, we click the **OK** button to close that window, and then close the **World Running** window that appears. We then click on the tab for **my_first_method** in the *editing area*, drag a **doInOrder** control up from the bottom of the pane, click on **world** in the *object tree*, and then drag the **playScene1()** message from the *details area* into the **doInOrder** statement, giving us the (short) program shown in Figure 2-5.

---

1.   Another approach is to have the method perform a **print()** statement, which is at the bottom of the *editing area*. When performed, this statement displays a message at the bottom of the **World Running** window, but it is awkward to view. (We had to resize the window and then scroll up to see the message.) The **print()** statement can also be used to view the value of a variable or parameter (see Chapter 3) when the statement is performed.

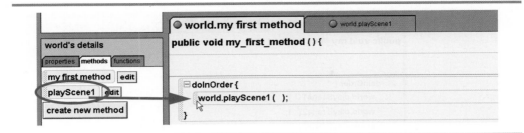

FIGURE 2-5   Sending `playScene1()` from `my_first_method()`

Now, when we click Alice's **Play** button, **world.my_first_method()** begins running. It sends the **playScene1()** message to **world**, which sends the **say()** message to the **ground**. If we've done everything correctly, we will see the **ground** "speak," as can be seen in Figure 2-6.

FIGURE 2-6   The **ground** speaks

Since the user story consists of three scenes, we can use this same approach to create new methods for the remaining two scenes, giving us the **my_first_method()** shown in Figure 2-7.

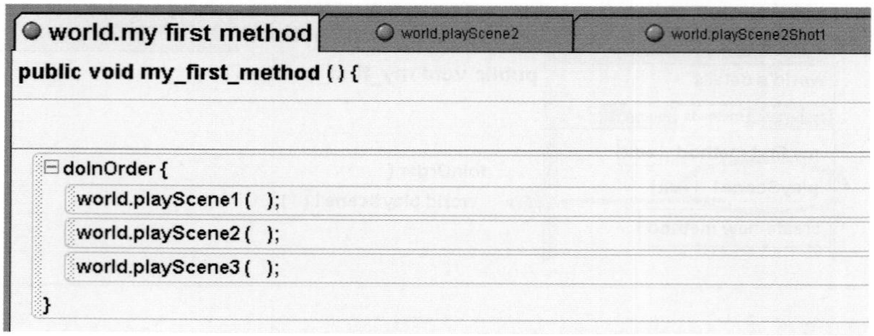

| ● world.my first method | ○ world.playScene2 | ○ world.playScene2Shot1 |

```
public void my_first_method ( ) {


    ⊟ doInOrder {
        world.playScene1 ( );
        world.playScene2 ( );
        world.playScene3 ( );

    }
```

FIGURE 2-7   Three new `playScene()` methods

Inside each new **playScene** method, we can send the **ground** a distinct **say()** message (for example, naming that scene). Clicking Alice's **Play** button should then display those messages in order. This is a simple way to test that the new methods are working properly. When we are confident that all is well, we can begin adding statements to **playScene1()** to perform the first scene, adding statements to **playScene2()** to perform the second scene, and so on.

2.1.2   Methods For Shots

We have just seen how a big, complicated project can be broken down into smaller, easier-to-program scenes. However in a *very* big project, a scene itself may be overwhelmingly complicated! In such situations, complex scenes can be divided into simpler (easier-to-program) **shots**. One good rule of thumb is:

> If you must use the scroll bar to view all the statements in a scene method, divide it into two or more shot methods.

The idea is that long methods are complicated, and therefore more error prone. If you keep your methods short and sweet, you'll be less likely to make a mistake — and if you do make one, it will be easier to find, since you won't have to scroll back and forth through lots of statements.

To illustrate this idea, suppose that the first scene is reasonably simple, and can be implemented in a method that requires no scrolling. However, suppose that the second scene is quite complicated, and we estimate that building it would require four or more screenfuls of statements. We can use an approach similar to what we did in Section 2.1.1 to create a method for each shot. Being systematic, we might name these methods **playScene2Shot1**, **playScene2Shot2**, **playScene2Shot3**, and **playScene2Shot4**.

As before, we select **world** in the *object tree*, and then click the **create new method** button in the *details area*. When asked to name the first method, we name it **playScene2Shot1**. As before, Alice (1) updates the *editing area* with a new pane containing an empty definition for the new method, and (2) adds the new method to the list of methods in the *details area*. To test that it works, we can again send the **ground** object a **say()** message, as shown in Figure 2-8.

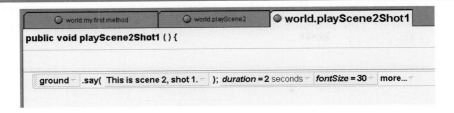

FIGURE 2-8 Testing a shot method

We can then select **world** in the *object tree*, click on the **world.playScene2** tab in the *editing area*, delete the **ground.say()** message from **playScene2()**, drag a **doInOrder** control into **playScene2()**, and finally drag the **playScene2Shot1()** message from the *details area* into the **doInOrder** statement, yielding the definition found in Figure 2-9.

```
○ world.my first method    ● world.playScene2    ○ world.playScene2Shot1
public void playScene2 () {


 doInOrder {
    world.playScene2Shot1 (  );
 }
```

FIGURE 2-9 Calling a shot method from a scene method

If we repeat this for each of the remaining shots in the scene, we get the definition shown in Figure 2-10.

```
○ world.playScene2Shot2    ○ world.playScene2Shot3    ○ world.playScene2Shot4
  ○ world.my first method    ● world.playScene2    ○ world.playScene2Shot1
public void playScene2 () {                           create new parameter
                                                      create new variable

 doInOrder {
    world.playScene2Shot1 (  );
    world.playScene2Shot2 (  );
    world.playScene2Shot3 (  );
    world.playScene2Shot4 (  );
 }
```

FIGURE 2-10 A scene method built from shot methods

Now we can add statements to each of the four shot methods to produce the animation required for that shot. When each is complete, we will have a complete animation for Scene 2!

If we were to draw a diagram of the structure of our program, it would be as shown in Figure 2-11.

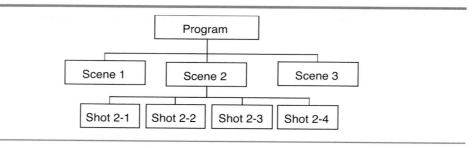

FIGURE 2-11   Structure diagram

Such a diagram or program can have as many pieces and levels as necessary to make your project manageable. If a shot is complicated, it can be further subdivided into **pieces**, and so on.

Scene and shot methods reflect the structure of the story we are telling, and hence belong to the world we are building. As such, they are properly stored in the *object tree*'s **world** object, since it represents the program as a whole. If you examine the *object tree* closely, you will see that all of the other objects in a world — including the **camera**, **light**, **ground**, and anything else we add to the world — are parts of the **world**. Because we store scene and shot messages in the **world** object, these messages must be sent to it, as we see in Figure 2-10.

In Alice, methods stored in the **world** are called **world methods**, because they define a message that is sent to the **world**. A method that affects the behavior of *multiple objects* (like a scene) should be defined as a world method.

2.2   Object Methods for Object Behaviors

An alternative to the world method is the **object method**, which is used to define a complex behavior for a *single object*. Where a world method usually controls the behavior of multiple objects (for example, each character in a scene), an object method controls the behavior of just one object — the object to which the corresponding message will be sent.

2.2.1   Example 1: Telling a Dragon to Flap Its Wings

To illustrate how to build an object method, let's create a new story starring a dragon who lives in the desert, as shown in Figure 2-12. Suppose that in one or more of this story's scenes, the dragon must flap its wings. Wing-flapping is a reasonably complex behavior, and it would be convenient if we could send a **flapWings()** message to a **dragon** object, but class **Dragon** does not provide a **flapWings()** method. In general, the following rule of thumb should be used in defining methods:

> Methods that control the behavior of a single object should be stored in that object.

From another perspective, a dragon is responsible for controlling its wings, so a **flapWings()** message should also be sent to a **dragon**. To do so, the **flapWings()** method must be stored in the **dragon** object. Conversely, it makes no sense to send the **world** a **flapWings()** message (since it has no wings to flap), so **flapWings()** should *not* be defined as a world method.

Assuming that we have added a **dragon** to the **world**, we can define a **dragon** method named **flapWings()** as follows. We first select **dragon** in the *object tree*, and click the *methods* tab in the *details area*. Above the list of **dragon** methods, we see the **create new method** button, as can be seen in Figure 2-12.

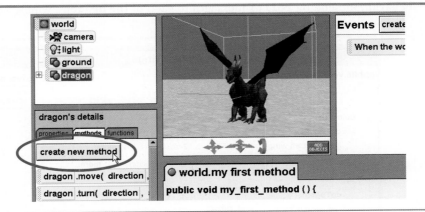

FIGURE 2-12   Creating a new class-level method

As we have seen before, clicking this button generates a dialog box asking us for the name of the new method, in which we can type **flapWings**. Alice then (1) creates a new tabbed pane in the *editing area* labeled **flapWings** containing an empty definition of a **flapWings()** method, and (2) creates an entry for the new method in the *details area* above the **create new method** button, as shown in Figure 2-13.

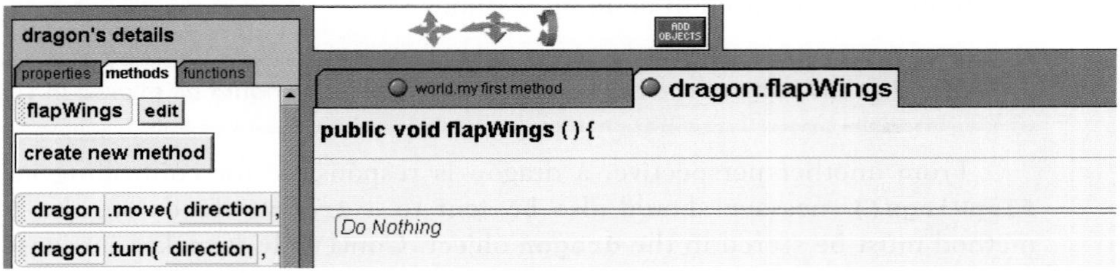

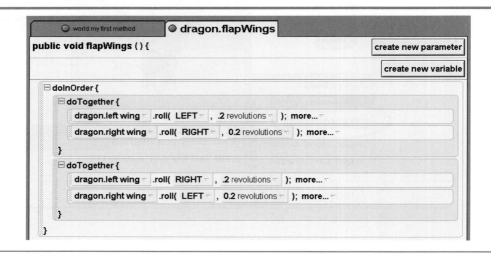

FIGURE 2-13   The empty `flapWings()` method

We can then fill this empty method definition with the statements needed to elicit the desired wing-flapping behavior. Figure 2-14 shows one way we might define such behavior, by sending **roll()** messages to each of the **dragon**'s wings.

FIGURE 2-14   One way to define a `flapWings()` method

Comments

It may take you some time to figure out why each statement that appears in Figure 2-14 is there. Puzzling out the purpose of statements consumes time that could be better spent on other activities.

To help human readers understand why a method's statements are there, good programmers insert **comments** into their methods to explain the purpose of tricky statements. Comments are ignored by Alice, so you can write whatever is needed by way of explanation.

To add a comment to a method in Alice, click on the *comment control* at the bottom of the *editing area*, drag the control upwards until the green bar appears above the statements you want to explain, and then drop the control, as shown in Figure 2-15.

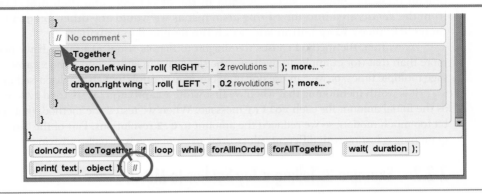

FIGURE 2-15   Dragging a comment

When you drop the comment, Alice gives it a **No comment** label. To edit a comment's explanation, you can either double-click its text, or click its list arrow and choose **other** from the menu that appears. Figure 2-16 shows a final, commented version of the **flapWings()** method.

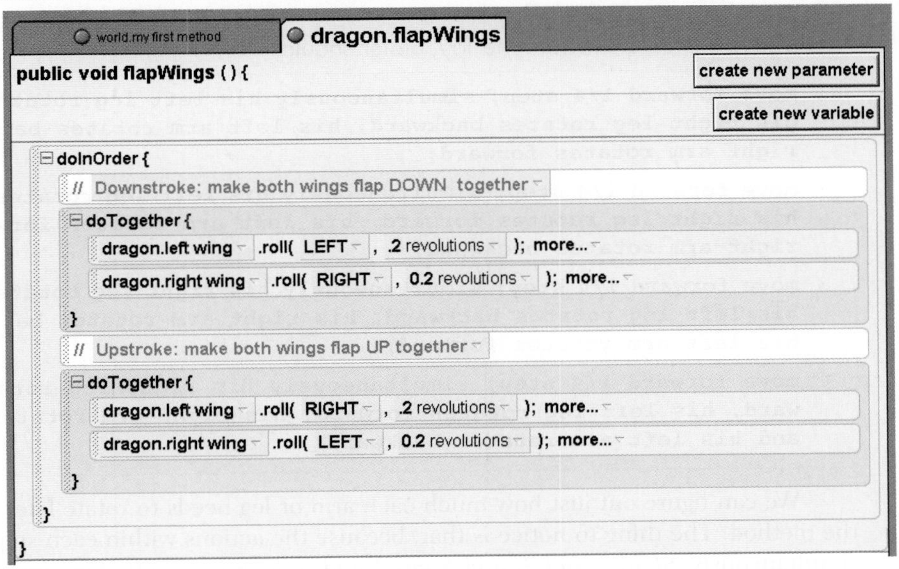

FIGURE 2-16   Final **flapWings()** method

Testing

To test the **flapWings()** method, we switch to **my_first_method()** — or to a world method that **my_first_method()** invokes, such as the scene method in which the dragon flaps its wings — select **dragon** in the *object tree*, and then drag **flapWings()** from the *details area* into the *editing area*, just as we would any other **dragon** method. We then click Alice's **Play** button and watch the dragon flap its wings!

As written, the method causes the dragon to flap its wings just once. If we need it to flap more than that (for example, to fly across the sky), we can either send it the **flapWings()** message multiple times, or we can use one of Alice's *loop* controls, which are discussed in Chapter 4.

It is worth mentioning that when we first wrote **flapWings()**, we tried **1/4 revolution** as the initial amount for each **roll()** message. When we tested the method, that seemed like a bit too much motion; so we reduced the amount to **0.2** revolutions. Part of the "art" of Alice programming is testing with different values until an animation is visually satisfying.

2.2.2   Example 2: Telling a Toy Soldier to March

Suppose we have a different story,[2] containing a scene in which a toy soldier is to march across the screen. There is a **ToySoldier** class in the Alice Gallery; unfortunately, this class contains no **march()** method. So let's build one! We can do so by defining an object method named **march()** in the **toySoldier**.

Design

It is always a good idea to spend time designing before we start programming, especially with a complex behavior like marching. If we think this behavior through step-by-step (Ha, ha! Get it? Step? Marching?), we might break it down into the following algorithm:

ALGORITHM 2-1   Behavior: The ToySoldier should:

```
1  move forward 1/4 step; simultaneously his left leg rotates forward,
   his right leg rotates backward, his left arm rotates backward, his
   right arm rotates forward;

2  move forward 1/4 step; simultaneously his left leg rotates backward,
   his right leg rotates forward, his left arm rotates forward, his
   right arm rotates backward;

3  move forward 1/4 step; simultaneously his right leg rotates forward,
   his left leg rotates backward, his right arm rotates backward, and
   his left arm rotates forward;

4  move forward 1/4 step; simultaneously his right leg rotates back-
   ward, his left leg rotates forward, his right arm rotates forward,
   and his left arm rotates backward.
```

We can figure out just how much each arm or leg needs to rotate later, when we test the method. The thing to notice is that, because the actions within each step are occuring simultaneously, *Steps 1 and 4, and Steps 2 and 3 describe exactly the same behaviors!* For

---

2.   Whenever we begin a new story or change to a different story, you will need to save your current world (using **File -> Save World**), and then open a new world (using **File -> New World**).

lack of better names, we might call Step 1 *marchLeft* and call Step 2 *marchRight*. If we were to write methods for these two steps, then the algorithm simplifies to this:

```
1  marchLeft;
2  marchRight;
3  marchRight;
4  marchLeft.
```

To move the soldier forward, we send him the **move()** message. To make his arms and legs rotate appropriately, we send **turn()** messages to his subparts. After some trial-and-error to find good **move()** and **turn()** distances, we get a definition like the one shown in Figure 2-17.

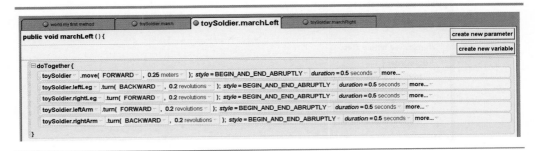

FIGURE 2-17 The **marchLeft()** method

The **marchRight()** method is similar, but with the behaviors reversed, as given in Figure 2-18.

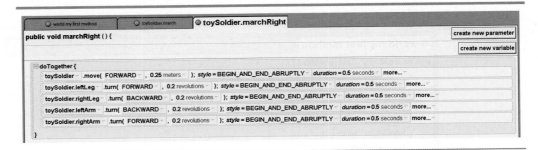

FIGURE 2-18 The **marchRight()** method

You may be wondering why in Figure 2-17 and Figure 2-18 we set each **move()** and **turn()** message's **style** attribute to **BEGIN_AND_END_ABRUPTLY**. The reason is that using this **style** smooths out the animation and makes it less "jerky." More precisely, by using this **style**, the first sending of **marchLeft()** will end abruptly, and since **marchRight()** begins abruptly, it will commence *immediately*. When it ends (abruptly), the second sending of **marchRight()** will begin without delay. And when it ends (abruptly), the second sending of **marchLeft()** will begin with no delay.

> If you find that your animations are moving in a "jerky" fashion, try setting the **style** of the animation's messages to **BEGIN_AND_END_ABRUPTLY**.

With these two methods in place, the **march()** method is quite simple, as shown in Figure 2-19.

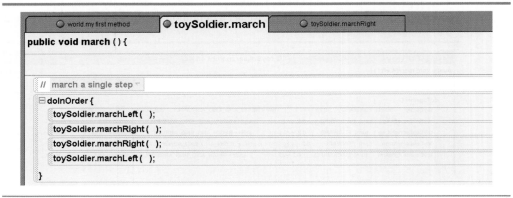

FIGURE 2-19   The **march()** method

To test the **march()** method, we can send the **toySoldier** the **march()** message, either from the scene in which it is needed or from **my_first_method()**. Figure 2-20 shows the latter.

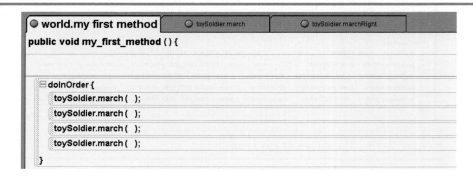

FIGURE 2-20   Testing the **march()** method

Now, when we click Alice's **Play** button, the soldier marches across the scene!

2.3   Alice Tip: Reusing Your Work

If you right-click on a statement, Alice displays a menu containing a **make copy** choice. Selecting this choice duplicates that statement. For example, in creating the program in Figure 2-20, we dragged **toySoldier.march();** into the *editing area* just once, and then used this right-click **make copy** mechanism to rapidly duplicate that statement three times.

This mechanism can also save time when you need to do similar, but not identical, things in a method. For example, to build the **flapWings()** method shown in Figure 2-16, we first built the top **doTogether** statement that makes the dragon's wings move down. We then made a copy of that statement, and in that copy, reversed the direction of the **roll()** messages, changing **LEFT** to **RIGHT** in the first message, and **RIGHT** to **LEFT** in the second message. This was much easier (and faster) than building the bottom **doTogether** statement from scratch.

In the rest of this section, we examine two other ways you can reuse existing work.

2.3.1   Using the Clipboard

The right-click **make copy** mechanism is useful when you have a statement that you want to duplicate *within* a particular method. But suppose you have written a statement in one method that you want to reuse in a different method.

For example, suppose you are programming a scene method, and producing the desired behavior takes more statements than anticipated. Viewing the method requires you to scroll back and forth, so you decide to break the scene up among two or more shot methods. How can you move the statements already in your scene method into a new (empty) shot method?

The answer is the **Alice clipboard**, located above the *events area* in the upper-right corner of the screen. From the *editing area*, you can drag any statement onto the clipboard and Alice will store a copy of it there for you, as shown in Figure 2-21.

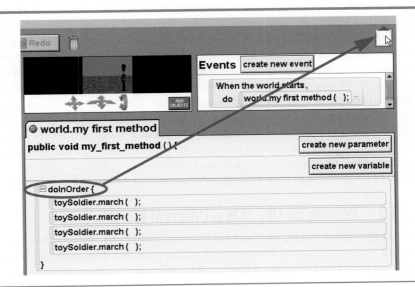

FIGURE 2-21   Dragging a statement to the clipboard

If we then create a new method (that is, for a scene or shot), we can drag the statement from the clipboard and drop it into that method, as shown in Figure 2-22.

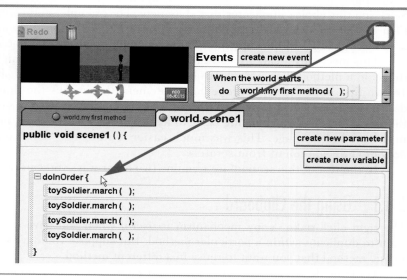

FIGURE 2-22   Dragging a statement from the clipboard

When we drag a statement from the clipboard and drop it in the *editing area*, Alice *copies* the statement from the clipboard. That is, a statement copied to the clipboard remains there until we replace it by dragging another statement onto the clipboard. In this case — where we are *moving* a statement from one method to another — we must then return to the first method and *delete* the original statement; Alice will not delete it for us.

The clipboard holds just one statement, whether it be a **doInOrder**, a **doTogether**, a message to an object, or one of the other Alice statements we will see later. If you find yourself in a situation where you need to store multiple statements, you can tell Alice to display more clipboards by selecting the **Edit -> Preferences** menu choice, selecting the **Seldom Used** tab, and then increasing the number of clipboards as necessary.

The ability to copy a statement to and from the clipboard is one advantage of placing all of a method's statements within a **doInOrder** statement. If for any reason we should later want to copy the method's statements into another method, we can just drag the outer **doInOrder** statement to the clipboard and then drag it from there into the other method. Otherwise, we would have to drag each statement to and from the clipboard individually.

2.3.2   Reusing an Object in a Different World

Writing a good object method takes time and effort. If you develop an object in one world, you may want to reuse it in a different world. For example, if we have spent time writing a method to make a dragon flap its wings — or a soldier to march, or a horse to gallop, or whatever — and we want to reuse that same character with the same behavior in a different world, we do not want to have to redo the work all over again.

Thankfully, Alice lets us reuse an object in different worlds. To do so, follow these steps:

1. In the world containing the original object, right-click it and **rename** it, choosing a new name that describes how it differs from the old object (for example, **marchingSoldier**).

2. Right-click the object again, but this time choose **save object...** Use the **Save Object** dialog box to save the object to your desktop (or anywhere you can find easily).

3. Open the world where you want to reuse the object.

4. Choose **File -> Import...** In the dialog box that appears, navigate to your saved object, select it, and click the **Import** button.

Let's go through these steps using the dragon we modified in Section 2.2.1.

1. First, we give the **dragon** a new name by right-clicking it, choosing **rename**, and then giving it a descriptive name, as shown in Figure 2-23.

FIGURE 2-23   Renaming an object

2. We right-click again, but, as shown in Figure 2-24, this time we choose **save object...** from the menu that appears:

FIGURE 2-24   Saving an object

As shown in Figure 2-25, a **Save Object** dialog box appears, with which we navigate to where we want to save the object (for example, the **Desktop**).

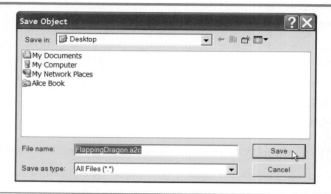

FIGURE 2-25   Saving an object

When we click the **Save** button, Alice saves the object in a special *.a2c* file (*a2c* stands for *a*lice-2.0-*c*lass). In our example, the file will be saved as **FlappingDragon.a2c**.[3]

3. Using Alice's **File** menu, we open the world into which we want to reuse the object. This can be either a new world, or an existing world. We will use a new, snowy world here.

4. With the new world open, we choose **Import...** from the **File** menu, as shown in Figure 2-26.

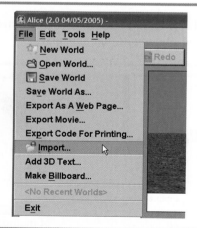

FIGURE 2-26   Importing an object

---

3.   The first letter of a *class* is capitalized, to help distinguish it from an *object*, whose first letter is lowercase.

In the dialog box that appears, we navigate to where we saved the object (for example, the **Desktop**), select the *.a2c* file we saved in Step 2, and click the **Import** button, as shown in Figure 2-27.

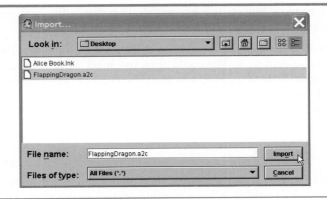

FIGURE 2-27 The import dialog box

Voila! the new world contains a copy of the **flappingDragon**, as shown in Figure 2-28!

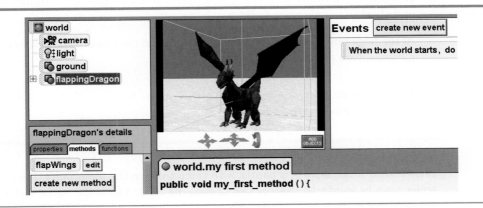

FIGURE 2-28 A reused object

As shown in Figure 2-28, the dragon in this new world includes the **flapWings()** method.

By saving an object from one world, and importing it into another, Alice provides us with a means of reusing the work we invest in building object methods.

2.4   Alice Tip: Using Dummies

As we mentioned earlier, scenes are often divided into shots, with each shot being a piece of a scene filmed with the camera in a different position. We have also seen that Alice places a **camera** object in every world. This raises the question: How do we move the camera from one position to another position within a scene?

Because the **camera** is an Alice object, any of the basic Alice messages from Appendix A can be sent to it. We could thus use a set of simultaneous **move()**, **turn()**, and other motion-related messages to shift the camera between shot methods. However, getting such movements right requires lots of trial and error and gets tedious. Thankfully, Alice provides a better way.

2.4.1   Dummies

The better way is to use a special Alice object called a **dummy**. A dummy is an invisible *marker* in your world that has a position and an orientation. The basic idea is as follows:

1. Manually move the camera (using the controls below the *world window*) until it is in the position and orientation where you want it for a given shot.

2. Drop a dummy at the **camera**'s position. This dummy has the **camera**'s point of view.

3. Rename the dummy something descriptive (for example, the number of the scene and shot).

4. At the beginning of the method for that shot, send the **camera** the **setPointOfView()** message, with the dummy as its target.

Let's illustrate these steps with a new example. Suppose that we have a user story whose second scene begins as follows:

Scene 2: The Wizard and the Trolls.

Shot 1: Wide-angle shot of a castle, with three trolls in the foreground. The leader of the trolls says he wants to destroy the castle. The other two trolls agree. Before they can act, a wizard materializes between them and the castle.

Shot 2: Zoom in: a half-body shot of the wizard. He cries, "YOU SHALL NOT PASS!"

Shot 3: Zoom out: the same wide angle shot as before. The trolls turn to the wizard ...

We can start by creating a new world, and creating empty world methods named **playScene2Shot1()**, **playScene2Shot2()**, **playScene2Shot3()**, and **playScene2()**, with this latter method invoking the first three. We then invoke **playScene2()** from **my_first_method()**, as we did in Section 2.1. We can then add the **castle**, **wizard**, and **trolls** to build the scene, as shown in Figure 2-29.

FIGURE 2-29   The set of "The Wizard and the Trolls"

With the *Add Objects* window still open, we click the **more controls** button, as shown in Figure 2-30.

FIGURE 2-30   The **more controls** button

Among the additional controls this button exposes is the **drop dummy at camera** button, as can be seen in Figure 2-31.

FIGURE 2-31   More controls

When we click this button, Alice adds a **dummy** object — an invisible marker — to the world, with the same position and orientation (point of view) as the **camera**. The first time we click this button, Alice creates a new folder named **Dummy Objects** in the *object tree*, in which all dummies are stored. If we open this folder (Figure 2-32), we can see the **Dummy** object inside it.

FIGURE 2-32   A dummy object

Since the name **Dummy** is not very descriptive, we can right-click on the object, select **rename** from the menu that appears, and rename the dummy **scene2Shot1**, as shown in Figure 2-33.

FIGURE 2-33   A renamed dummy

By doing so, we will know exactly which scene and shot this dummy is for, and not confuse it with the dummies we create for other scenes and shots.

Now that we have a dummy in place for the first shot, the next step is to manually position the **camera** where we want it for the second shot, using the controls beneath the *world window*. Using these controls, we can zoom in until we get a nice half-body shot of the wizard, leaving space above his head for his dialog-balloon to appear. See Figure 2-34.

FIGURE 2-34   A half-body shot of the wizard

When we have the **camera** just where we want it, we again press the **drop dummy at camera** button to drop a second dummy at the **camera**'s current position. As before, we rename it, as shown in Figure 2-35.

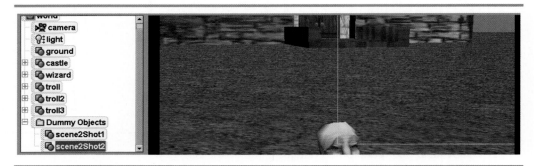

FIGURE 2-35   A second dummy

Since the third shot is back in the camera's original position, we can reuse the **scene2Shot1** dummy for the third shot and avoid creating an additional dummy.

With dummies for all three of the shots, we then click the *Add Objects* window's **DONE** button and turn our attention to programming these shots.

2.4.2   Using **setPointOfView()** to Control the Camera

Now that we have dummies for each of the shots, how do we make use of them? The key is the method *obj*.**setPointOfView(***obj2***)**, which changes the position and orientation of **obj** to that of **obj2**. If we send the message **setPointOfView(***aDummy***)** to the **camera**, then the **camera**'s position and orientation will change to that of *aDummy*!

Back in the *editing area* with the **playScene2Shot1()** method open, we start by dragging a **doInOrder** statement into the method. We then click on the **camera** in the *object tree*, scroll down to the **setPointOfView()** method in the *details area*, and then drag **setPointOfView()** to make it the first statement in the **playScene2Shot1()** method. For its target, we select **Dummy Objects -> scene2Shot1**, as shown in Figure 2-36.

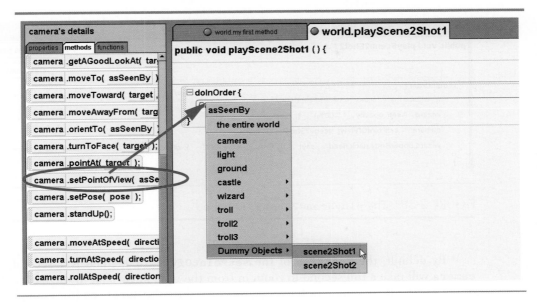

FIGURE 2-36   Setting the **camera**'s point of view to a dummy

When we have chosen **scene2Shot1** as its target, we then set the statement's **duration** to zero (so that the camera moves to this position and orientation instantly). We can then add the rest of the statements for the shot, resulting in a method definition like that shown in Figure 2-37.

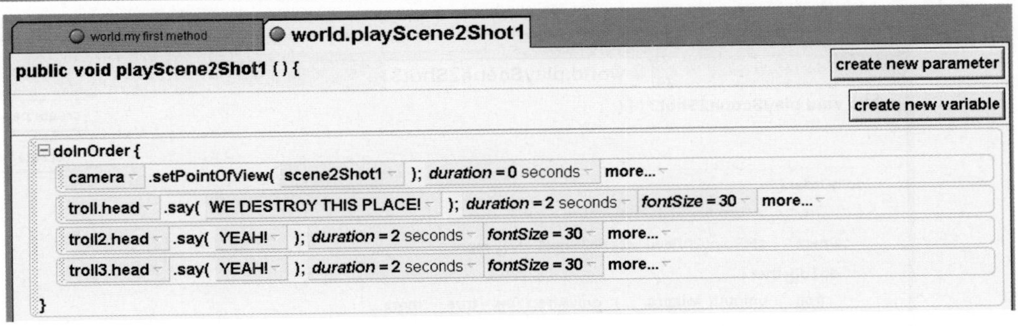

FIGURE 2-37   Using the **setPointOfView()** method with a dummy

We then use the same approach in **playScene2Shot2()** to move the **camera** to the position and orientation of the **scene2Shot2** dummy near the start of that method (Figure 2-38).

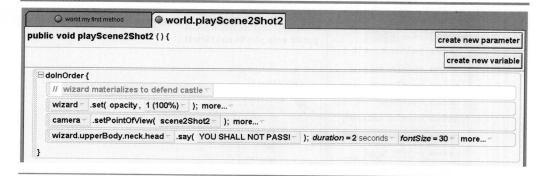

FIGURE 2-38   The `playScene2Shot2()` method

By default, the **duration** of the **setPointOfView()** method is 1 second, so the **camera** will take a full second to zoom in from the wide angle shot to the half-body shot of the wizard. If we want a faster zoom, we can reduce the **duration** (for example, 0 seconds causes an instantaneous cut). If we want a slower zoom, we can set the **duration** to 2 or more seconds.

Note also that to make the **wizard** materialize, the **playScene2Shot2()** method sets his **opacity** property to 1, using the approach described in Section 1.5.1. To make him initially invisible, we manually set his **opacity** to 0 in the *properties* pane.

For the third shot, we use the **setPointOfView()** message to reset the **camera**'s position and orientation back to the wide-angle shot, using the **scene2Shot1** dummy. Figure 2-39 shows the code at this point.

```
world.my first method    ◉ world.playScene2Shot3    ○ world.playScene2
public void playScene2Shot3 ( ) {                                        create new parameter
                                                                         create new variable
  ⊟ doInOrder {
      // The trolls turn towards the wizard...
      camera ▾ .setPointOfView( scene2Shot1 ▾ ); more... ▾
    ⊟ doTogether {
        troll ▾ .pointAt( wizard ▾ ); onlyAffectYaw = true ▾ more... ▾
        troll2 ▾ .pointAt( wizard ▾ ); onlyAffectYaw = true ▾ more... ▾
        troll3 ▾ .pointAt( wizard ▾ ); onlyAffectYaw = true ▾ more... ▾
    }
  }
}
```

FIGURE 2-39   The `playScene2Shot3()` method

Now, when we click the **Play** button, we see the first shot from the wide angle view and see the trolls speak. The camera then zooms in to the half-body view of the wizard, and we see his dialog. The camera then zooms back out to the wide-angle view, and the trolls turn toward the wizard.... What happens next? It's up to you! (See the Chapter 3 problems for one possibility.)

You may have noticed that when we used the **pointAt()** message to make the trolls turn to the wizard, we set that message's **onlyAffectYaw** attribute to **true**. Every object in a 3D world has six attributes that determine its position and orientation in the world. **Yaw** is one of these six attributes, which we examine in the next section.

2.5   Thinking in 3D

Most of us are not used to thinking carefully about moving about in a three-dimensional world, any more than we think carefully about grammar rules when we speak our native language. However, to use Alice well and understand the effects of some of its methods, we need to conclude this chapter by thinking about how objects move in a 3D world.

Every object in a 3D world has the following two properties:

- An object's **position** determines its *location* within the 3D world.
- An object's **orientation** determines *the way it is facing* in the 3D world, determining what is in front of and behind the object, what is to the left and right of the object, and what is above and below the object.

In the rest of this section, we will explore these two properties in detail.

2.5.1   An Object's Position

Pretend that you are a pilot flying the seaplane in Figure 2-40.

FIGURE 2-40   A seaplane

As you fly the seaplane, it can move along any of the arrows shown in Figure 2-41.

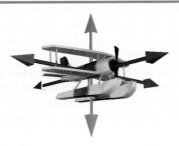

FIGURE 2-41   The seaplane and 3D axes

Each pair of opposite-facing arrows (from the pilot's perspective: *LEFT-RIGHT* [red], *UP-DOWN* [green], *FORWARD-BACKWARD* [blue]) is called an **axis**. Two or more of these arrows are called **axes**.

Every Alice object has its own three axes. For example, from a "downward-looking" angle, we might imagine the three axes of our three-dimensional world as shown in Figure 2-42.

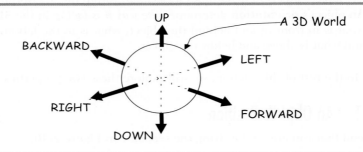

FIGURE 2-42   The three-dimensional world

Once we create a world and start adding objects to it, every object is located somewhere within that 3D world. To determine each object's exact location, we can use the world's axes.

To illustrate, the seaplane's position along the world's *LEFT-RIGHT* axis specifies its location in the world's *width* dimension. We will call this axis the **LR axis**.

Similarly, the seaplane's position along the world's *UP-DOWN* axis specifies its location in the world's *height* dimension. We will call this axis the **UD axis**.

Finally, the seaplane's position along the world's *FORWARD-BACKWARD* axis specifies its location in the world's *depth* dimension. We will call this axis the **FB axis**.

An object's **position** within a three-dimensional world thus consists of three values — *lr*, *ud*, and *fb* — that specify its location measured using the world's three axes.[4]

---

4.   These axes are usually called the X, Y, and Z axes, but we'll use the more descriptive LR, UD, and FB.

Changing Position

To change an object's position, Alice provides a method named **move()** (see Appendix A). When we drop Alice's **move()** method into the *editing area*, Alice displays a menu of the directions the object may move, shown in Figure 2-43.

FIGURE 2-43 The directions an object may move

If you compare Figure 2-41 and Figure 2-43, you'll see that Alice's **move()** message allows an object to move along any of that object's three axes:

- Moving **LEFT** or **RIGHT** changes the object's location along its LR-axis.
- Moving **UP** or **DOWN** changes the object's location along its UD-axis.
- Moving **FORWARD** or **BACKWARD** changes its location along its FB-axis.

Alice's **move()** message thus changes the *position* of the object to which the message is sent with respect to the world's axes, but the directional values that we specify for the movement (**LEFT**, **RIGHT**, **UP**, **DOWN**, **FORWARD**, and **BACKWARD**) are given with respect to *that object's axes*, not the world's axes.

2.5.2 An Object's Orientation

When an object moves, its axes move with it. For example, if we send the seaplane of Figure 2-41 the message **turn(RIGHT, 0.25)**, the picture would change to that shown in Figure 2-44.

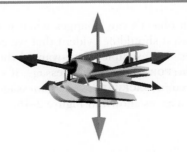

FIGURE 2-44 The seaplane turned 1/4 revolution right

If we now send the turned seaplane a message to **move(FORWARD, ...)**, the seaplane will move forward according to the new direction its FB axis points.

Yaw

If you compare the axes in Figure 2-41 and Figure 2-44 carefully, you'll see that a **turn(RIGHT, 0.25)** message causes the seaplane to *rotate* about its UD-axis. A **turn(LEFT, 0.25)** message causes a rotation about the same axis, but in the opposite direction. If we were to position ourselves "above" the plane's UD-axis and look down, we might visualize the effects of such **turn()** messages as shown in Figure 2-45.

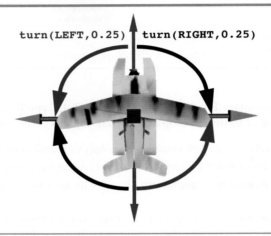

turn(LEFT,0.25)   turn(RIGHT,0.25)

FIGURE 2-45   Changing yaw: turning left or right

In 3D terminology, an object's **yaw** is how much it has rotated about its UD axis from its original position. For example, when you shake your head "no," you are changing your head's yaw. Alice's **turn(LEFT, ...)** and **turn(RIGHT, ...)** messages change an object's yaw.

Pitch

We just saw that an object's yaw changes when it rotates around its UD axis. Since an object has three axes, it should be evident that we could also rotate an object around one of its other two axes. For example, if we wanted the seaplane to dive toward the sea, we could send it a **turn(FORWARD, ...)** message; if we wanted it to climb toward the sun, we could send it a **turn(BACKWARD, ...)** message. These messages cause an object to rotate about its LR-axis, as shown in Figure 2-46.

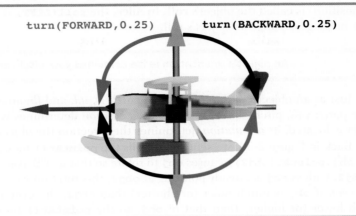

FIGURE 2-46 Turning forward or backward

An object's **pitch** is how much it has rotated about its LR axis from its original position. For example, when you shake your head "yes," you change your head's pitch. In Alice, a **turn(FORWARD, ...)** or **turn(BACKWARD, ...)** message changes an object's pitch.

Roll

An object can also rotate around its FB axis. For example, if we were to send the seaplane the **roll(LEFT, 0.25)** or **roll(RIGHT, 0.25)** message, it would rotate as shown in Figure 2-47.

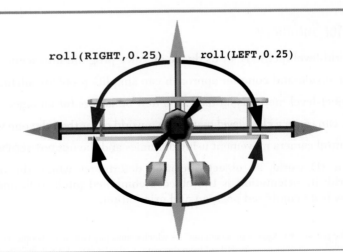

FIGURE 2-47 Rolling left or right

The amount by which an object has rotated about its FB axis (compared to its original position) is called the object's **roll**. In Alice, the `roll(LEFT, ...)` and `roll(RIGHT, ...)` messages change an object's roll.

> **An object's *orientation* is its combined yaw, pitch, and roll.**

Just as an object's *position* has three parts: *lr*, *ud*, and *fb*; an object's *orientation* has three parts: yaw, pitch, and roll. An object's *position* determines where in the world that object is located; its *orientation* determines the direction the object is facing.

Back in Figure 2-39, we sent three trolls the `pointAt()` message. By default, a message `obj.pointAt(obj2);` causes `obj` to rotate so that its FB axis is pointing at the *center* of `obj2`. Unless `obj` is already pointing at `obj2`, this rotation will change the yaw of `obj`. However, if `obj` is much taller (or shorter) than `obj2`, then the center of `obj2` will be much lower (or higher) than that of `obj`, so the `pointAt()` message will also change `obj`'s pitch. This would cause the trolls to lean forward at an unnatural angle. By setting the message's `onlyAffectYaw` attribute to `true`, we ensured that each troll's pitch remained unchanged.

The message `obj.turnToFace(obj2);` is a shorthand for `obj.pointAt(obj2)` with `onlyAffectYaw=true`, and we will use it in future examples.

2.5.3   Point of View

In Alice, an object's combined position and orientation are called that object's **point of view**. An object's point of view thus consists of six values: [(*lr*, *ud*, *fb*), (yaw, pitch, roll)]. Alice's `move()`, `turn()`, and `roll()` messages let you change any of these six values for an object, giving Alice objects *six degrees of freedom*.[5] Alice's `setPointOfView()` message (see Appendix A) lets you set an object's point of view.

2.6   Chapter Summary

❏ World-level methods let us divide an Alice program into scenes and shots.

❏ The divide-and-conquer approach can simplify problem solving.

❏ Object-level methods let us define new behaviors for an object.

❏ We can reuse a class-level method in a world other than the one where we defined it.

❏ Control camera movement using dummies and the `setPointOfView()` message.

❏ In a 3D world, an object's position determines where the object is located in the world; its orientation is the object's combined pitch, roll, and yaw; and its point of view is its combined position and orientation.

---

5.   The phrase "six degrees of separation" — which claims any two living people are connected by a chain of six or fewer acquaintances — is derived from this phrase "six degrees of freedom." The "Six Degrees of Kevin Bacon" game — that claims that the actor Kevin Bacon and any other actor are linked by a chain of six or fewer film co-stars — is further derived from "six degrees of separation." See **www.cs.virginia.edu/oracle/**.

2.6.1 Key Terms

axis	position
comment	reusable method
divide and conquer	roll
dummy	scene
object method	shot
orientation	world method
pitch	yaw
point of view	

Programming Projects

2.1 Revisit the programs you wrote for Chapter 1. If any of them require scrolling to view all of their statements, rewrite them using divide-and-conquer and world-level methods whose statements can be viewed without scrolling.

2.2 The director Sergio Leone was famous for the extreme closeups he used of gunfighters' eyes in "western" movies like *For a Fistful of Dollars*; *The Good, the Bad, and the Ugly*; and *Once Upon a Time in the West*. Watch one of these films; then modify the **playScene2()** method we wrote in Section 2.4, using Leone's camera techniques to heighten the drama of the wizard's confrontation with the trolls.

2.3 Build an undersea world containing a **goldfish**. Build a **swim()** method for the **goldfish** that makes it swim forward one meter in a realistic fashion. Add a **shark** to your world, and build a similar **swim()** method for it. Build a program containing a scene in which the **shark** chases the **goldfish**, and the **goldfish** swims to its giant cousin goldfish that chases the **shark** away. (Hint: Make the giant cousin goldfish by Saving and Importing your modified **goldfish**.)

2.4 Choose a hopping animal from the Alice Gallery (for example, a frog, a bunny, etc.). Write a **hop()** method that makes it hop in a realistic fashion. Add a building to your world, then write a program that uses your **hop()** method to make the animal hop around the building. Write your program using divide-and-conquer so that **my_first_method()** contains an **Inorder** control and no more than four statements.

2.5 Build a world containing a flying vehicle (for example, a biplane, a helicopter, etc.). Build a class-level **loopDeeLoop()** method for your flying vehicle that makes it move in a vertical loop. Using the Torus class (under Shapes), build a world containing a giant arch. Then write a program in which your flying vehicle does a **loopDeeLoop()** through the arch.

2.6 *Boom, Boom, Ain't It Great To Be Crazy* is a silly song with the lyrics on the next page. Create an Alice program containing a character who sings this song. Use divide-and-conquer to write your program as efficiently as possible.

A horse and a flea and three blind mice sat on a curbstone shooting dice. The horse he slipped and fell on the flea. "Whoops," said the flea, "there's a horse on me." Boom, boom, ain't it great to be crazy? Boom, boom, ain't it great to be crazy? Giddy and foolish, the whole day through, boom, boom, ain't it great to be crazy?	Way down south where bananas grow, a flea stepped on an elephant's toe. The elephant cried, with tears in his eyes, "Why don't you pick on someone your size." Boom, boom, ain't it great to be crazy? Boom, boom, ain't it great to be crazy? Giddy and foolish, the whole day through, boom, boom, ain't it great to be crazy?
Way up north where there's ice and snow, there lived a penguin whose name was Joe. He got so tired of black and white, he wore pink pants to the dance last night. Boom, boom, ain't it great to be crazy? Boom, boom, ain't it great to be crazy? Giddy and foolish, the whole day through, boom, boom, ain't it great to be crazy?	

2.7 Using appropriately colored **Shapes** from the Alice Gallery, build a checker-board. Then choose an object from the Gallery to serve as a checker. Build class-level methods named **moveLeft()**, **moveRight()**, **jumpLeft()**, and **jumpRight()** for the character. Then make copies of the object for the remaining checkers. Build a program that simulates the opening moves of a game of checkers, using your board and checkers.

2.8 Using the **heBuilder** or **sheBuilder** (or any of the other persons with enough detail in the Alice Gallery), build a person and add him or her to your world. Using your person, build an aerobic exercise video in which the person leads the user through an exercise routine. Use world- and/or class-level methods in your program, as appropriate.

2.9 In Section 2.4, we developed a program consisting of Scene 2, in which a wizard faces off against three trolls. Create your own Scene 1 and Scene 3 for this program to show what happened before and after the scene we developed.

2.10 Write an original story consisting of at least two characters, three scenes, and dummies to position your characters in the different scenes. Each scene should have multiple shots. Use world- and class-level methods to create your story efficiently.

Chapter 3
Variables and Functions

The first step towards wisdom is calling things by their right names.

OLD CHINESE PROVERB

Figuratively speaking, killing two birds with one stone may be good, but killing three, four, or even more birds with one stone is even better.

V. OREHCK III

Stop! Who would cross the Bridge of Death must answer me these questions three, ere the other side he see.

THE BRIDGEKEEPER (TERRY GILLIAM), IN *MONTY PYTHON AND THE HOLY GRAIL*

Objectives
Upon completion of this chapter, you should be able to:

- ❏ Use variables to store values for use later in a method
- ❏ Use a variable to store the value of an arithmetic expression
- ❏ Use a variable to store the value produced by a function
- ❏ Use parameters to write methods that are more broadly useful
- ❏ Define and access property variables
- ❏ Use the **vehicle** property to synchronize the movements of two objects
- ❏ Create functions — messages that return a value to their sender

In Chapter 2, we saw how to define world and object methods. In this chapter, we turn our attention to **variables**, the use of which can make it easier to define methods. In computer programming, *a variable is a name that refers to a piece of the program's memory, in which a value can be stored, retrieved, and changed.*

Alice provides several different kinds of variables that we will examine in this chapter. The first kind is the **method variable**, which lets us store a value within a method for later use. The second kind is the **parameter**, which lets us write methods that are more broadly useful. These first two kinds of variables are created using the two buttons that appear on the right edge of every Alice method, as shown in Figure 3-1.

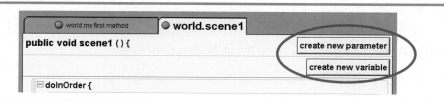

FIGURE 3-1   The buttons to create variables and parameters

The third and final kind of variable is the **object variable** or **property variable**, which lets us store a property of an object. Object variables are created using the `create new variable` button under the *properties* pane of the *details area*.

In this chapter, we'll see how to create and use all three kinds of variables.

3.1   Method Variables

Method variables are names defined within a method that refer to program memory in which values can be stored. When we click the `create new variable` button within a method, Alice asks us what we want to *name* the variable, the *type* of information we want to store in it, and its initial value. When we have told it these things, Alice reserves as much program memory as is needed for that type of information, and associates the name with that memory, which is called **defining** the variable. Method variables are often called **local variables**, because they can only be accessed from within the method in which they are defined — they are *local* to it.

One common use of method variables is to compute and store values that will be used later, especially values that will be used more than once. Another common use is to store values that the user enters. In the rest of this section, we present these two uses.

3.1.1   Example 1: Storing a Computed Value

Suppose that in Scene 2 of a story, a girl and a horse are positioned as seen in Figure 3-2.

FIGURE 3-2 Girl and horse: initial positions

Suppose our scene calls for the girl to move toward the horse and stop when she is directly in front of it. We can send the girl the **move()** message to move her toward the horse, but how far should we ask her to move? One way would be to use trial-and-error to find a suitable value. But trial-and-error is tedious, especially when there is a better way. The better way is to:

1. Define a variable to store the distance from the girl to the horse.

2. Ask the girl how far she is from the horse, and store her reply in the variable.

3. Use that variable in the **move()** message to get her to move the right distance.

To accomplish the first step, we just click the **create new variable** button we saw in Figure 3-1. To get the information it needs to define the variable, Alice pops up a **Create New Local Variable** dialog box in which we can enter the variable's **name**, **type**, and **initial value**.

A variable's name should be a noun that describes the value it stores.

For example, this variable is storing the distance from the girl to the horse, so we will **name** it **distanceToHorse**. Like method names, variable names always use lower-case letters, capitalizing the first letter of words after the first word.

A variable's **type** describes the kind of value we intend to store in it. Alice provides four basic types:

- **Number**, for storing numeric values (for example, **-3**, **-1.5**, **0**, **1**, **3.14159**, and so on)
- **Boolean**, for storing logical (**true** or **false**) values
- **Object**, for storing references to Alice objects (for example, **troll**, **wizard**, **castle**, and so on)
- **Other**, for storing things like **String**s, **Color**s, **Sound**s, and other kinds of values

Since the distance from the girl to the horse is a numerical value, **Number** is the appropriate type for this variable.

As its name suggests, the **initial value** is the value the variable will contain when the method begins. We will usually use a value like 0 or 1, as shown in Figure 3-3.

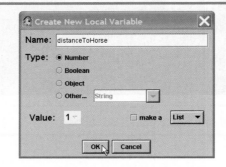

FIGURE 3-3   The **Create New Local Variable** dialog box

When we click the **OK** button, Alice defines a new variable in the method, in the space above the *editing area*, as shown in Figure 3-4.

FIGURE 3-4   The **distanceToHorse** variable

Next, we want to ask the girl how far she is from the horse, and set the value of this variable to her response. In Alice, it is easiest to do these steps in reverse order.

Setting the value of a variable is done in a way similar to how we set the value of a property back in Chapter 1: we drag its definition into the *editing area*, and Alice generates a menu of potential values, as shown in Figure 3-5.

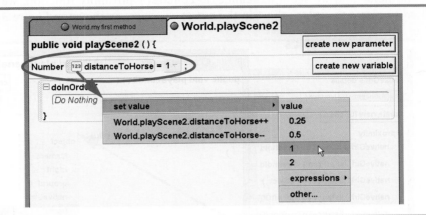

FIGURE 3-5   Setting a variable's value (part I)

If we wished to add 1 to **distanceToHorse**, we would choose **World.playScene2.distanceToHorse++** from the menu (**++** is called the **increment operator**). If we wanted to subtract 1 from its value, we would choose **World.playScene2.distanceToHorse--** (**--** is called the **decrement operator**). Since we want to *set* the variable's value, we choose the **set value** choice.

The value to which we want to set **distanceToHorse** is the result of asking the girl how far she is from the horse. Unfortunately, this value is not present in the menu. In this situation, we can choose any value from the menu to act as a **placeholder** for the function. (In Figure 3-5, we are choosing **1** as the placeholder.) The result is the **set()** statement shown in Figure 3-6.

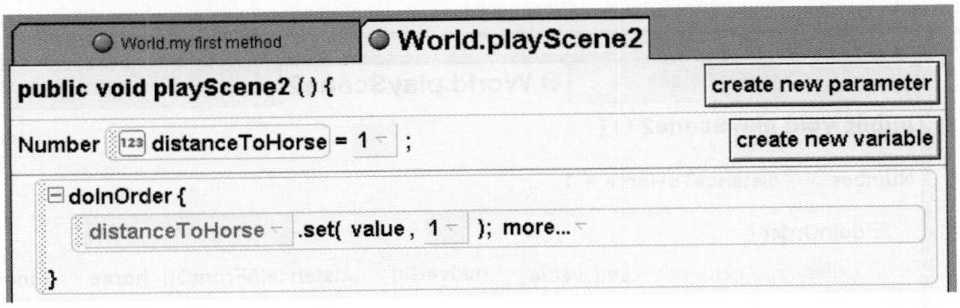

FIGURE 3-6   Setting a variable's value using a placeholder

With a **set()** statement in place, we are ready to ask the girl how far she is from the horse. To do so, we make sure we have the girl selected in the *object tree*, and then click the *functions* tab in the *details area*. "How far are you from the horse?" is a proximity question, so we look in the proximity section of the functions. Since the girl is in front of the horse and we see a **distanceInFrontOf()** proximity function, we drag it into the *editing area* to replace the **1** in the **set()** message, as shown in Figure 3-7.

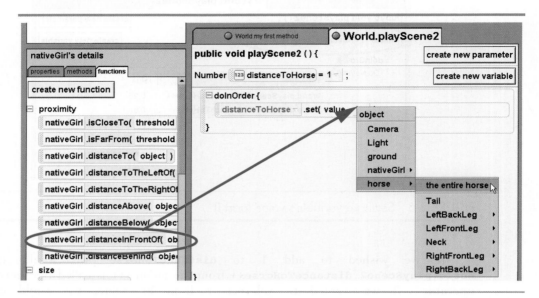

FIGURE 3-7   Setting a variable's value to a function's answer

When we drag the function onto the placeholder (**1**), the box around the **1** turns green, indicating we can drop it. Alice then asks us for the object whose distance we want to compute, and displays a menu of the available options. When we select **horse -> the entire horse** (see Figure 3-7), Alice replaces the placeholder **1** with the function, as can be seen in Figure 3-8.

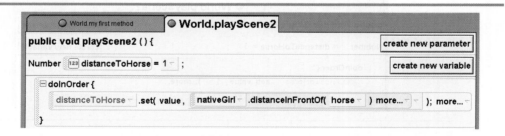

FIGURE 3-8   Setting a variable's value (part III)

You may be wondering why we used the **distanceInFrontOf()** function instead of the **distanceTo()** function. The reason is that the **distanceTo()** function returns the distance from the *center* of one object to the *center* of the other object. If we moved the girl that far, she and the horse would occupy the same space, which looks really weird! (Try it and see.) By contrast, the other proximity methods all measure from the *outer edge* of one object's bounding box to the *outer edge* of the other object's bounding box.

Once we have a variable containing the distance from the girl to the front of the horse, we can use it in the **move()** message. When we drag the **move()** message into the *editing area*, we can specify that we want the girl to move forward the value of the variable by selecting **expressions -> distanceToHorse**. Alice's **expressions** menu usually contains a list of all the variables (and parameters, and functions we define) that are available for use within the current method. Figure 3-9 illustrates this.

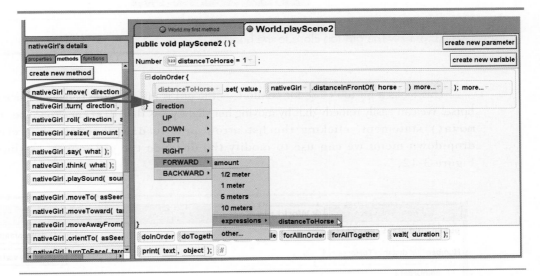

FIGURE 3-9   Using a variable's value in a message (part I)

Figure 3-10 shows the statement Alice generates when we select **distanceToHorse**.

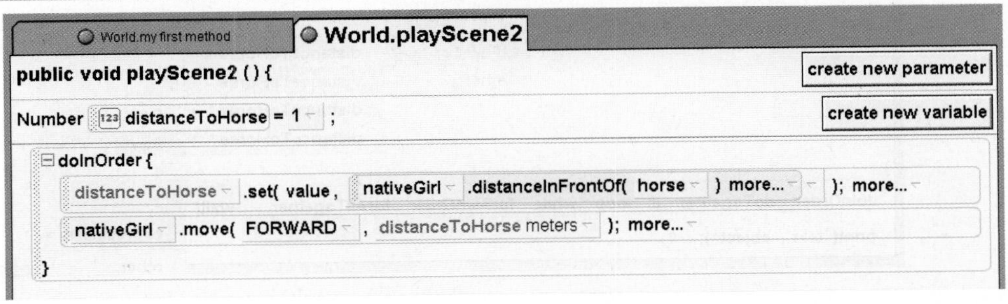

FIGURE 3-10   Using a variable's value in a message (part II)

When we play this method, we get the result shown in Figure 3-11.

FIGURE 3-11   The girl too close to the horse

This looks a bit too close for comfort — the girl is invading the personal space of the horse! We can easily remedy that by moving her slightly less than **distanceToHorse**. In the **move()** statement, clicking the list arrow next to **distanceToHorse** reveals a drop-down menu we can use to modify the distance the girl moves, as shown in Figure 3-12.

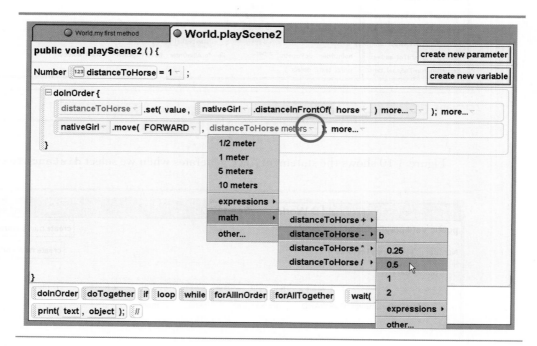

FIGURE 3-12   Adjusting a value in a message

As can be seen in Figure 3-12, Alice's **math** menu choice provides the basic arithmetic calculations of addition, subtraction, multiplication, and division. Selecting **distanceToHorse – 0.5** produces the statement shown in Figure 3-13.

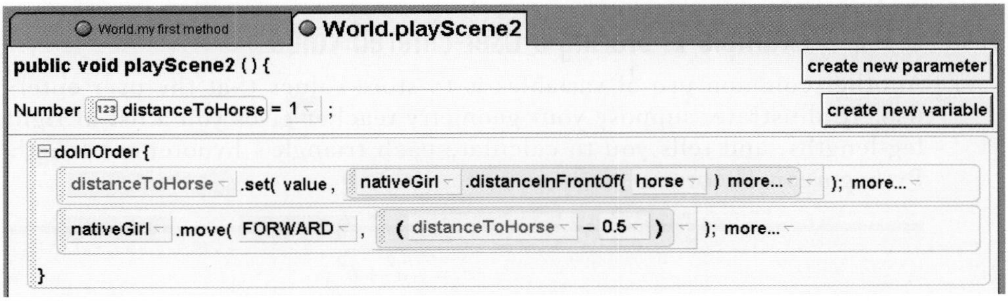

FIGURE 3-13   Decreasing how far she moves

Now, when we play the method, the girl stops a comfortable distance from the horse, as shown in Figure 3-14.

FIGURE 3-14   Stopping a comfortable distance from the horse

Using functions and variables has a major advantage over trial-and-error: it yields the right behavior even if we reposition the girl or the horse! If we had used trial-and-error to find the exact distance to move the girl, and then later repositioned the girl or horse, the value we had found using trial-and-error would no longer be correct, so we would have to fix it (either with another round of trial-and-error, or by getting smart and using a variable and a function).

Once you get used to using variables and functions, they often provide a much better way to make a character move a distance relative to another object.

3.1.2   Example 2: Storing a User-Entered Value

Another common use of variables is to store values that the user enters, for later use. To illustrate, suppose your geometry teacher gives you a list of right triangles' leg-lengths, and tells you to calculate each triangle's hypotenuse length using the Pythagorean Theorem:

$$c = \sqrt{a^2 + b^2}$$

We could either get out our calculators and grind through the list, or we could write an Alice program to help us. Which sounds like more fun? (Writing an Alice program, of course!)

As always, we start with a user story. We might write something like this:

Scene: There is a girl on the screen. She says, "I can calculate hypotenuse-lengths in my head!" Then she says, "Give me the lengths of the two edges of a right triangle..." A dialog box appears, prompting us for the first edge length. When we enter it, a second dialog box appears, prompting us for the second edge length. When we enter it, the girl says, "The hypotenuse-length is X." (Where X is the correct answer.)

The nouns in our story include girl, hypotenuse-length, first edge length, second edge length, and two dialog boxes. For the girl, we will use the **skaterGirl** from the Alice Gallery. For the hypotenuse-length, first edge length, and second edge length, we will create **Number** variables named **hypotenuse**, **edge1**, and **edge2**, respectively. For the dialog boxes, Alice provides a function that will build and display dialog objects for us (see below).

Since the scene has just one object (girl), we will create a **skaterGirl** object method named **computeHypotenuse()** to animate her with the desired behavior. Within this method, we declare the three **Number** variables, and then begin programming the desired behavior. Using what we have seen so far, we can get to the point shown in Figure 3-15:

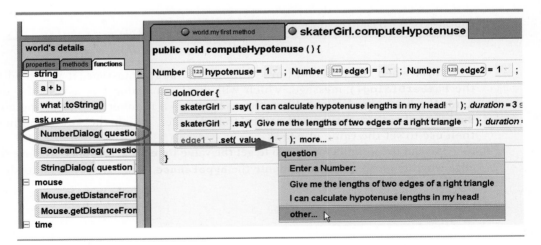

FIGURE 3-15   Getting started

But how do we generate a dialog box to set the value of **edge1**? The trick is to look in the **World**'s functions! The **World**'s *functions* pane provides an entirely different set of function-messages from those we can send to an object. If we scroll down a bit, we find the **NumberDialog** function that we can drag over to replace the **1** placeholder, as we saw in Figure 3-7. When we drop it on the **1**, Alice displays a menu of questions we can have the dialog box ask, as shown in Figure 3-16.

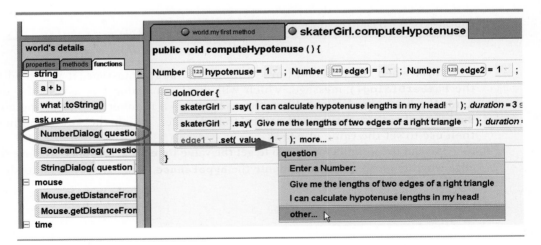

FIGURE 3-16   Dragging a dialog function

In this case, we want the dialog box to ask for the length of one edge of a right triangle, so we choose **other...** Alice then lets us enter the prompt to be displayed, as shown in Figure 3-17.

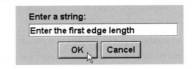

FIGURE 3-17   Customizing a dialog box's prompt message

This yields the **set()** message shown at the bottom of Figure 3-18.

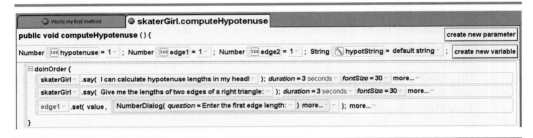

FIGURE 3-18   Setting a variable to a dialog box's result

Now, when the program flows through the **set()** message, it will send **World** the **NumberDialog()** message, which will display a dialog box asking the user to enter the first edge length. When the user enters a number in that dialog box, the **NumberDialog()** function will return that number, which the **set()** method will then use to set the value of **edge1**.

We can use a similar approach to get the value for **edge2**, and once we have the two edge lengths, we are ready to compute the **hypotenuse** value. We get as far as shown in Figure 3-19 before we hit a snag.

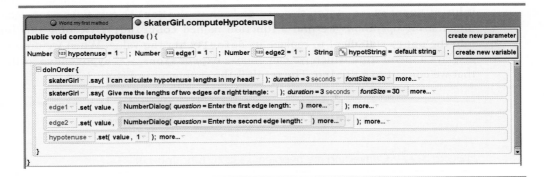

FIGURE 3-19   How to compute the hypotenuse

Looking back at the Pythagorean Theorem, we see that we need the square root function. Like the dialog box function, square root is available in the **World**'s *functions* pane, under the *advanced math* category. We thus drag and drop **Math.sqrt()** to replace the placeholder **1** in the **set()** message. From there, we can use the list arrow, the **expressions** menu choice, and the **math** menu choice several times to build the **set()** statement shown in Figure 3-20.

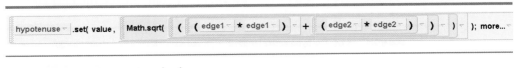

FIGURE 3-20   Computing the hypotenuse

Now that we have the **hypotenuse** calculated, how do we get the **skaterGirl** to say it? We can easily get her to say **"The hypotenuse length is "**, but how do we get her to say the value of **hypotenuse** at the same time? The answer has to do with *types*. As you know, the type of hypotenuse is **Number**. The type of the value we send with the **say()** message must be a **String**. Resolving this dilemma takes several steps.

The first step is to declare a new variable that will contain the value of **hypotenuse**, converted to a **String**. We'll call it **hypotString**, make its type **String**, and leave its initial value as **<None>**. We can then set its value to a placeholder value, like any other variable.

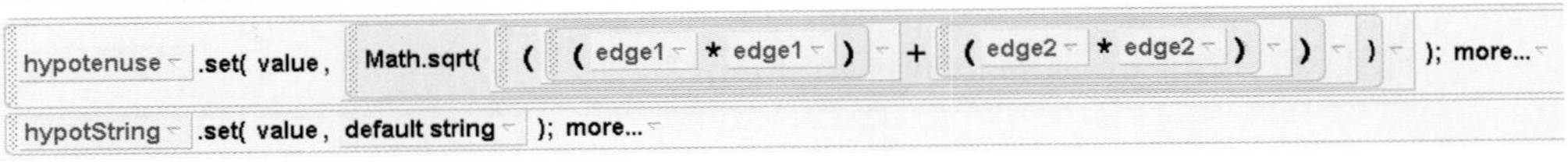

FIGURE 3-21   Converting the hypotenuse to a string (part I)

The next step is to use this variable to store a **String** representation of the (**Number**) value of **hypotenuse**. To do this, we go back to the **World**'s *functions* pane again, and under *string operations* we find a function named **toString()**. We drag this function into the **set()** statement to replace its **default string** value. When we drop it, Alice displays a menu from which we can choose **expressions -> hypotenuse** as the thing that we convert to a **String**. The result is the statement in Figure 3-22.

hypotString ▾ .set(value ,   hypotenuse ▾ .toString() ▾   ); more... ▾

FIGURE 3-22   Converting the hypotenuse to a string (part II)

We now have a **String** version of the **hypotenuse**. The next step in the algorithm is for the **skaterGirl** to say "The hypotenuse length is X" where X is **hypotString**. To make this happen, we need a way to combine **"The hypotenuse is "** with **hypotString**. In programming, combining two strings **a** and **b** into a single string **ab** is called **concatenating** the strings, and for **String** values, the + sign is called the **concatenation operator**. In a concatenation **a + b**, the order of **a** and **b** matters: **"en"** + **"list"** makes **"enlist"**, but **"list"** + **"en"** makes **"listen"**.

We can start by having **skaterGirl** say the first part of what we want her to say: **"The hypotenuse length is "**. It doesn't show up well in Figure 3-23, but we must take care to leave a space after the word **is**, to separate it from the next part.

skaterGirl ▾ .say(The hypotenuse length is ▾); *duration* = **5** seconds ▾ *fontSize* = **30** ▾ more... ▾

FIGURE 3-23   Converting the hypotenuse to a string (part III)

To make her also say the second part, we make a final trip to the **World**'s *functions* pane, from which we drag the other **String** function (**a+b**) onto **"The hypotenuse length is "** in the **set()** statement. When we drop the **a+b** function onto **"The hypotenuse length is "** in Figure 3-23, Alice takes the **String** that's there (**"The hypotenuse length is "**) as its **a** value. Alice then displays the menu we have seen before, from which we can select **expressions -> hypotString** as the (**a+b**) function's **b** value, as shown in Figure 3-24.

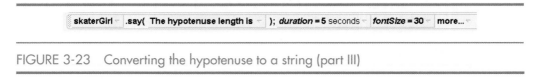

skaterGirl ▾ .say(The hypotenuse length is ▾ + hypotString ▾   ▾); *duration* = **5** seconds ▾ *fontSize* = **30** ▾ more... ▾

FIGURE 3-24   Concatenating two strings

Since that is the last step, the method is done! The complete method is shown in Figure 3-25.

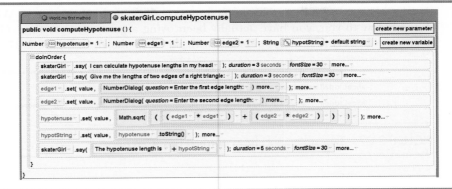

FIGURE 3-25   The `computeHypotenuse()` method (final version)

We then send **skaterGirl** the **computeHypotenuse()** message in **my_first_method()** to finish the program.

To test our work, we enter commonly known values. Figure 3-26 shows the result after we have entered edge lengths of 3 and 4 (the corresponding hypotenuse length is 5).

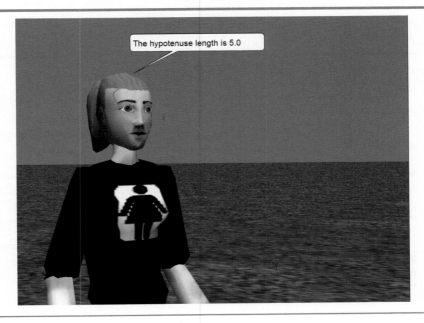

FIGURE 3-26   Testing `computeHypotenuse()`

Variables thus provide a convenient way to store values for later use in a program.

3.2   Parameters

A value that we pass to an object via a message is called an **argument**. While the word may be new to you, you have actually been using arguments ever since Chapter 1. For example, our very first program began with the code shown in Figure 3-27.

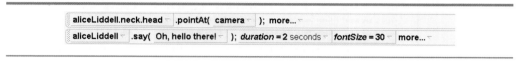

FIGURE 3-27   Two statements from our first program

In the first statement, **camera** is an argument being passed to **aliceLiddell.neck.head** — the *value* at which **aliceLiddell.neck.head** should point. Each of the statements in Figure 3-27 has a single argument: **camera** (an **Object**) in the first statement, and **Oh, hello there!** (a **String**) in the second statement. Other methods we have seen require us to pass multiple arguments, as shown in Figure 3-28.

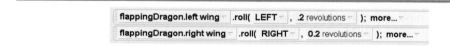

FIGURE 3-28   The **roll()** message requires two arguments

Here, we see that the **roll()** message requires two arguments: the *direction* the object is to roll, and the *amount* it is to roll.

When you send an object a message accompanied by an argument, that argument must be stored somewhere so that the receiving object can access it.

A parameter is a variable that stores an argument, so that the receiver of the message can access it!

Thus, the **pointAt()** and **say()** methods each have a single parameter, while the **roll()** method has two parameters. There is no limit to the number of parameters a method can have.

To make all of this a bit more concrete, let's see some examples.

3.2.1 Example 1: Old MacDonald Had A Farm

Suppose we have a user story containing a scene in which a scarecrow is supposed to sing the song "Old MacDonald," one line at a time. Some of the lyrics to this song are below:

Old MacDonald had a farm, E-I-E-I-O. And on this farm he had a cow, E-I-E-I-O. With a moo-moo here, and a moo-moo there, here a moo, there a moo, everywhere a moo-moo. Old MacDonald had a farm, E-I-E-I-O.	Old MacDonald had a farm, E-I-E-I-O. And on this farm he had a duck, E-I-E-I-O. With a quack-quack here, and a quack-quack there, here a quack, there a quack, everywhere a quack-quack. Old MacDonald had a farm, E-I-E-I-O.
Old MacDonald had a farm, E-I-E-I-O. And on this farm he had a horse, E-I-E-I-O. With a neigh-neigh here, and a neigh-neigh there, here a neigh, there a neigh, everywhere a neigh-neigh. Old MacDonald had a farm, E-I-E-I-O.	Old MacDonald had a farm, E-I-E-I-O. And on this farm he had a dog, E-I-E-I-O. With a ruff-ruff here, and a ruff-ruff there, here a ruff, there a ruff, everywhere a ruff-ruff. Old MacDonald had a farm, E-I-E-I-O.

Subsequent verses introduce other farm animals (for example, chicken, cat, pig, etc.). For now, we will just have the character sing these four verses.

Clearly, we *could* use divide-and-conquer to have the scarecrow sing four verses; in each verse we send the scarecrow five **say()** messages. For example, **singVerse1()** would contain statements like these:

```
scarecrow.say("Old MacDonald had a farm, E-I-E-I-O.");
scarecrow.say("And on this farm he had a cow, E-I-E-I-O.");
scarecrow.say("With a moo-moo here and a moo-moo there,");
scarecrow.say("here a moo, there a moo, everywhere a moo-moo.");
scarecrow.say("Old MacDonald had a farm, E-I-E-I-O.");
```

However, this approach has several disadvantages. One is that if later we want to add a fifth verse, then we must write a new method, containing five more **say()** messages, and add it to the program. With this approach, every new verse we want the scarecrow to sing will require a new method containing five more statements. This seems like a lot of repetitive work.

A related disadvantage of this approach is that each verse-method we write is identical, except for (1) the animal, and (2) the noise it makes.

> **Whenever you find yourself programming the same thing more than once, there is usually a better way to write the program.**

In this case, the better way is to write a single "generic" **singVerse()** method, to which we can pass a given animal and its noise as arguments. That is, we want a message like this:

```
scarecrow.singVerse("cow", "moo");
```

to make the scarecrow sing the first verse; a message like this:

```
scarecrow.singVerse("horse", "neigh");
```

to make him sing the second verse, and so on.

The trick to making this happen is to build a method with a generic *animal* parameter to store whatever animal we want to pass, and a generic *noise* parameter to store the noise it makes. The statements of this method then contain the lyrics that are common to each verse, but using the *animal* parameter in place of the specific cow, duck, horse, or dog; and using the *noise* parameter in place of the specific moo, quack, neigh, or ruff.

Assuming we have created a world containing a **scarecrow** (from Alice's Web Gallery) and whatever other farm-related objects we desire, we can start by creating a new **scarecrow** method named **singVerse()**. With this method open, we click the **create new parameter** button we saw back in Figure 3-1. When clicked, this button generates a **Create New Parameter** dialog box similar to the **Create New Local Variable** dialog box we saw in Figure 3-3. As in that dialog box, we can specify the *name* of the parameter and its *type*. When we click this dialog box's **OK** button, it defines a new parameter with the given *name* and *type* between the method's parentheses. In Figure 3-29, we have used this button to create the **animal** and **noise** parameters.

FIGURE 3-29   Parameters for animal and noise

With the parameters defined, we can proceed to add statements to the method to make the scarecrow sing a verse. Like a variable, a parameter's name appears in the **expressions** menu choice that appears when we drag and drop a statement into the method. Figure 3-30 shows one way we might define the **singVerse()** method.

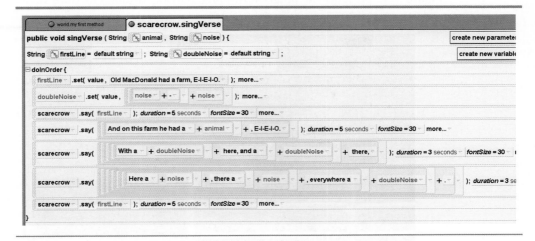

FIGURE 3-30 The `singVerse()` method

Recognizing that the first and last lines are the same, we defined a variable named **firstLine** to store those lines, so that we need not write them twice. Also, seeing that a verse uses the string *noise-noise* three times, we defined a variable named **doubleNoise**, and defined its value as **noise + "-" + noise**, using the string concatenation operator (+) we saw in the last section. In fact, we used the concatenation operator *14 times* in building this method, most often in the statements in which the scarecrow sings the 3rd and 4th lines of the verse.

Given this method, we can now define a **singOldMacDonald()** method quite simply (Figure 3-31).

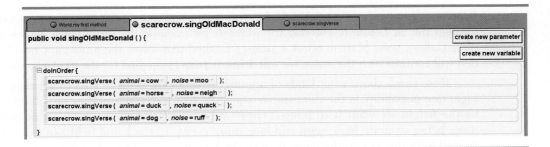

FIGURE 3-31 The `singOldMacDonald()` method

Figure 3-32 presents the program running, partway through its third verse.

FIGURE 3-32   Testing `singOldMacDonald()`

If we should subsequently decide to add a new verse, doing so is as easy as sending the **scarecrow** another **singVerse()** message, with the desired *animal* and *noise* arguments.

3.2.2   Example 2: Jumping Fish!

Suppose we have a user story in which a fish jumps out of the water, tracing a graceful arc through the air before re-entering the water. If we examine the various fish classes in the Alice Gallery, none of them offers a **jump()** method that solves the problem. Choosing one that will contrast with the water, we will define a **jump()** method for the **Pinkminnow** class.

If we think about what kinds of arguments we might want to pass to a **jump()** message, one possibility is the *distance* we want the fish to jump. Another possibility would be the *height* we want it to jump. (These are very different behaviors, as indicated by there being separate *high jump* and *long jump* events in track and field.) In this section, we will have the fish do the equivalent of the long jump, and pass the *distance* we want it to jump.

If we think through the behavior this method should provide, we might sketch it as the sequence of steps shown in Figure 3-33.

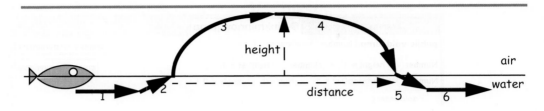

FIGURE 3-33   Sketching a fish's jumping behavior

We can write out these steps as an algorithm as follows:

> 1 fish swims forward a starting distance (to get its speed up)
> 2 fish angles upward
> 3 fish moves upward the height and half the distance, angling upward
> 4 fish moves downward the height and forward half the distance, angling downward
> 5 fish angles upward (levels off)
> 6 fish swims forward a stopping distance (coasting to a stop)

If we consider how an animal jumps, when an animal jumps a short distance, it doesn't spring very high; but if it jumps a longer distance, it springs higher. The height and distance of an animal's jump are thus related. For the sake of simplicity, we will approximate the height as 1/3 of the distance. (If this proves too simplistic, we can always change it.) Similarly, if a fish is to jump farther, it may need a longer starting distance to get its speed up, and the distance it glides before it stops will be greater. For simplicity's sake, we will assume that the starting and stopping distances are 1/4 of the distance to be jumped.

Using our algorithm and our sketch, we might identify these objects: fish, height, distance, half the distance, angle, starting distance, and stopping distance. We have already selected the **Pinkminnow** class for the fish. Since we intend to pass the distance to be jumped as an argument, and such a value is numeric, we will create a **Number** parameter to store this value using the **create new parameter** button. The remaining objects are all numeric values, so we will define a **Number** variable for each of them, using the **create new variable** button we saw in Figure 3-1. We will use the names **height**, **halfDist**, and **angle** for three of these objects. If we assume that the starting and stopping distances are the same, we can use one variable for both, which we will name **startStopDist**, as shown in Figure 3-34.

FIGURE 3-34   The **jump()** parameter and variables

Given our algorithm and these variables, building the method consists of setting their values appropriately, and then dragging the right statements into the method to elicit the behavior required by our algorithm. Figure 3-35 shows the completed definition.

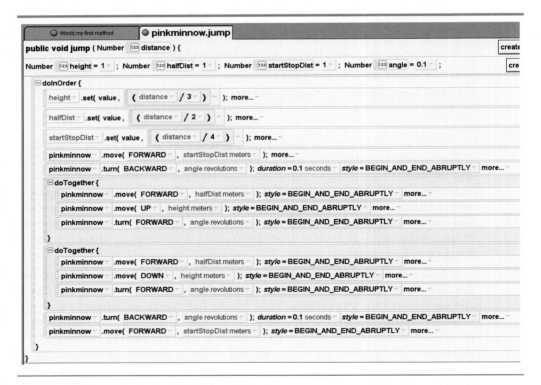

FIGURE 3-35   The **jump()** method (complete)

We can see in Figure 3-35 that each variable's value is accessed multiple times. One of the benefits of using variables this way is that if we later decide to change a value (for example the height of the jump, or its angle), we only have to change it in one place, instead of in several places. This can be a big time-saver when you are using trial-and-error to find just the right value.

To test our program, we send **pinkminnow** the **jump()** message. To test it thoroughly, we use a variety of argument values (for example, 0.25, 0.5, 1, 2, ...), to check that its behavior is appropriate in each case. Figure 3-36 shows a test using one of these values.

FIGURE 3-36   Testing the **jump()** method

Figure 3-37 is a montage of snapshots, showing the behavior produced by the **jump()** method.

FIGURE 3-37   A jumping fish

Parameters are thus variables through which we can pass arguments to a method. By passing different arguments to the same method, that method can produce different (related) behaviors. For example, the **singVerse()** method allows the **scarecrow** to sing different verses of the same song, depending on what *animal* and *noise* values we pass it. Similarly, the **jump()** method makes the **pinkminnow** jump different distances, depending on what *distance* we pass it.

The key to using parameters well is to anticipate that you will want to pass different values to the method as arguments, and then create a parameter to store such values. A well-written method with parameters is like a stone that (figuratively speaking) lets you kill multiple birds.

3.3   Property Variables

Now that we have seen method variables and parameters, it is time to take a brief look at Alice's third kind of variable: **object variables**, which are also known as **instance variables** or **properties**. Whereas method variables and parameters are defined within a method, an object variable is defined within an object. More precisely, an object variable is defined within the *properties* pane of an object's *details area*.

An object variable allows an object to *remember* one of its properties. Each object has its own variable for the property, in which it can store a value distinct from any other object.

To clarify this, let's look at a concrete example. Suppose a user story calls for twin wizards named *Jim* and *Tim*, and each wizard needs to know his own name. One way to make this happen is to add a **wizard** to our world and define within it an object variable whose name is **myName**, whose type is **String**, and whose value is **"Jim"**. If we then make a copy of the **wizard**, the new wizard will have its own **myName** variable, whose value we can change to **"Tim"**.

To define an object variable in the wizard, we click on **wizard** in the *object tree*, click the *properties* tab in the *details area*, and then click the **create new variable** button we see there[1], as shown in Figure 3-38.

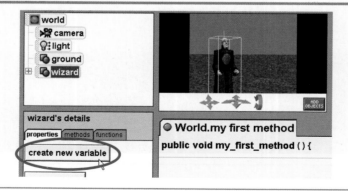

FIGURE 3-38   The properties pane's `create new variable` button

---

1.   Just below the **create new variable** button is a **capture pose** button. When pressed, this button saves the object's current *pose* (the positions+orientations of its subparts) in a new property variable of type **Pose**. If you want to pose your character manually before running your program, this button lets you save such poses. You can use the **setPose()** method within your program to change an object's pose to a saved pose. (The **getCurrentPose()** function can be used to retrieve an object's current pose while your program is running.)

Clicking this button causes the **create new variable** dialog box to appear, which is almost identical to the **Create New Local Variable** dialog box we saw back in Figure 3-3. In it, we enter **myName** for the name, select **Other -> String** as its type, and enter **Jim** for its value. When we click the dialog box's **OK** button, Alice creates a new **String** variable named **myName** whose value is **Jim** in the wizard's *properties* pane, as shown in Figure 3-39.

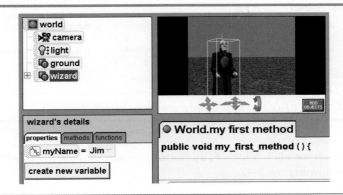

FIGURE 3-39   A new property variable

To make the wizard's twin, we can use the **copy** button (the rightmost control in the **Add Objects** window), as was covered in the Alice Tutorial. Copying the wizard this way gives us two wizards named **Jim**, so we close the **Add Objects** window, click on the second wizard in the *object tree*, click the *properties* tab in the *details area*, and there change the value of the new wizard's **myName** property from **Jim** to **Tim**. See Figure 3-40.

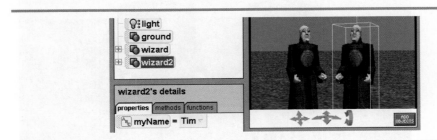

FIGURE 3-40   Twin wizards

A program can now access each wizard's name, as shown in Figure 3-41.

World.my first method

public void my_first_method ( ) {

doTogether {

wizard .say(My name is + wizard.myName); *duration* = 2 seconds *fontSize* = 30 more...

wizard2 .say(My name is + wizard2.myName); *duration* = 2 seconds *fontSize* = 30 more...

}

FIGURE 3-41   Accessing property variables

When we click Alice's **Play** button, we see that each wizard "knows" his own name, as shown in Figure 3-42.

My name is Jim

My name is Tim

FIGURE 3-42   The twin wizards introduce themselves

A property variable thus provides a place for us to store an *attribute* of an object, such as its name, its size, its weight, and anything else we want an object to know about itself.

As we have seen, each Alice object has a number of predefined property variables. These variables store the object's **color** (essentially a filter through which we see the object), its **opacity** (what percentage of light the object reflects), its **vehicle** (what can move this object?), its **skinTexture** (the graphical appearance of the object), its **fillingStyle** (how much of the object gets drawn), its **pointOfView** (the object's position and orientation), and its **isShowing** property (whether or not the object is visible). If you have not done so already, take the time to experiment with each of these properties, to get a feel for what role each plays.

In the next section of this chapter, we will take a closer look at the **vehicle** property.

3.4 Alice Tip: Using the Vehicle Property

In some user stories, it may be desirable to **synchronize** the movements of two objects, so that when one of the objects moves, the other moves with it. To illustrate, let us return to the example from Section 3.1.1, in which Scene 2 had a girl approaching a horse. Suppose that Scene 4 calls for her to ride the horse across the screen. We might set the scene as shown in Figure 3-43.

FIGURE 3-43   The girl on the horse

With the girl on the horse, we can use a **move()** message to move the horse across the screen (Figure 3-44).

○ World.my first method	● **world.playScene4**

public void playScene4 ( ) {

⊟ **doInOrder {**
    `horse ⌄` `.move( FORWARD ⌄` `, 5 meters ⌄` `);  more... ⌄`
}

FIGURE 3-44   Moving the horse across the screen

However, as shown in Figure 3-45, when we do so, the horse moves, leaving the girl hanging suspended in mid-air!

FIGURE 3-45   Moving the horse leaves the girl hanging

We could solve this problem using a **doTogether** block, in which we make the girl and the horse move together. But doing so would force us to write twice as many statements anytime we wanted her to ride the horse, and the additional statements to move the girl will be virtually identical to those we are using to move the horse. It would be much better if we could somehow make the girl "ride" the horse, so that if the horse moves, the girl moves with it.

The way to achieve this better solution is by using the **vehicle** property. As its name implies, an object's **vehicle** is the thing on which it "rides," which is by default, the **world**. If we want the girl to ride the horse, we need to change her **vehicle** property. This can be done by setting her **vehicle** property (using the approach we saw back in Section 1.5.1) at the beginning of the scene, as shown in Figure 3-46.

```
○ World.my first method        ● world.playScene4

public void playScene4 ( ) {


  ⊟ doInOrder {
       nativeGirl⁻ .set( vehicle , horse⁻ ); more...⁻
       horse⁻ .move( FORWARD⁻ , 5 meters⁻ ); more...⁻
  }
```

FIGURE 3-46   Changing the girl's **vehicle** property

As soon as we have made this change, playing the scene causes the girl to "ride" the horse across the screen, as shown in Figure 3-47.

FIGURE 3-47   The girl rides the horse across the screen

By setting the **vehicle** of the girl to the horse, any **move()** messages we send to the horse will cause her to move as well, effectively synchronizing her movements with those of the horse.

Note that if a subsequent scene calls for the girl and the horse to move independently, we will need to reset her **vehicle** to be the **World**. If we neglect to do this, then **move()** messages we send to the horse will make her move too, since their movements will still be synchronized.

3.5   Functions

We have seen how to use a function to send an object a message in order to get information from it. Suppose we wanted to be able to get information from an object, but there was no predefined function providing that information? In such circumstances, we can define our own function.

3.5.1   Example: Retrieving an Attribute From an Object

Let us return to the twin wizards we met in Section 3.3. Suppose that in addition to their names, the wizards have titles that, together with their names, they use on formal occasions. For example, suppose that the wizard *Jim* goes by the title *The Enchanter*, while the wizard *Tim* goes by the title *The Magus*. (Yes, these sound pretentious to me, too.) It should be evident that we can use the same approach we used in Section 3.3 to define a second property variable for each of the wizards to store his title. We will name this property variable **myTitle**, and define it to be of type **String**. Once we have defined this property, we can set its value to the appropriate value in each of the wizards, as shown in Figure 3-48.

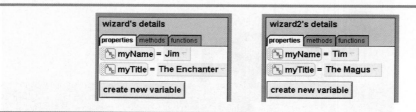

FIGURE 3-48   The wizards' **myTitle** properties

Now suppose that, at times, we need to access a wizard's name, at other times we need to access a wizard's title, and at other times we need to access a wizard's full name (that is, title plus name). In the first case, we can retrieve the wizard's name using the **myName** property. In the second case, we can retrieve the wizard's title using the **myTitle** property. But how can we access the wizard's full name?

One approach would be to concatenate **myTitle** and **myName** with a space in between:

```
wizard.say("I am " + myTitle + " " + myName);
```

This approach is okay, so long as we don't have to access the full name very often. If we have to access it frequently, it can get tiresome to have to repeatedly rebuild the wizard's full name. In such a situation, we can define a function that, when sent to a wizard, produces his full name as its value. To do so, we select the wizard in the *object tree*, click the *functions* tab in the *details area*, and then click the **create new function** button, as shown in Figure 3-49.

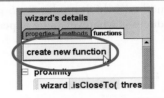

FIGURE 3-49   The **create new function** button

Alice then displays a **New Function** dialog box in which we can enter the name of the function and select the type of value it should produce. We will call the function *getFullName*, and the value it produces is a **String**, as shown in Figure 3-50.

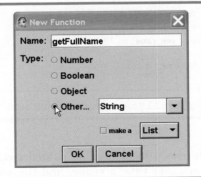

FIGURE 3-50   The **New Function** dialog box

When we click the **OK** button, Alice adds the new function to the wizard's *functions* in the *details area* and opens this function in the *editing area*, as shown in Figure 3-51.

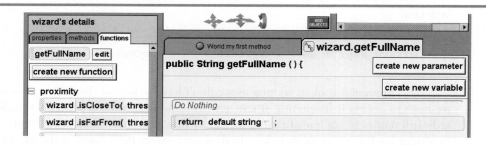

FIGURE 3-51   An "empty" string-returning function

Unlike an Alice method (which produces no value), *a function produces a value*. The value the function produces is whatever value appears in the function's **return statement**, whose form is:

```
return Value ;
```

When Alice performs this statement, the function produces **Value**, sending it back to the place from which the function-message was sent. Note that when Alice defines an "empty" function, it supplies the **return** statement with a default **Value** appropriate for the function's type.

Figure 3-52 shows one way we could define the function.

FIGURE 3-52   The getFullName() function (version 1)

This approach uses a local variable named **fullName** to store the computation of concatenating the wizard's title, a space, and the wizard's name, and then returns the value of **fullName**. Alternatively, we can eliminate the local variable and just return the value produced by the concatenation operators. Figure 3-53 uses this approach to define `getFullName()` for `wizard2`.

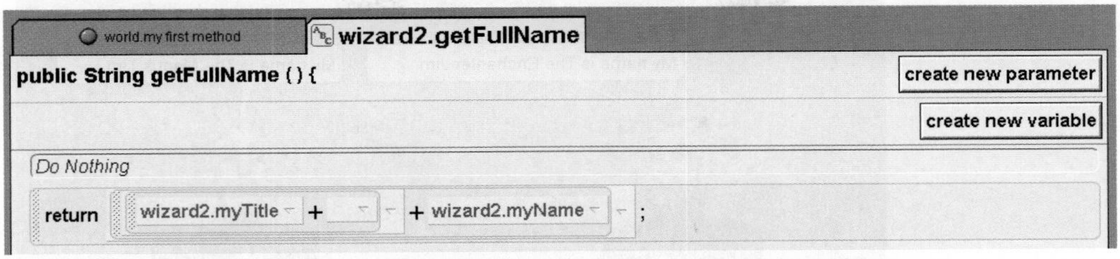

FIGURE 3-53 The `getFullName()` function (version 2)

This version is equivalent to that in Figure 3-52, but it requires no local variable. Now, we can use these functions in a program like that shown in Figure 3-54.

FIGURE 3-54 The wizards introduce themselves

The behavior these functions produce can be seen in Figure 3-55.

FIGURE 3-55   The wizards introducing themselves

3.5.2   Functions With Parameters

Like methods, functions can have parameters to store arguments passed by the sender of the message. The arguments can then be accessed through the parameters. To illustrate, recall that in Section 3.1.2, we built a world in which **skaterGirl** could compute hypotenuse-lengths in her head. The method we wrote there inputs values for the two leg lengths, computes the hypotenuse, and then outputs the result. There might be situations where we just want to calculate the numerical hypotenuse-length, without the input or output:

```
hypotenuse.set(value, skaterGirl.calculateHypotenuse(3, 4) );
```

To define such a function, we make sure **skaterGirl** is selected in the *object tree*, click the *functions* tab in the *details area*, and then click the **create new function** button as before. When the **New Function** dialog box appears, we enter its name (*calculate-Hypotenuse*), but this time we select **Number** as the type of value it produces, as shown in Figure 3-56.

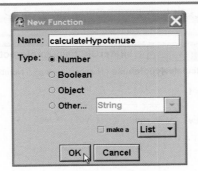

FIGURE 3-56   Creating a number-producing function

When we click the **OK** button, Alice adds **calculateHypotenuse** to **skaterGirl**'s *functions* in the *details area*, and opens the new function in the *editing area*, as shown in Figure 3-57.

skaterGirl's details		○ world.my first method	123 **skaterGirl.calculateHypotenuse**

skaterGirl's details
properties | methods | **functions**
calculateHypotenuse | edit
create new function
⊟ proximity
  skaterGirl .isCloseTo(threshold

public Number calculateHypotenuse ( ) {
create new parameter
create new variable

Do Nothing
return 1 ▾ ;

FIGURE 3-57   An empty number-returning function

To store whatever arguments the sender of this message passes for the two leg lengths, we need two parameters, which we can make using the function's **create new parameter** button. This displays a dialog box like the one shown in Figure 3-3, in which we can enter a parameter's name and its type. Doing this for each of the two parameters gives us the function shown in Figure 3-58.

○ world.my first method   123 **skaterGirl.calculateHypotenuse**

public Number calculateHypotenuse (Number 123 **leg1 , Number** 123 **leg2) {**
create new parameter
create new variable

Do Nothing
return 1 ▾ ;

FIGURE 3-58   A function with parameters

To finish the function, we add the necessary operations to make it compute the hypotenuse length using its parameters. Figure 3-59 shows one way to do so.

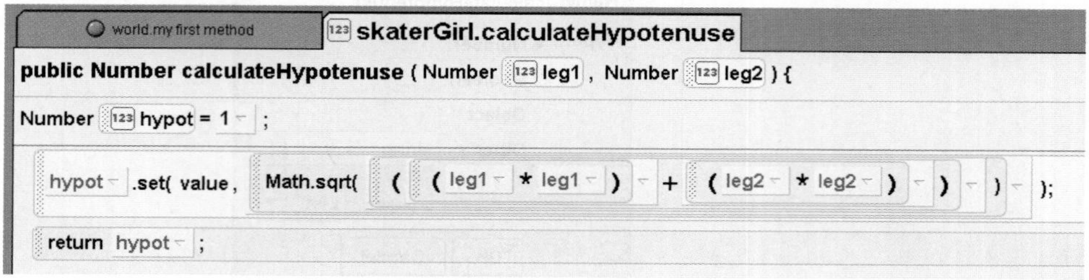

FIGURE 3-59   Calculating the hypotenuse

Given this function, we can now send **skaterGirl** the **calculateHypotenuse()** message, and pass it arguments for the leg lengths. Figure 3-60 shows a revised version of Figure 3-25.

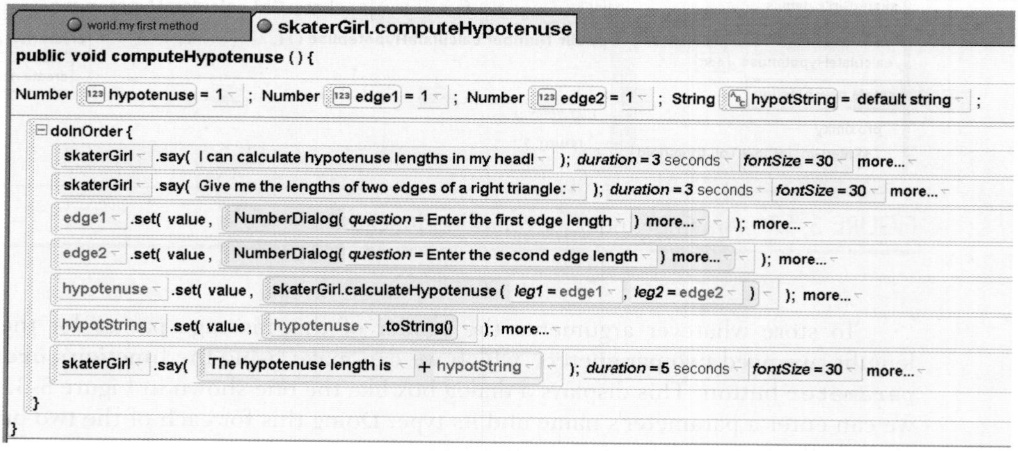

FIGURE 3-60   Sending a function-message

When this program is performed, it prompts the user to enter the lengths of the two tri-angle legs, and then **skaterGirl** "says" the corresponding hypotenuse length. For example, if the user enters **3** and **4** for the leg lengths, the program behaves as shown in Figure 3-61.

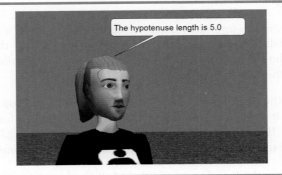

FIGURE 3-61   Testing the function

Functions are thus much like methods. We can create parameters and local variables within each of them, and perform just about any computation we can envision. The difference between the two is that a function-message returns a value to its sender, while a method-message does not. Because of this difference, a function-message must be sent from a place where a *value* can appear, such within a `set()` statement. By contrast, a method-message can only be sent from a place where a *statement* can appear.

Being able to define messages — both method and function — is central to object-based programming. In the chapters to come, we will see many more examples of each.

3.6   Chapter Summary

❏ Method variables let us store computed and user-entered values for later use.

❏ Parameters let us store and access arguments passed by the sender of a message.

❏ Properties (object variables) let us store and retrieve an object's attributes.

❏ Alice's `vehicle` property lets us synchronize the movements of two objects.

❏ A function lets us send a message to an object, and get a value in response.

3.6.1   Key Terms

argument
concatenation
define a variable
function
initial value
local variable
method variable
object variable
parameter

placeholder
property variable
return statement
synchronized movements
variable
variable name
variable type
vehicle
world functions

Programming Projects

3.1 Following the approach used in Section 3.1.1, build a scene containing two people who walk toward each other from opposite sides of the screen. When they meet, they should turn and walk off together toward a building, and enter the building when they get there.

3.2 Using the horse we used in Section 3.4, build a **gallop()** method for the horse that makes its legs move realistically through the motions for one stride of a gallop. Then modify the **playScene4()** method so that the horse gallops across the screen. (For now, you may send the **gallop()** message multiple times.)

3.3 Using the **heBuilder** or **sheBuilder**, build a person. For your person, define an object method named **walkInSquare()** that has a parameter named **edgeLength**. When **walkInSquare(dist)** is sent to your person, he or she should walk in a square with edges that are each *dist* meters long. Make certain your person begins and ends at the same spot. When the person is done, have the person say the area and perimeter of the square.

3.4 Using the ideas in this chapter, build a world containing a person who can calculate Einstein's formula $e = m^*c^2$ in his or her head, where the user enters the m value (mass, in kilograms), and c is the speed of light (299,792,458 meters per second). Define descriptive variables for each quantity, and use the **World** function **pow()** to compute c^2.

3.5 Choose a hopping animal from the Alice Gallery (for example, a frog, a bunny, etc.). Write a **hop()** method that makes it hop in a realistic fashion, with a parameter that lets the sender of the message specify how far the animal should hop. Using your **hop()** method, have your animal hop around a building in four hops.

3.6 *The Farmer in the Dell* is an old folk song with the lyrics below. Create an Alice program containing a character who sings this song. Use a **singVerse()** method, parameters, and variables to write your program efficiently.

The farmer in the dell. The farmer in the dell. Heigh-ho, the derry-o. The farmer in the dell.	The farmer takes a wife. The farmer takes a wife. Heigh-ho, the derry-oh. The farmer takes a wife.
The wife takes a child. The wife takes a child. Heigh-ho, the derry-oh. The wife takes a child.	The child takes a nurse. The child takes a nurse. Heigh-ho, the derry-oh. The child takes a nurse.
The nurse takes a cow. The nurse takes a cow. Heigh-ho, the derry-oh. The nurse takes a cow.	The cow takes a dog. The cow takes a dog. Heigh-ho, the derry-oh. The cow takes a dog.

The dog takes a cat. The dog takes a cat. Heigh-ho, the derry-oh. The dog takes a cat.	The cat takes a rat. The cat takes a rat. Heigh-ho, the derry-oh. The cat takes a rat.
The rat takes the cheese. The rat takes the cheese. Heigh-ho, the derry-oh. The rat takes the cheese.	The cheese stands alone. The cheese stands alone. Heigh-ho, the derry-oh. The cheese stands alone.

3.7 Using the **heBuilder** or **sheBuilder** (or any of the other persons in the Alice Gallery with enough detail), build male and female persons and add them to your world. Using your persons, build a program in which your people dance the waltz (or a similar dance in which the partners' movements are synchronized). Have your world play music while your people dance.

3.8 Build a world in which two knights on horseback joust, using the techniques from this chapter.

3.9 In Section 2.4, we developed Scene 2 of a program, in which a wizard confronts three trolls. Write a wizard method **castChangeSizeSpell(obj, newSize)**, that takes an object **obj** and a number **newSize** as arguments. The method should cause the wizard to turn towards **obj**, raise his arms, say a magic word or phrase, and then lower his arms. The method should resize **obj** the amount specified by **newSize**, and then make certain **obj** is standing on the ground. Create a scene 3 in which the wizard uses the **castChangeSizeSpell()** message to defeat the trolls by shrinking most of them to 1/10 their original size.

3.10 Alice provides the **Pose** type, which can be used to store the position of each of an object's subparts. Under the *properties* pane, the **capture pose** button allows you to save an object's current **Pose** in a property variable before the program is run. The function named **getCurrentPose()** can be used (as the value of a **set()** message) to save an object's pose in a **Pose** variable as the program is running. The **setPose()** method can be used to set an object's pose to a pose stored in a **Pose** variable. Rewrite the **march()** method we wrote in Section 2.2.2. Discard the **moveLeftLegForward()** and **moveRightLegForward()** methods we used, using three **Pose** variables instead.

Chapter 4
Flow Control

Controlling complexity is the essence of computer programming.

BRIAN KERNIGHAN

When you get to the fork in the road, take it.

YOGI BERRA

If you build it, he will come.

THE VOICE (JAMES EARL JONES), IN *FIELD OF DREAMS*

While you're at it, why don't you give me a nice paper cut and pour some lemon juice on it?

MIRACLE MAX (BILLY CRYSTAL), IN *THE PRINCESS BRIDE*

Objectives

Upon completion of this chapter, you will be able to:

❏ Use the **Boolean** type and its basic operations

❏ Use the **if** statement to perform some statements while skipping others

❏ Use the **for** and **while** statements to perform (other) statements more than once

❏ Use **Boolean** variables and functions to control **if** and **while** statements

❏ Use the **wait()** message to temporarily suspend program execution

In Chapter 1, we saw that the flow of a program is the sequence of steps the program follows in performing a story. From the perspective of an Alice program, we can think of a flow as the sequence of statements that are performed when we click the **Play** button.

In the preceding chapters, the programs we have written have mostly used the **doInOrder** statement, which produces a sequential execution. However, we sometimes used a **doTogether** statement, which produces a parallel execution. If we consider a group of N statements within a **doInOrder** statement compared to a **doTogether** statement, we can visualize the difference in behavior of these two statements in a **flow diagram** like the one shown in Figure 4-1.

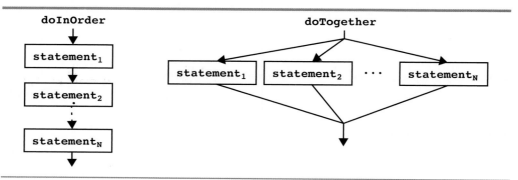

FIGURE 4-1   The flows produced by the **doInOrder** and **doTogether** statements

The **doInOrder** and **doTogether** are thus **flow control** statements, because their effect is to *control the flow* of the program through the statements within them. Computer scientists often describe flow control statements as **control structures**.

In this chapter, we will examine several of Alice's flow control statements, including the following:

- the **if** statement, which directs the flow through one group of statements and away from another group of statements
- the **for** statement, which directs the flow through a group of statements a fixed number of times
- the **while** statement, which directs the flow through a group of statements an arbitrary number of times

Before we examine these statements, let's briefly look at a related topic: the **Boolean** type.

4.1   The **Boolean** Type

You may recall from Chapter 3 that **Boolean** is one of Alice's basic types (for defining variables). The **Boolean** type is named after George Boole, a 19th century English mathematician who studied *true/false* values and the kinds of operations that can be used with them.

Whereas a **Number** variable can have any of millions of (numeric) values, and an **Object** variable can refer to any Alice object, a **Boolean** variable can have either of just two values: **true** or **false**. At first, this may seem rather limiting: what good is a type that only provides two values? As we shall see, the **Boolean** type is extremely useful when we want the program to make decisions. Decision-making depends on current circumstances or *conditions*, so a piece of a program that produces a **true** or **false** value is called a **boolean expression** or **condition**.

4.1.1 Boolean Functions

The *functions* pane of Alice's *details area* contains questions we can ask an object. When the answer to a question is **true** or **false**, the function is a condition. Many of the questions we can ask an object produce a **Boolean** value for their answer, including those shown in Figure 4-2.

Function	Value Produced
obj.isCloseTo(*dist*, *obj2*)	**true**, if *obj2* is within *dist* meters of *obj*; **false**, otherwise.
obj.isFarFrom(*dist*, *obj2*)	**true**, if *obj2* is at least *dist* meters away from *obj*; **false**, otherwise.
obj.isSmallerThan(*obj2*)	**true**, if *obj2*'s volume exceeds that of *obj*; **false**, otherwise.
obj.isLargerThan(*obj2*)	**true**, if *obj*'s volume exceeds that of *obj2*; **false**, otherwise.
obj.isNarrowerThan(*obj2*)	**true**, if *obj2*'s width exceeds that of *obj*; **false**, otherwise.
obj.isWiderThan(*obj2*)	**true**, if *obj*'s width exceeds that of *obj2*; **false**, otherwise.
obj.isShorterThan(*obj2*)	**true**, if *obj2*'s height exceeds that of *obj*; **false**, otherwise.
obj.isTallerThan(*obj2*)	**true**, if *obj*'s height exceeds that of *obj2*; **false**, otherwise.

FIGURE 4-2   Boolean functions

continued

Function	Value Produced
obj.isToTheLeftOf(obj2)	**true**, if *obj*'s position is beyond *obj2*'s left edge; **false**, otherwise.
obj.isToTheRightOf(obj2)	**true**, if *obj*'s position is beyond *obj2*'s right edge; **false**, otherwise.
obj.isAbove(obj2)	**true**, if *obj*'s position is above *obj2*'s top edge; **false**, otherwise.
obj.isBelow(obj2)	**true**, if *obj*'s position is below *obj2*'s bottom edge; **false**, otherwise.
obj.isInFrontOf(obj2)	**true**, if *obj*'s position is before *obj2*'s front edge; **false**, otherwise.
obj.isBehind(obj2)	**true**, if *obj*'s position is beyond *obj2*'s rear edge; **false**, otherwise.
obj.isToTheLeftOf(obj2)	**true**, if *obj*'s position is beyond *obj2*'s left edge; **false**, otherwise.

FIGURE 4-2   Boolean functions *(continued)*

Note that most of these functions refer to an object's bounding box. For example, the function **obj.isBehind(obj2)** uses the rear edge of **obj2**'s bounding box.

These functions can be used with an **if** or **while** statement (see below) to make a decision or otherwise control an object's behavior.

4.1.2 **Boolean** Variables

Another kind of condition is the **Boolean** variable or parameter. **Boolean** variables, parameters, or properties can be created by clicking the appropriate **create new variable** (or **parameter**) button, and then specifying **Boolean** as the type of the new variable (or parameter). Such variables can be used to store **true** or **false** values until they are needed, and can serve as a condition in an **if** or **while** statement, which we describe below.

4.1.3 Relational Operators

Another kind of condition is produced by an *operator* that computes a **true** or **false** value. The six most common operators that produce **Boolean** values are called the **relational operators**, and they are shown in Figure 4-3.

Relational Operator	Name	Value Produced
`val1 == val2`	equality	**true**, if `val1` and `val2` have the same value; **false**, otherwise.
`val1 != val2`	inequality	**true**, if `val1` and `val2` have different values; **false**, otherwise.
`val1 < val2`	less-than	**true**, if `val1` is less than `val2`; **false**, otherwise.
`val1 <= val2`	less-than-or-equal	**true**, if `val1` is less than or equal to `val2`; **false**, otherwise.
`val1 > val2`	greater-than	**true**, if `val1` is greater than `val2`; **false**, otherwise.
`val1 >= val2`	greater-than-or-equal	**true**, if `val1` is greater than or equal to `val2`; **false**, otherwise.

FIGURE 4-3   The relational operators

In Alice, the six relational operators are located in the *functions* pane of the **world**'s *details area*. These are most often used to compare **Number** values. For example, suppose a person is to receive overtime pay if he or she works 40 hours or more in a week. If **hoursWorked** is a **Number** variable in which a person's weekly working hours are stored, then the condition

```
hoursWorked > 40
```

will produce **true** if the person should receive overtime pay, and **false** if he or she should not. Relational operators compare two values and produce an appropriate **true** or **false** value.

Beyond numeric values, the equality (**==**) and inequality (**!=**) operators can be used to compare **String**, **Object**, and **Other** values. We will see an example of this in Section 4.2.

4.1.4   **Boolean** Operators

The final three conditional operators are used to combine or modify relational operations. These are called the **boolean operators**, and they are shown in Figure 4-4.

Boolean Operation	Name	Value Produced
`val1 && val2`	AND	*true*, if *val1* and *val2* are both **true**; **false**, otherwise.
`val1 || val2`	OR	*true*, if either *val1* or *val2* is **true**; **false**, otherwise.
`!val`	NOT	*true*, if *val* is **false**; **false**, if *val* is **true**.

FIGURE 4-4   The boolean operators

Like the relational operators, Alice provides the boolean operators in the *functions* pane of the **World**'s *details area*. To illustrate their use, suppose we want to know if a person is a teenager, and their age is stored in a **Number** variable named **age**. Then the condition

```
age > 12 && age < 20
```

will produce the value **true** if the person is a teenager; otherwise it will produce the value **false**. Similarly, suppose that a valid test score is in the range 0 to 100, and we want to guard against data-entry mistakes. If the score is in a **Number** variable named **testScore**, then we can decide if it is invalid with the condition

```
testScore < 0 || testScore > 100
```

since the condition will produce **true** if either **testScore < 0** or **testScore > 100** is **true**, but will produce **false** if neither of them is **true**.

Now that we have seen the various ways to build a condition, let's see how we can make use of them to control the flow of a program.

4.2   The if Statement

4.2.1   Introducing Selective Flow Control

Suppose we have a user story in which the following scene occurs:

Scene 3: A princess meets a mute dragon, and says "Hello." The dragon just looks at her. She asks it, "Can you understand me?" The dragon shakes its head up and down to indicate yes. She says, "Can you speak?" The dragon shakes its head sideways to indicate no. She says, "Can you only answer yes or no questions?" The dragon shakes its head yes. She says, "Are you a tame dragon?" The dragon shakes its head no.

The co-star of the scene is a mute dragon, who answers yes-or-no questions by shaking his head up and down for *yes*, and shaking it sideways for *no*. We could write two separate **dragon** methods, one named **shakeHeadYes()**, and another named **shakeHeadNo()**. Instead, let's "kill two birds with one stone" and write one **shakeHead()** method providing both behaviors.

As we saw in Chapter 3, the key to making one method do the work of two (or more) is to use a parameter to produce the different behaviors. In this case, we will pass the argument **yes** when we want the dragon to shake its head up and down, and pass the argument **no** when we want it to shake its head sideways. To store this argument, we will need a parameter whose type is **String**. For lack of a better name, we will name the parameter **yesOrNo**.

If we write out the behavior this method should produce, we might write the following:

Parameter: yesOrNo, a String.

If *yesOrNo* is equal to "yes", the dragon shakes his head up and down;

Otherwise, the dragon shakes his head sideways.

The key idea here is that if the parameter has one value, we want one thing to happen; otherwise, we want something else to happen. That *if* is the magic word. Any time we use the word *if* to describe a desired behavior, we can use Alice's **if statement** to produce that behavior.

To build this method in Alice, we might start by opening a world, adding a **playScene3()** method to the world, adding a dragon to the world; positioning the camera so that we can see the dragon's head clearly; selecting **dragon** in the *object tree*; creating a new method named **shakeHead()**; and then within this method, creating a new parameter named **yesOrNo**, whose type is **String**. The result is shown in Figure 4-5.

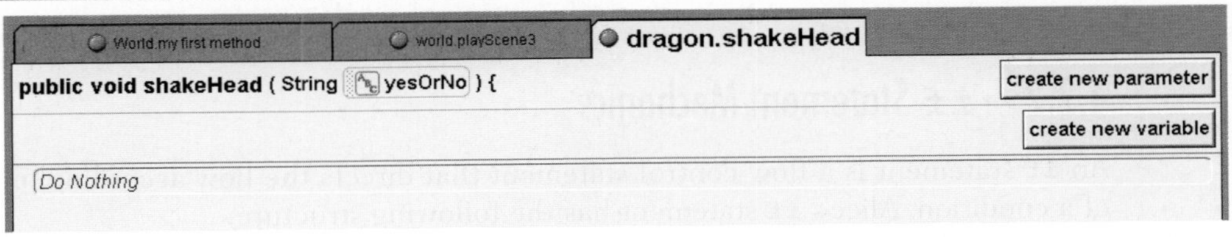

FIGURE 4-5 The empty **shakeHead()** method

Looking at the algorithm for this method, we see the magic word *if*. There is a control named **if** at the bottom of Alice's *editing area*, so we drag it into the method. When we drop it, Alice produces a **condition** menu, with the choices **true** or **false**, as shown in Figure 4-6.

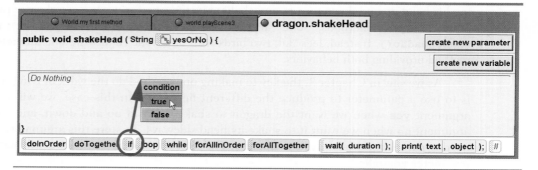

FIGURE 4-6   Dragging the `if` control

For the moment, we will just choose **true** as a *placeholder* value. Alice then generates an **if** statement in the method, as shown in Figure 4-7.

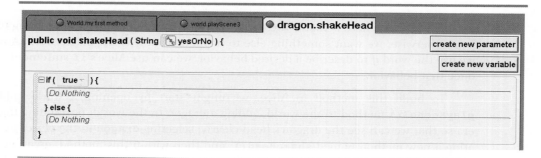

FIGURE 4-7   The Alice `if` statement

4.2.2   `if` Statement Mechanics

An **if** statement is a flow control statement that directs the flow according to the value of a condition. Alice's **if** statement has the following structure:

```
if ( Condition ) {
    Statements₁
} else {
    Statements₂
}
```

and we might visualize the **if** statement's flow-behavior as shown in Figure 4-8.

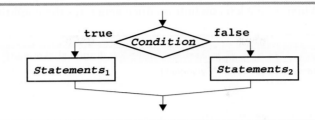

FIGURE 4-8   Flow through an `if` statement

Figure 4-8 shows that when the flow reaches an **if** statement, it reaches a "fork" in its path. Depending on its **Condition**, the flow proceeds one way or the other, but not both. That is, when the flow first reaches an **if** statement, its **Condition** is evaluated. If the value of the **Condition** is **true**, then the flow is directed through the first group of statements (and the second group is ignored); if the **Condition**'s value is **false**, then the flow is directed through the second group of statements (ignoring the first group). Put differently, when the **if** statement's **Condition** is **true**, then the first group of statements is *selected* and the second group is skipped; otherwise, the second group of statements is *selected* and the first group is skipped. The **if** statement's behavior is sometimes called **selective flow**, or **selective execution**.

4.2.3   Building `if` Statement Conditions

Back in the user story, we want the dragon to shake its head up and down if **yesOrNo** is equal to **yes**; otherwise, it should shake its head sideways. We saw in Figure 4-3 that the **equality operator** is ==, so that is what we need. To use it, we can click on the **yesOrNo** parameter, drag it into the *editing area*, and drop it on the placeholder in the **if** statement's condition. Alice will display a menu from which we can choose **yesOrNo** == , followed by a second menu from which we can choose the **b**-value, as shown in Figure 4-9.

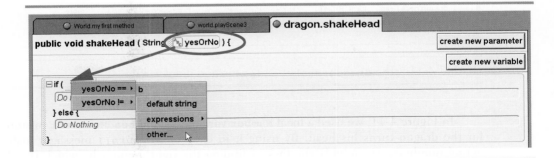

FIGURE 4-9   Dragging a parameter to an `if` statement's condition

Choosing **other** for the **b**-value produces a dialog box into which we can type **"yes"**. When we click its **OK** button, Alice generates the condition shown in Figure 4-10.

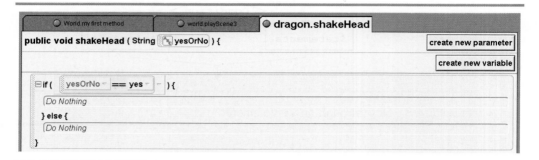

FIGURE 4-10   An **if** statement's condition using a parameter

With the condition in place, finishing the method consists only of placing messages in the top *Do Nothing* area to shake the dragon's head up and down, and placing messages in the bottom *Do Nothing* area to shake its head sideways. Figure 4-11 shows the finished method.

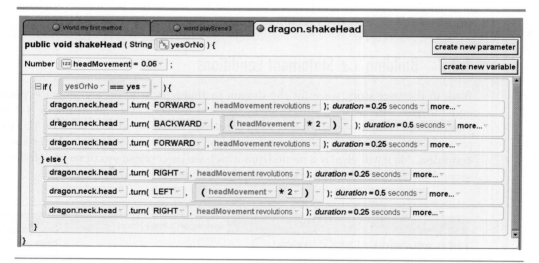

FIGURE 4-11   The **dragon.shakeHead()** method (final version)

In Figure 4-11, we used a local **Number** variable named **headMovement** to store how far the dragon turns his head. By using it in each of the **turn()** messages instead of actual numbers, we simplify the task of finding the right amount by which the dragon should shake his head, since trying a given value only requires one change (to the variable) instead of six changes.

To test the **shakeHead()** method, we build the scene method, as shown in Figure 4-12.

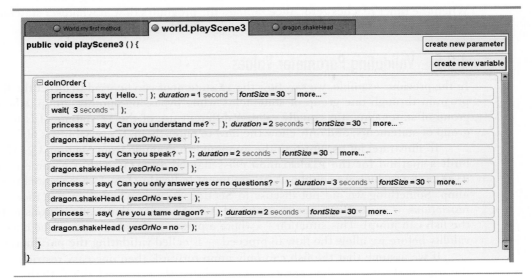

FIGURE 4-12   Testing `shakeHead()` in `playScene3()`

When we click Alice's **Play** button, we see that the **shakeHead()** method works as intended, as shown in Figure 4-13.

FIGURE 4-13   Testing the `shakeHead()` method

4.2.4 The `wait()` Statement

To introduce a time delay between the princess's first and second statements in Figure 4-12, we used another flow control statement named **wait()**, whose form is as follows:

```
wait(numSecs);
```

When the flow reaches this statement, Alice *pauses* the program's flow, sets an internal timer to **numSecs** seconds, and starts this timer counting down towards zero. When the timer reaches zero, Alice *resumes* the program's flow at whatever statement follows the **wait()**.

4.2.5   Validating Parameter Values

In the previous example, we saw how the **if** statement can be used to direct the flow of a program through one group of statements while bypassing another group, where each group of statements was equally valid. A different use of the **if** statement is to *guard* a group of statements, and only allow the flow to enter them if "everything is ok."

To illustrate, let us return to the jumping fish example from Section 3.2. There, we built a method for the **Pinkminnow** class named **jump()**, with a parameter named **distance** to which we could pass an argument indicating how far we wanted the fish to jump. Something we did not discuss in Section 3.2 was whether or not there are any *restrictions* or *preconditions* on the value of this argument (that is, limitations to how *far* the fish can jump). This situation — where a parameter's value needs to be checked for validity before we allow the flow to proceed — is called **validating the parameter**.

If we assume that the fish can only jump forward, then one easy restriction is that the argument passed to **distance** must be positive. We can check this with the condition **distance > 0**. Passing an argument that is 0 or less can be treated as an error.

There may also be an upper bound on how far a **PinkMinnow** can jump, but identifying such a bound is more difficult. Minnows are rather small fish, so 2 meters might be a reasonable upper bound. However if a minnow were bigger than normal, or were super-strong, maybe it could jump farther, so we want to make this upper bound easy to change. We can do so by defining a variable named **MAX_DISTANCE**, and then using the condition **distance   <= MAX_DISTANCE** to check that the argument passed to parameter **distance** is within this bound.

> If a variable's value will not change, and its purpose is to improve a program's readability, name it with all uppercase letters, to distinguish it from normal variables.

We now have two conditions that need to be met in order for the argument passed to the parameter to be deemed valid: **distance > 0** and **distance <= MAX_DISTANCE**. Since *both* of these must be true in order for our argument to be acceptable, we use the boolean AND operator (**&&**) to combine them: **distance > 0 && distance <= MAX_DISTANCE**.

We will use these ideas to revise the **jump()** method, as follows:

```
if (distance > 0 && distance <= MAX_DISTANCE) {
   // ... statements performed when distance is valid
   // (make the fish jump)
} else {  // ... distance is invalid
   if (distance <= 0) {
      // ... statements performed when distance is too low
   } else {
      // ... statements performed when distance is too high
   }
}
```

Here, we are using an **if** statement with a second **if** statement nested within its **else** statements. The first **if** is often called the **outer if**, and the second **if** is often called the **inner if**, or the **nested if**.

Figure 4-14 presents a revised version of the **jump()** method, using this approach to validate the parameter.

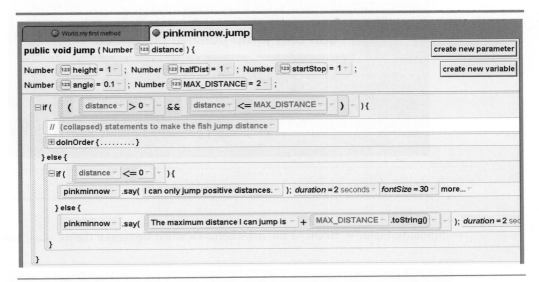

FIGURE 4-14   Validating a parameter's value with nested **if** statements

To save space, we have collapsed the **doInOrder** statement that contains the statements that make the fish jump, using the plus (**+**) sign at the beginning of the statement.

Let us take a moment to trace the program flow through the revised method:

- When **distance** is valid, the outer **if**'s condition will be **true**, so flow will proceed into the statements that make the fish jump, as we saw in Figure 3-36 in Chapter 3.

- When **distance** is invalid, the first condition will be **false**, so flow will proceed into the **else** statements of the outer **if**. The only statement there is the inner **if** statement, which determines *why* **distance** is invalid (too small or too large?):

  - If **distance** is zero or less, the flow proceeds to the statement in which we send the fish the first **say()** message.

  - Otherwise, **distance** must be greater than **MAX_DISTANCE**, so the flow proceeds to the statement in which we send the fish the second **say()** message.

To illustrate, Figure 4-15 shows the fish's behavior when we send it the message **jump(-2)**.

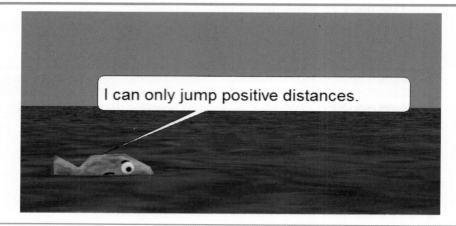

FIGURE 4-15   Asking the fish to jump a negative distance

Similarly, Figure 4-16 shows the fish's behavior when we send it the message **jump(3)**.

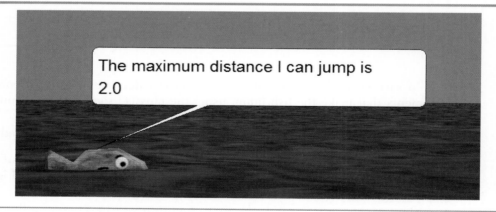

FIGURE 4-16   Asking the fish to jump too far

When building a method with a parameter, think about whether there are any "bad" arguments that could be passed to the parameter. If so, use an **if** statement to guard against such values.

The **if** statement thus provides a way to build **if-then-else logic** into a method. When such logic uses a method's parameter for its condition, then the method can produce different behaviors, based on what argument is passed to that parameter when the message is sent.

4.3   The `for` Statement

4.3.1   Introducing Repetition

In Section 2.2.1, we built a **flapWings()** method for the dragon, and in Section 2.3, we saw how to rename, save, and import the dragon as a **flappingDragon**. One drawback to the **flapWings()** method is that the **flappingDragon** will only flap its wings once. Now that we have learned about parameters, we might improve this method by passing it an argument specifying how many times the dragon should flap its wings. To store this argument, we will need a **Number** parameter, which we will name **numTimes**. We might describe the behavior we want this way:

Parameter: *numTimes*, a Number.

For each value count = 1, 2, ..., *numTimes*:

      The dragon flaps its wings once.

Since we already know how to make the dragon flap its wings once, the idea is to have the method redirect the flow so as to *repeat* the wing-flapping behavior **numTimes** times.

We can start by opening the **flapWings()** method from Figure 2-16. To make the dragon's wing-flapping seem more realistic, we might adjust the **duration** values of the wing movements, so that downstrokes (that is, beating against the air) take longer than upstrokes (that is, resetting for a downstroke). In the version below, we've made the complete cycle (down-stroke and up-stroke) require 1 second.

To make the **flapWings()** method flap the dragon's wings more than once, we define a **Number** parameter named **numTimes**, as shown in Figure 4-17. Next, we drag the **loop** control from the bottom of the *editing area* into the method. Since we want to repeat the method's wing-flap behavior, we drop the **loop** control at the very beginning of the method. When we drop it, Alice displays an **end** menu from which we can choose the number of repetitions we want, as shown in Figure 4-17.

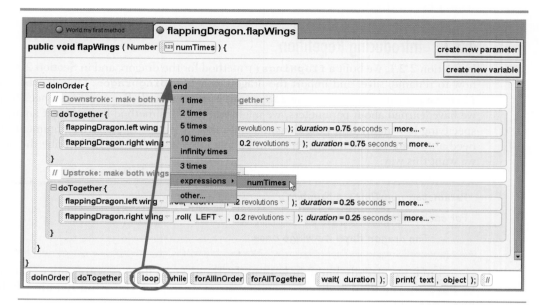

FIGURE 4-17   Dragging the `loop` control

When we select **numTimes**, Alice inserts an empty **for statement** in the method, as shown in Figure 4-18.

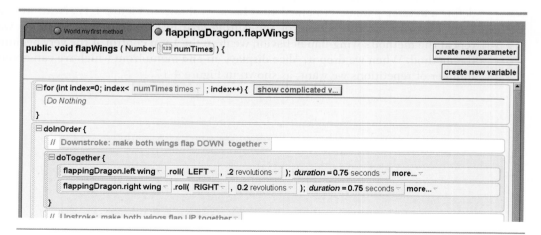

FIGURE 4-18   An empty `for` loop

To finish the method, we drag the **doInOrder** statement below the **for** statement into the **for** statement, resulting in the method definition shown in Figure 4-19.

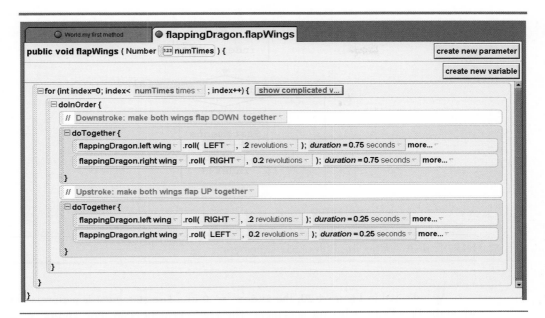

FIGURE 4-19 The revised `flapWings()` method

With this definition, if we send the **dragon** the message **flapWings(3)**, then it will flap its wings three times. If we send it the message **flapWings(8)**, it will flap its wings eight times.

4.3.2 Mechanics of the `for` Statement

The **for** statement is a flow control statement whose purpose is to direct the program's flow through the statements within it, while *counting* through a range of numbers. For this reason, it is sometimes called a **counting loop**. If we were to send the **dragon** the message **flapWings(3);** then the **for** statement would count **0, 1, 2** (performing the statements within it once for each number), and then quit. If we were to send **dragon.flapWings(8);** then the **for** statement would count **0, 1, 2, 3, 4, 5, 6, 7** (again, performing the statements within it once for each number), and then quit. More generally, the **for** statement in **flapWings()** will always count from **0** to **numTimes-1**.

How does it work? Alice's "simple" **for** statement has the structure shown below:

```
for (int index = 0; index < limit; index++ ) {
    Statements
}
```

When the program's flow reaches this statement, the flow behaves as shown in Figure 4-20.

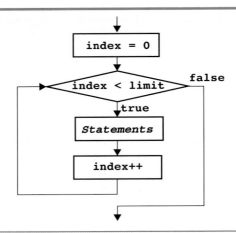

FIGURE 4-20   Flow through a `for` statement

As indicated in Figure 4-20, the **index = 0** in a **for** statement is performed just once, when the flow first reaches the statement. The **for** statement's condition **index < limit** is then checked. If the condition is **false**, then the flow is directed *around* the **Statements** within it to whatever statement follows the **for** statement. If the condition is **true**, then the **Statements** within the **for** statement are performed, followed by the **index++** (recall that **++** is the **increment operator**). The flow is then redirected *back* to the condition, restarting the cycle.

In Figure 4-21, we trace the behavior of the **for** statement in Figure 4-19 when we send **dragon** the message **flapWings(3)**.

Step	Flow is in...	Effect	Comment
1	`index = 0;`	Initialize **index**	**index**'s value is **0**
2	`index < numTimes` `(0 < 3)`	The condition is **true**	Flow is directed into the loop
3	`doInOrder`	Flap wings	The first repetition
4	`index++`	Increment **index**	**index**'s value changes from **0** to **1**
5	`index < numTimes` `(1 < 3)`	The condition is **true**	Flow is directed into the loop
6	`doInOrder`	Flap wings	The second repetition
7	`index++`	Increment **index**	**index**'s value changes from **1** to **2**

FIGURE 4-21   Tracing the flow of `flapWings(3)`

continued

Step	Flow is in...	Effect	Comment
8	index < numTimes (2 < 3)	The condition is **true**	Flow is directed into the loop
9	doInOrder	Flap wings	The third repetition
10	index++	Increment **index**	**index**'s value changes from **2** to **3**
11	index < numTimes (3 < 3)	The condition is **false**	Flow is directed *out of* the loop
12	Flow leaves the **for** statement, moving to the end of the method		

FIGURE 4-21   Tracing the flow of `flapWings(3)` *(continued)*

The simple version of the Alice **for** statement always begins counting with **0**, uses **index < limit** as the condition (for whatever **limit** value we specify), and uses **index++** as the way to increase the index. If we want different values for any of these, we can click the **show complicated version** button on the first line of the **for** statement. (The button appears as **show complicated v...** in Figure 4-19). Clicking this button "expands" the first line of the **for** statement into the form shown in Figure 4-22.

```
for (int [123] index = 0 ⊽ ; index< numTimes times ⊽ ; index += 1 ⊽ ){   show simple version
```

FIGURE 4-22   The complicated `for` loop

Where the simple version just lets you modify the **limit** value, the complicated version also lets you set the initial value of **index** to a value other than zero, and increase **index** by a value other than **1** each repetition.

In our experience, the simple version of the **for** loop is sufficient most of the time, but Alice provides the complicated version for situations where the simple version is inadequate. Both versions will only count up; if you need to count down, you will need to use a **while** statement (see Section 4.4) with a **Number** variable that you explicitly set, test, and decrement.

4.3.3   Nested Loops

Suppose the first scene of a user-story is as follows:

A castle sits in a peaceful countryside. A dragon appears, flying toward the castle. When it gets close, it circles the castle's tower three times, and then descends, landing on the castle's drawbridge.

Using divide-and-conquer, we might divide this scene into three shots:

1. A castle sits in a peaceful countryside. A dragon appears, flying toward the castle.

2. When it gets close, it circles the castle's tower three times.

3. It then descends, landing on the castle's drawbridge.

The first shot can be built several ways. One way is to position the dragon off-screen, store the distance from the dragon to the castle's drawbridge in a variable, and then use a **move()** statement to move the dragon that distance, as we have seen before. Another way is to go into the **Add Objects** window, position the dragon above the castle's drawbridge, move it upwards until it is even with the castle's tower, and then (using **more controls**) click the **drop dummy at selected object** button. If we then drag the dragon off-screen, the program can move it to the dummy's position above the drawbridge using the **setPointOfView()** message.

The third shot can also be built in several ways. Section 4.4 presents one approach.

To build the second shot, we will use a **for** statement controlling other statements that make the dragon fly around the castle tower, as shown in Figure 4-23.

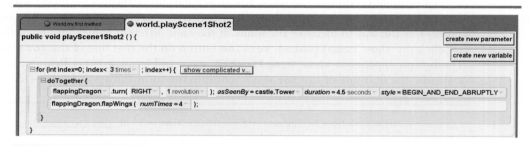

FIGURE 4-23   Making the dragon circle the castle

As defined in Figure 4-23, the **for** statement contains a **doTogether** statement that causes the dragon to simultaneously fly around the castle (taking 4.5 seconds per circuit), and flap its wings four times. As shown above, this behavior will repeat three times. If, after testing the method, we were to decide that two circuits around the castle tower would be preferable, all we need to do is change the **for** statement's **limit** value from **3** to **2**.

Figure 4-23 is deceptively simple. It contains several subtleties that we discuss next.

Nested **for** Statements

One subtlety is that this method is actually using *two* **for** statements: the one visible in Figure 4-23, plus the one that is hidden within the **flapWings()** method. This situation — where one **for** statement is controlling another **for** statement — is called **nested for statements,** because one **for** statement is nested within another.

In Figure 4-23, the **inner for statement** (the one hidden within **flapWings()**) repeats 4 times for every 1 repetition of the **outer for statement** (the one that is visible). With the outer statement repeating 3 times, the dragon flaps its wings a total of 3 × 4 = 12 times. Nested loops thus have a **multiplying effect**: if the outer loop repeats **i** times and the inner loop repeats **j** times, then the statements in the inner loop will be repeated a total of **i** × **j** times.

The `asSeenBy` Attribute

The second subtlety is how the **turn()** message in Figure 4-23 causes the dragon to circle the tower. Alice's **turn()** message has a special **asSeenBy** attribute. Normally, this attribute is set to **None**, in which case **turn()** just causes its receiver to revolve about its **LR** axis or its **FB** axis. However, if we specify another object (like **castle.tower**) as the value of the **asSeenBy** attribute, then the **turn()** message causes its receiver to *revolve around that object*. Figure 4-23 uses this trick to make the dragon revolve around the castle tower once for each repetition of the outer **for** statement.

The `duration` Attribute

In testing the method, we initially set the **duration** of the **turn()** message to **4** seconds, to match the dragon's 4 wing-flaps (1 per second) per circuit of the tower. This produced a "hitch" in the animation as the dragon finished each circuit. The problem is that while each wing-flap takes 1 second to complete, the **flapWings(4)** message consumes slightly longer than 4 seconds.[1] As a result, the 4-second **turn()** message was finishing before the 4 wing-flaps. We were able to smooth the animation by increasing the **duration** of the **turn()** message slightly, and setting the message's **style** attribute to **BEGIN_AND_END_ABRUPTLY**, as shown in Figure 4-23.

4.4   The `while` Statement

The **for** statement is a means of causing flow to repeatedly move through the same group of statements a fixed number of times. For this reason, the **for** statement is often called a counting statement, or a **counting loop**. The program must "know" (that is, be able to compute) how many repetitions are needed when flow reaches the **for** statement, to set its **limit** value.

This raises a problem: What do we do when we encounter a situation for which we need repetitive flow-behavior, but we do not know in advance how many repetitions are required? For such statements, Alice (and other programming languages) provides the **while** statement.

4.4.1   Introducing the `while` Statement

In Section 4.3.3, we began work on a scene consisting of three shots:

1. A castle sits in a peaceful countryside. A dragon appears, flying toward the castle.

2. When it gets close, it circles the castle's tower three times.

3. It then descends, landing on the castle's drawbridge.

---

1.   For each repetition of a **for** statement, its **index++** statement and the **index < limit** condition must be processed, which consumes time. A **flapWings(n)** message thus consumes more than **n** seconds.

We have seen how to build the first two shots, and it is possible to build the third shot using a variable, a function, and a **doTogether** statement containing a **move()** message and the **flapWings()** method. The drawback to this approach is that we must coordinate the **move()** and **flapWings()** messages, so that the duration of the **move()** (that is, how long the descent will take) coincides with the wing-flaps of the dragon. If we later change the elevation of the dragon above the drawbridge, we will have to recoordinate the **move()** and **flapWings()** messages.

In this section, we will see an alternative way to build this shot, using a **while** statement, a function, and a **doTogether** statement containing a **move()** message and the **flapWings()** message. The idea is to repeatedly (1) have the dragon flap its wings, and (2) move it downwards whatever distance it drops in one wing-flap, so long as it is above the drawbridge.

We begin by moving the camera closer (via a dummy we'll rename shot1-3, using the techniques described in Section 2.4.), to better see the dragon's descent, as shown in Figure 4-24.

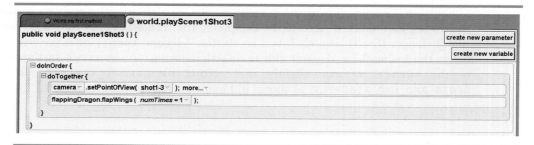

FIGURE 4-24   Moving the camera closer

With the camera in position, we are ready to make the dragon descend. To do so, we click the **while** control at the bottom of the *editing area*, drag it into the method, and drop it at the last position within the **doInOrder** statement. See Figure 4-25.

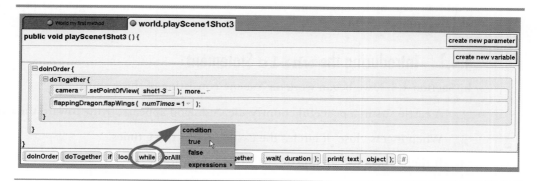

FIGURE 4-25   Dragging the **while** control

When we drop it there, Alice generates a **condition** menu from which we can choose a condition to control the **while** statement. For the moment, we just choose **true** as a *placeholder*. Alice then generates the empty **while** statement shown in Figure 4-26.

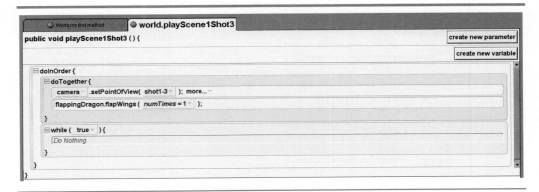

FIGURE 4-26   An empty **while** statement

For each repetition of the **while** statement, we want the dragon to flap its wings once and move downward a short distance (still to be determined). We want this behavior to repeat as many times as necessary, so long as the dragon is above the drawbridge. For the **while** statement's condition, we can thus drag the dragon's **isAbove()** function into the **while** statement's placeholder condition, and when we drop it, choose the castle's drawbridge as its argument, as shown in Figure 4-27.

FIGURE 4-27   Repeating so long as the dragon is above the drawbridge

Any statements we place within the **while** statement will be repeated so long as the condition **flappingDragon.isAbove(castle.Bridge)** produces the value **true**. Those statements must ensure that the condition eventually becomes **false**, or else an **infinite loop** will result. That is, if the flow reaches the **while** statement shown in Figure 4-27, the flow will remain there sending **flappingDragon** the **isAbove()** message over and over forever, or until we terminate the program, whichever comes first. Any time the flow reaches a **while** loop whose statements do not cause its condition to eventually become **false**, this infinite looping behavior is the result.

To avoid an infinite loop, the loop's statements should flap the dragon's wings and move it down a small distance, so that its bounding box eventually touches that of the bridge. When that happens, the **isAbove()** condition will become **false** and the loop will terminate. We can use these ideas to complete the method as shown in Figure 4-28.

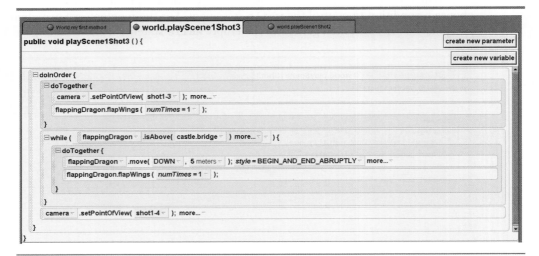

FIGURE 4-28   The `playScene1Shot3()` method (final version)

Each repetition of the **while** statement in Figure 4-28 takes 1 second, during which the dragon simultaneously flaps its wings and moves down 5 meters. If we decide this descent is too slow, we can double its descent rate by changing the **5** to a **10**; or if it seems too fast, we can slow the descent by changing the **5** to a **4**, a **2**, or a **1**. The key decision in this approach is how far a dragon should descend in 1 second (which is simpler than the use-a-variable approach).

The final statement in the method zooms the camera in (using another dummy) for a closer shot of the dragon on the bridge after its descent, yielding the shot in Figure 4-29.

FIGURE 4-29   The dragon on the drawbridge

4.4.2 `while` Statement Mechanics

Where the **for** statement is a counting loop, the **while** statement is a **general**, or **indefinite loop**, meaning the number of repetitions to be performed need not be known in advance. The structure of the Alice **while** statement is as follows:

```
while ( Condition ) {
    Statements
}
```

When flow reaches a **while** statement, it proceeds as shown in Figure 4-30.

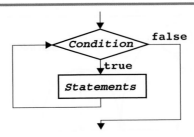

FIGURE 4-30   Flow through a `while` statement

In Figure 4-30, when flow first reaches a **while** statement, its **Condition** is evaluated. If it is **false**, then the flow leaves the **while** statement, bypassing its **Statements**. However, if it is **true**, then the **Statements** within the **while** statement are performed, after which the flow is redirected back to recheck its **Condition**, where the process begins again.

4.4.3   Comparing the `for` and `while` Statements

If you compare Figure 4-30 to Figure 4-20, you will see that the **while** statement's behavior is actually much simpler than that of the **for** statement. This is because the **while** is the more general flow-control statement; whereas the **for** statement is useful mainly in counting situations, the **while** statement can be used in any situation where repetition is required.

So when should you use each statement? Whenever you are working to produce a behavior that needs to be repeated, ask yourself this question: "Am I counting something?" If the answer is "yes," then use a **for** statement; otherwise, use a **while** statement. For example, in Figure 4-19 and Figure 4-23, we counted wing-flaps and tower-circuits, respectively. By contrast, in Figure 4-28, we were not counting anything, just controlling the dragon's descent.

Both the **while** and the **for** statements test their condition *before* the statements within the loop are performed. In both cases, if the condition is initially **false**, then statements within the loop will be bypassed (that is, not performed). If you write a program containing a loop statement that seems to be having no effect, it is likely that the loop's condition is **false** when flow reaches it. To remedy this, either choose a different condition, or ensure that its condition is **true** before flow reaches the loop.

4.4.4   A Second Example

As a second example of the **while** statement, suppose that Scene 1 of a story has a girl named Jane dropping a soccer ball (that is, a football everywhere outside of the U.S.). Jane lets it bounce until it stops on its own. Our problem is to get it to bounce realistically.

When dropped, a ball falls until it strikes a surface beneath it. It then rebounds upwards some distance (depending on some bounce factor that combines its elasticity, the hardness of the surface it hits, etc.), drops again, rebounds again, drops again, rebounds again, and so on. We can sketch the behavior as being something like that shown in Figure 4-31.

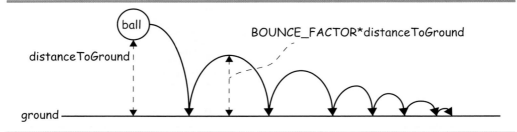

FIGURE 4-31   Sketch of the up-down motion of a bouncing ball

For simplicity, we will just have the soccer ball bounce straight up and down.

Using the **sheBuilder** (located in the **People** folder in the Alice Gallery), the **SoccerBall** class from Alice's **Web Gallery**, and the **quad-view** window, we might start by building a scene like the one shown in Figure 4-32.

FIGURE 4-32   Jane with the soccer ball

To produce the desired bouncing behavior, we can write a **dropAndBounce()** method for the **soccerBall**, which is shown in Figure 4-33.

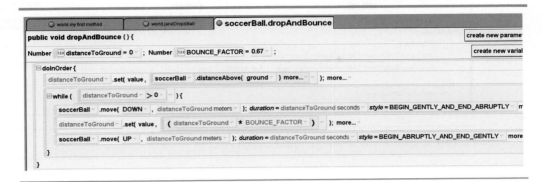

FIGURE 4-33   Method `soccerBall.dropAndBounce()`

When Jane drops the ball, we do not know in advance how many times it is going to rebound, so we have used a **while** statement instead of a **for** statement. The condition controlling the loop is this: the ball should continue to bounce so long as its distance above the ground exceeds zero.

We have assumed that on each bounce, the ball will rebound to 2/3 of the distance it fell previously. (If this proves to be a poor assumption, we have made it easy to change by storing the 2/3 in a variable called **BOUNCE_FACTOR**.) By storing the (initial) distance from the ball to the ground in a variable named **distanceToGround**, then for each repetition of the loop, we

1. move the ball *down* **distanceToGround** meters

2. change the value of **distanceToGround** to **distanceToGround*BOUNCE_FACTOR**

3. move the ball *up* **distanceToGround** meters (which is now 2/3 of its previous value)

To make the ball's behavior seem more realistic, we set the **duration** of each bounce-movement to the current value of the **distanceToGround** variable. Thanks to this, each successive bounce-movement will occur faster as **distanceToGround** gets smaller.

Another refinement to increase the realism was to set the style of the **move()** causing the ball's drop to **BEGIN_GENTLY_AND_END_ABRUPTLY**, and set the style of the **move()** causing the ball's rebound to **BEGIN_ABRUPTLY_AND_END_GENTLY**. The net effect is to make a fast down-to-up transition when the ball bounces, and to make a slow up-to-down transition as the ball reaches the peak of its bounce.

Given the method in Figure 4-33, we can easily build a world method (since it animates two different objects) in which Jane drops the ball, as shown in Figure 4-34.

FIGURE 4-34   Method `world.janeDropsBall()`

Try this yourself, and experiment with the statements and settings shown in Figure 4-33, to see how each one affects the ball's behavior. (There's always the **Undo** button!)

4.5   Flow-Control in Functions

At the end of Chapter 3, we saw that if we want to ask an object a question for which there is not already a function, we can define our own function to provide the answer. The functions we wrote there used sequential flow, and were fairly simple. The flow-control statements we have seen in this chapter allow us to build functions that answer more complex questions.

4.5.1   Spirals and the Fibonacci Function

Suppose that we have a story in which a girl finds an old book. The book tells her that there is a treasure hidden near a certain palm tree in the middle of the desert. The book contains a map showing how to find the tree, plus instructions for locating the treasure from the tree. Suppose that Scene 1 of the story has the girl finding the old book and reading its contents. In Scene 2, the girl uses the map to locate the palm tree. In Scene 3 she follows the instructions:

Scene 3: The girl is at the tree, her back to the camera. She says, "Now that I am at the tree, I turn to face North." She turns to face the camera. "Then I walk in a spiral of six quarter turns to the left, and then say the key phrase." She walks in a spiral of six quarter turns to her left, says a key phrase, and an opening appears in the ground at her feet.

The main challenge in building this user story is getting the girl to move in a spiral pattern. Mathematicians have discovered that many of the spirals that occur in nature — for example, the spiraling chambers inside a nautilus shell, the spiral of petals in a rose, and the spiraling seeds in sunflowers and pinecones — all use a pattern given in the following numbers:

1, 1, 2, 3, 5, 8, 13, 21, 34, 55, 89, 144, ...

Can you see a pattern in these numbers? The first known mention of them is by the Indian scholar Gospala sometime before 1135 AD. The first European to discover them was Leonardo Pisano, a 13th century mathematician who found that they predict the growth of rabbit populations. Leonardo was the son of Guglielmo Bonaccio, and often called himself Fibonacci (short for "son of Bonaccio"). Today, these numbers are called the **Fibonacci series.**

To draw a spiral from the series, we draw a series of squares whose lengths and widths are the Fibonacci numbers. Starting with the smallest square, we draw a series of quarter turn arcs, crossing from one corner of the square to the opposite corner, as shown in Figure 4-35.

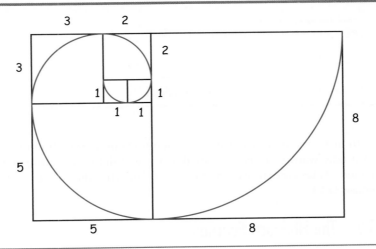

FIGURE 4-35   A Fibonacci spiral pattern

To move the girl in the story in a spiral pattern, we can use a similar approach. More precisely, we can move her in a close approximation of the Fibonacci spiral as follows:

1.   move her forward 1 meter while turning left 1/4 revolution

2.   move her forward 1 meter while turning left 1/4 revolution

3.   move her forward 2 meters while turning left 1/4 revolution

4.   move her forward 3 meters while turning left 1/4 revolution

5.   move her forward 5 meters while turning left 1/4 revolution

6.   move her forward 8 meters while turning left 1/4 revolution

More concisely, we can have her move 6 times, each time moving a distance equal to the next Fibonacci number while turning left 1/4 revolution. That is, if we had a function that, given a positive number *i*, computes the ith Fibonacci number, we could write the **playScene3()** method as shown in Figure 4-36.

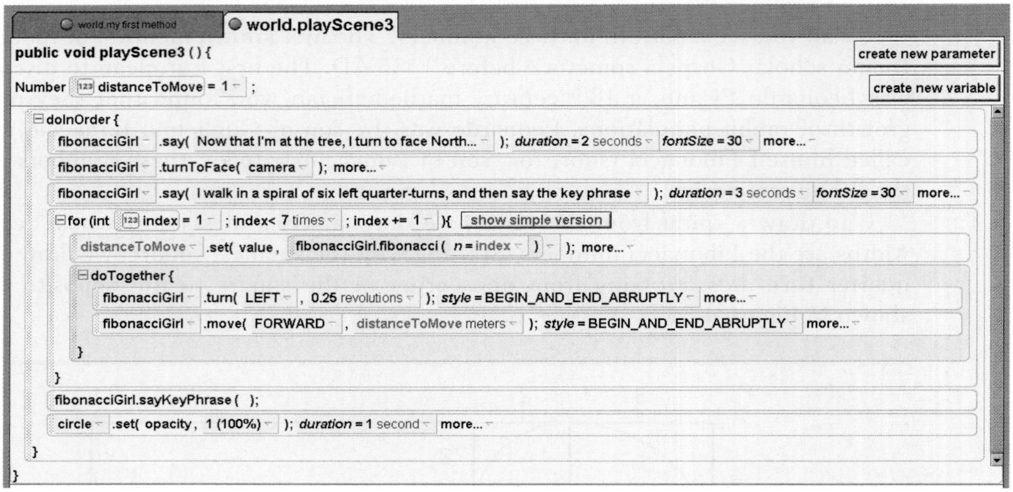

FIGURE 4-36   The **playScene3()** Method

In just a moment, we will build such a **fibonacci()** function. Since it seems possible we may want to reuse it someday, we will define it within the girl, whom we have renamed **fibonacciGirl** in Figure 4-36. (In the Alice Gallery, her name was **RandomGirl3**).

4.5.2   The Fibonacci Function

To create the **fibonacci()** function that is invoked in Figure 4-36, we select the girl in the *object tree*, click the *functions* tab in her *details area*, and then click the **create new function** button. Alice prompts us for the name of the function, so we enter **fibonacci**.

To invoke this function, we must pass it a positive **Number** argument indicating which Fibonacci number we want it to return. To store this argument, the function must have a **Number** parameter. We will name this parameter **n**.

Design

The question the function must answer is this: Given *n*, what is the nth Fibonacci number? If we look at the series carefully

1, 1, 2, 3, 5, 8, 13, 21, 34, 55, 89, 144, ...

we can see this pattern: after the initial two 1s, every subsequent number is the *sum of the preceding two numbers*. That is, there are two cases we must deal with:

> if (n is 1 or n is 2) the function's result is 1;
>
> otherwise, the function's result is the sum of the preceding two values in the series.

The tricky part is figuring out "the preceding two values in the series." As we have seen before, let's first try doing this by hand. For example, to compute **fibonacci(9)**:

```
  1        1        2        3        5        8       13
 +1       +2       +3       +5       +8      +13      +21
 ---      ---      ---      ---      ---      ---      ---
  2        3        5        8       13       21       34
```

Since we are doing the same thing over and over, we can do this using a loop. To do so, we store each value used per iteration in a variable: one for the next-to-last term, one for the last term, and one for the result; we can then use a **for** loop to count from 3 to **n**. When **n** is 9:

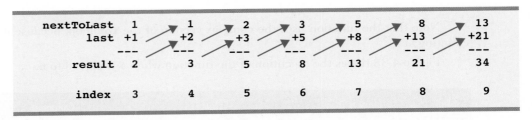

Putting all of this together yields the following algorithm for the function:

```
1  Parameter: n, a Number.
2  Number result = 0; Number nextToLast = 1; Number last = 1;
3  if (n == 1 or n == 2) {
4      result = 1;
5  } else {
6      for (int index = 3; index < n+1; index++) {
7          result = last + nextToLast;
8          nextToLast = last;
9          last = result;
10     }
11 }
12 return result;
```

Coding in Alice

We can encode the algorithm in Alice as shown in Figure 4-37.

```
○ world.my first method      ○ world playScene3     123 fibonacciGirl.fibonacci

public Number fibonacci ( Number 123 n ) {                              create new parameter

Number 123 result = 0 ; Number 123 last = 1 ; Number 123 nextToLast = 1 ;    create new variable

☐if (   (   n ══ 1   ||   n ══ 2   )  ){

    result .set( value, 1 );

} else {

    ☐for (int 123 index = 3 ; index<  ( n + 1 )  ; index += 1 ){  show simple version

        result .set( value,  ( nextToLast + last )  );

        nextToLast .set( value, last );

        last .set( value, result );

    }

}

return result ;
```

FIGURE 4-37   The `fibonacci()` function

Note that the function uses the complex version of the **for** loop, because it begins counting at 3.

Figure 4-38 traces the execution of the function when **4** is passed to **n**.

Step	Flow is in...	Effect	Comment
1	if *Condition*	*Condition* is **false**	Control flows to the **if**'s **else** branch
2	index = 3	For loop is initialized	**index** is **3**
3	index < n+1	The condition is **true**	Flow is directed into the loop
4	result = ...	Compute fibonacci(3)	**result** is **2**
5	nextToLast = ...	Update **nextToLast**	**nextToLast** is **1**
6	last = ...	Update **last**	**last** is **2**
7	index++	Increase **index**	**index** is **4**
8	index < n+1	The condition is **true**	Flow is directed into the loop
9	result = ...	Compute fibonacci(4)	**result** is **3**

FIGURE 4-38   Tracing the `fibonacci()` function

continued

Step	Flow is in...	Effect	Comment
10	`nextToLast = ...`	Update `nextToLast`	`nextToLast` is 2
11	`last = ...`	Update `last`	`last` is 3
12	`index++`	Increase `index`	`index` is 5
13	`index < n+1`	The condition is `false`	Flow is directed out of the loop
14	`return result;`	The function terminates	`result` is 3, the 4th Fibonacci number
15	Flow leaves the function, returning `result` to the point where the function was invoked.		

FIGURE 4-38   Tracing the `fibonacci()` function *(continued)*

Note that we initialize `result` to zero. If the user passes an invalid argument (for example, zero or a negative number), then the function returns this zero. First, control flows into the `if` statement's `else` branch. However when its `for` loop tests the condition `(3 < (n+1))`, that condition will be `false` if `n` is negative or zero, so the body of the `for` loop will be skipped. Control then flows to the `return` statement, and since `result` has not been modified, the function returns zero.

Using this function, the `for` loop in Figure 4-35 will cause `fibonacciGirl` to move in a spiral pattern, after which she says the key phrase and a dark opening appears in the ground at her feet. What happens next? It's up to you!

4.6   Chapter Summary

❏ `Boolean` operators allow us to build *conditions*.

❏ The `if` statement uses a condition to direct program flow *selectively* through one group of statements while bypassing others.

❏ The `for` statement uses a condition to direct program flow through a group of statements *repeatedly*, a fixed number of times.

❏ The `while` statement uses a condition to direct program flow through a group of statements *repeatedly*, where the number of repetitions is not known in advance.

❏ The `wait()` message lets us suspend a program's flow for a fixed length of time.

❏ The `asSeenBy` attribute alters the behavior of the `turn()` message.

4.6.1 Key Terms

boolean expression
boolean operators
  (&&, ||, !)
Boolean type
boolean variables
condition
control structure
counting loop
flow control
flow diagram
general loop
if-then-else logic
if statement

indefinite loop
infinite loop
nested statement
  (inner statement, outer statement)
relational operators
  (==, !=, <, >, <=, >=)
repetitive control
selective control
selective execution
selective flow
validating parameter values
wait() statement
while statement

Programming Projects

4.1 Choose a hopping animal from the Alice Gallery (for example, a frog or a bunny). Write a **hop()** method that makes it hop in a realistic fashion, with a (validated) parameter that lets the sender of the message specify how far the animal should hop. Then build a method containing just one **hop()** message that causes your animal to hop around a building.

4.2 *Johnny Hammers* is a traditional song with the lyrics below. Create an Alice program containing a character who sings this song. Write your program using as few statements as possible.

Johnny hammers with 1 hammer, *1 hammer, 1 hammer.* *Johnny hammers with 1 hammer,* *all day long.*	*Johnny hammers with 2 hammers,* *2 hammers, 2 hammers.* *Johnny hammers with 2 hammers,* *all day long.*
Johnny hammers with 3 hammers, *3 hammers, 3 hammers.* *Johnny hammers with 3 hammers,* *all day long.*	*Johnny hammers with 4 hammers,* *4 hammers, 4 hammers.* *Johnny hammers with 4 hammers,* *all day long.*
Johnny hammers with 5 hammers, *5 hammers, 5 hammers.* *Johnny hammers with 5 hammers,* *all day long.*	*Johnny's very tired now,* *tired now, tired now.* *Johnny's very tired now,* *so he goes to sleep.*

4.3 Using the horse we used in Section 3.4, build a **gallop()** method for the horse that makes its legs move realistically through the motions of a gallop, with a (validated) parameter that specifies the number of strides (or alternatively, the distance to gallop). Then create a story containing a scene that uses your method to make the horse gallop across the screen.

4.4 *The Song That Never Ends* is a silly song with the lyrics below. Create an Alice program containing a character who sings this song, using as few statements as possible. (If your computer has a microphone, get your character to "sing" a recording of the song as well as "say" the lyrics. If you do not know the tune, find and listen to the song on the World Wide Web.)

This is the song that never ends, and it goes on and on my friends. Some people started singing it not knowing what it was, and now they'll keep on singing it forever just because.	This is the song that never ends, and it goes on and on my friends. Some people started singing it not knowing what it was, and now they'll keep on singing it forever just because.
This is the song that never ends, and it goes on and on my friends. Some people started singing it not knowing what it was, and now they'll keep on singing it forever just because.	... (ad infinitum, ad annoyeum, ad nauseum)

4.5 Build a world containing a person who can calculate the average of a sequence of numbers in his or her head. Have the person ask the user how many numbers are in the sequence, and then display a **NumberDialog** that many times to get the numbers from the user. When all the numbers have been entered, have your person "say" the average of those numbers.

4.6 Proceed as in Problem 4.5, but instead of having your person ask the user in advance how many numbers are in the sequence, have your person and each **NumberDialog** tell the user to enter a special value (for example, -999) after the last value in the sequence.

4.7 *99 Bottles of Pop* is a silly song with the lyrics below. Create an Alice program in which a character sings this song. Use as few statements as possible. (Hint: Even though this is a counting problem, you will need to use a **while** statement instead of a **for** statement. Why?)

99 bottles of pop on the wall, 99 bottles of pop, take one down, pass it around, 98 bottles of pop on the wall.	98 bottles of pop on the wall, 98 bottles of pop, take one down, pass it around, 97 bottles of pop on the wall.
(96 verses omitted) ...	1 bottle of pop on the wall, 1 bottle of pop, take one down, pass it around 0 bottles of pop on the wall.

4.8 Using the **heBuilder** or **sheBuilder** (or any of the other persons in the Alice Gallery with enough detail), build a person and add him or her to your world. Using your person, build an aerobic exercise video in which the person leads the user through an exercise routine. Using repetition statements, your person should do each exercise a fixed number of times. (Hint: Use **Pose** variables and the **capture pose** button.)

4.9 Proceed as in Problem 4.8, but at the beginning of the program, ask the user to specify the difficulty level of the workout (1, 2, 3, 4, or 5). If the user specifies 1, have your person do each exercise 10 times. If they specify 2, 20 times. If they specify 3, 40 times, If they specify 4, 80 times. If they specify 5, 100 times.

4.10 From the Alice Gallery, choose a clock class that has subparts for the minute and hour hands.

    a. Build a clock method named **run()** that moves the minute and hour hands realistically (that is, each time the minute hand completes a rotation, the hour hand should advance 1 hour). Define a parameter named **speedUp** that controls the **duration**s of the hand movements, such that **run(0)** will make the clock run at normal speed, **run(60)** will make the clock run at 60 times its normal speed, **run(3600)** will make the clock run at 3600 times its normal speed, and so on.

    b. Build a clock method **setTime(h, m)** that sets the clock's time to **h:m** (**m** minutes after hour **h**).

    c. Build three functions for your clock: one that returns its current time (as a **String**), one that returns its current hours value (as a **Number**), and one that returns its current minutes value (as a **Number**).

    d. Build a clock method **setAlarm(h, m)** that lets you set the clock's alarm to **h:m**. Then modify your **run()** method so that when the clock's current time is equal to **m** minutes after hour **h**, the clock plays a sound (for example, Alice's **gong** sound).

4.11 Using appropriately colored **Shapes** from the Alice Gallery, build a chessboard. Then choose objects from the Gallery to serve as chess pieces. Build a class-level method named **chessMove()** for each piece that makes it move appropriately (for example, a bishop should move diagonally). For pieces that can move varying distances, the definition of **chessMove()** should have a (validated) parameter indicating the distance (in squares) of the move, plus any other parameters necessary. When your "pieces" are finished, build a program that simulates the opening moves of a game of chess, using your board and pieces.

4.12 Design an original 3–5 minute story that uses each of the statements presented in this chapter at least once.

Chapter 5
Lists and Arrays

He's making a list, checking it twice. 'Gonna find out who's naughty or nice ...

SANTA CLAUS IS COMING TO TOWN

For seven men she gave her life. For one good man she was his wife. Beneath the ice by Snow White Falls, there lies the fairest of them all.

VIRGINIA (KIMBERLY WILLIAMS), IN *THE 10TH KINGDOM*

The generation of random numbers is too important to be left to chance.

ROBERT R. COVEYOU

When a cat is dropped, it always lands on its feet, and when toast is dropped, it always lands with the buttered side down. I propose to strap buttered toast to the back of a cat; the 2 will hover, inches above the ground. With a giant buttered-cat array, a high-speed monorail could easily link New York with Chicago.

JOHN FRAZEE

Objectives

When you complete this chapter, you will be able to:

❏ Use a list to store multiple items

❏ Use Alice's **forAllInOrder** and **forAllTogether** statements

❏ Use random numbers to vary the behavior of a program

❏ Use an array to store multiple items

In the preceding chapters, we have often used variables to store values for later use. Each variable we have seen so far has stored a *single* value, which might be a **Number**, a **Boolean**, a **String**, an **Object**, a **Sound**, a **Color**, or any of the other types that Alice supports. For example, if we have three variable definitions like this in our program:

```
Number result = 0.0;
Boolean done = false;
String name = "Jo";
```

then we might (simplistically) visualize these three variables as shown in Figure 5-1.

FIGURE 5-1   Storing three values in three variables

Each variable stores a single value (of a given type) that can be changed by the program.

It is sometimes convenient to be able to define a variable that can store *multiple* values. For example, suppose you have 12 songs (call them $s_0 \ldots s_{11}$) in your music player that you want to represent in a program. You could define 12 single-value variables (for example, $song_0$, $song_1$, $song_2$, ..., $song_{10}$, $song_{11}$), but it would be more convenient if you could define one variable capable of storing all 12 songs, as shown in Figure 5-2.

FIGURE 5-2   Storing 12 values in one variable

One advantage of this approach is that if I need to pass my song collection to a method, I only have to pass one argument (**playList**) instead of 12. Also, my method needs only one parameter.

A variable like this is called a **data structure** — a structure for storing a group of data values. In this chapter, we will examine two data structures that are available in Alice:

- The **list**, which stores a group of values where the group's size changes frequently
- The **array**, which stores a group of values where the group's size does not change

Each structure is used for storing *sequences* of values, but the two have very different properties.

5.1   The List Structure

5.1.1   List Example 1: Flight of the Bumble Bees

Suppose Scene 2 of a story requires a dozen bees to take off, one at a time, to defend the honor of their queen bee. We might begin by using the Alice Gallery to build the scene as shown in Figure 5-3.

FIGURE 5-3   The queen and her 12 bees

To make the bees take off one at a time, we could use 12 separate statements:

```
bee.move(UP, verticalDistance);
bee2.move(UP, verticalDistance);
...
bee12.move(UP, verticalDistance);
```

Note, however, that although the bee to which we are sending the **move()** message changes, each statement is otherwise the same. Remember: *any time you find yourself programming the same thing over and over, there is usually a better way*. In this case, the better way is to create a data structure variable named **bees** that stores references to the 12 bees, and which we might visualize as shown in Figure 5-4.

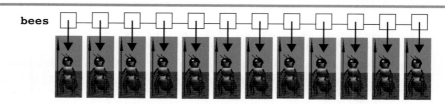

FIGURE 5-4   A list of 12 bees

As indicated in the caption of Figure 5-4, this kind of data structure is called a **list**, as in *shopping list*, *guest list*, or *play list*. Alice's list data structure can store a sequence of **items**, which can be any Alice type (for example, **Number**, **Boolean**, **Object**, **String**, **Color**, etc.).

Given a list variable, we can use Alice's **forAllInOrder** statement to send each item in the list the message **move(UP, verticalDistance)**:

```
for all bees, one item_from_bees at a time {
    item_from_bees.move(UP, verticalDistance);
}
```

We will look at each of these steps separately.

Defining a List Variable

We can begin by defining a **playScene2()** method, and then defining a list variable within it. To create a list variable, we click the **create new variable** button as usual. Because the things we want to store in the list (bees) are objects, we select **Object** as the type in the dialog box that appears. We then click the checkbox labeled **make a List**, which expands the dialog box with a **Values** pane, as shown in Figure 5-5.

FIGURE 5-5   Creating a list variable

To store the bees in the list, we click the **new item** button visible in Figure 5-5. Alice then adds an item to the list whose value is **<None>**, as shown in Figure 5-6 (left side).

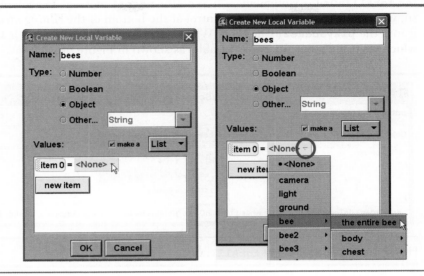

FIGURE 5-6   Defining initial values in a list variable

To make the value of this new item the first bee, we click the list arrow next to **<None>**, choose the **bee** from the menu that appears, and select **the entire bee**, as shown in Figure 5-6 (right side). We then repeat these steps to create new items for each additional bee in the story, and finally click the dialog's **OK** button. The result is the list variable shown in Figure 5-7.

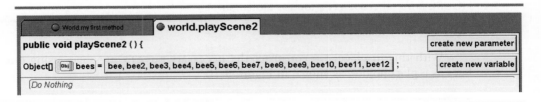

FIGURE 5-7   A list variable definition

While Alice's choice of font makes it a bit difficult to see, the form of this definition is:

```
Object [] bees = bee, bee2, ... bee12;
```

Alice uses square brackets (**[** and **]**) to distinguish data structures from "normal" variables.

Processing List Entries

Now that we have defined a list variable, the next step is to use a new Alice statement — the **forAllInOrder** statement — to send the **move()** message to each of its items. To do so, we click the **forAllInOrder** control at the bottom of the *editing area*, and then drag it into the **playScene2()** method. When we drop it, Alice generates a **list** menu from which we can choose the **bees** variable, as shown in Figure 5-8.

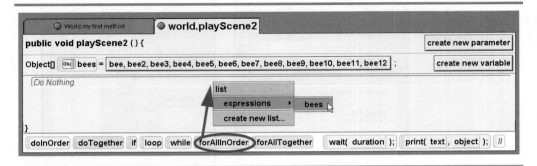

FIGURE 5-8   Dragging the **forAllInOrder** statement

When we choose **bees** from this menu, Alice generates the **forAllInOrder** statement shown in Figure 5-9.

```
⊟For all  bees ⁻ , one  Obj  item_from_bees  at a time {
    Do Nothing
}
```

FIGURE 5-9   The **forAllInOrder** statement

With this in place, we construct the necessary **move()** message, using one of the bees as a placeholder, as shown in Figure 5-10.

```
⊟For all  bees ⁻ , one  Obj  item_from_bees  at a time {
    bee2 ⁻ .move( UP ⁻ , 5 meters ⁻ ); more... ⁻
}
```

FIGURE 5-10   The **forAllInOrder** statement with a bee placeholder

We then replace the placeholder with an item from the **bees** list. To do so, we drag **item_from_bees** onto the placeholder and drop it, as shown in Figure 5-11.

FIGURE 5-11   The **forAllInOrder** statement with an item from **bees**

The resulting loop will send the **move()** message to each bee in the list, one at a time, causing them to "take off." We can similarly add statements to make the queen bee turn to face each bee and order it to take off. Figure 5-12 shows the completed scene method.

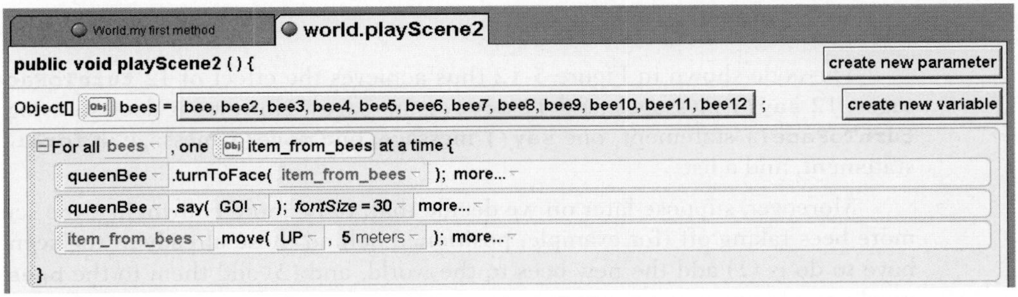

FIGURE 5-12   The **playScene2()** method (final version)

With Figure 5-4 as the starting scene, we can trace the flow through this loop as follows:

- In the first repetition of this loop, the **queenBee** faces **bee** and says **Go!**; then **bee** moves up five meters, because **item_from_bees** refers to **bee**.

- In the second repetition of the loop, the **queenBee** faces **bee2** and says **Go!**; then **bee2** moves up five meters, because **item_from_bees** refers to **bee2**.

- In the third repetition of the loop, the **queenBee** faces **bee3** and says **Go!**; then **bee3** moves up five meters, because **item_from_bees** refers to **bee3**.

- This process repeats for each bee, up to the eleventh bee.

- In the eleventh repetition of the loop, the **queenBee** faces **bee11** and says **Go!**; then **bee11** moves up five meters, because **item_from_bees** refers to **bee11**.

- In the twelfth (and final) repetition of the loop, the **queenBee** faces **bee12** and says **Go!**; then **bee12** moves up five meters, because **item_from_bees** refers to **bee12**.

Figure 5-13 shows the scene during the loop's first, third, and last repetitions.

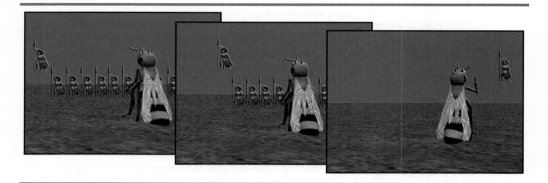

FIGURE 5-13   Repetitions 1, 3, and 12 of the loop

The code shown in Figure 5-12 thus achieves the effect of 12 **turnToFace()** messages, 12 **say()** messages, and 12 **move()** messages. However it does so using only one **turnToFace()** statement, one **say()** message, one **move()** message, a **forAllInOrder** statement, and a list!

Moreover, suppose later on we decide that, to be more convincing, the scene needs more bees taking off (for example, positioned behind those already in the scene). All we have to do is (1) add the new bees to the world, and (2) add them to the **bees** list.[1] We need not add any new **turnToFace()**, **say()**, or **move()** statements to **playScene2()**.

In any situation for which you need to do the same thing to multiple items, a data structure can save you a lot of work!

5.1.2   List Operations

The preceding example illustrates how the **forAllInOrder** statement can be used to process each of the items in a list in turn. It provides a very simple way to **iterate** (or loop) through the entries in the list, doing the same thing to each item in the list.

You may have noticed that there is also a **forAllTogether** control at the bottom of the editing pane. This can be used to create **forAllTogether** statements. Like the **forAllInOrder** statement, the **forAllTogether** statement operates on a list. However, where the **forAllInOrder** statement performs the statements within it once for each item in the list *sequentially*, the **forAllTogether** statement performs the statements within it once for each item in the list *simultaneously*, or in parallel.

To illustrate, if we wanted all of the bees in Figure 5-3 to take off at the same time instead of one at a time, we could rewrite the **playScene2()** method using the **forAllTogether** statement, as shown in Figure 5-14.

---

1.   To add new values to a list variable, just click the box of values (for example, **bee**, **bee2**, ... **bee12**) in its definition.

```
○ world.my first method    ● world.playScene2

public void playScene2 ( ) {                              create new parameter

Object[]  [Obj] bees = bee, bee2, bee3, bee4, bee5, bee6, bee7, bee8, bee9, bee10, bee11, bee12 ;    create new variable

  ☐ For all bees ▾ , every [Obj] item_from_bees together {
      queenBee ▾ .say( GO! ▾ ); fontSize = 30 ▾  more... ▾
      item_from_bees ▾ .move( UP ▾ , 5 meters ▾ ); more... ▾
  }
```

FIGURE 5-14   Making the bees take off together

Using this version of **playScene2()**, clicking Alice's **Play** button produces the screen shown in Figure 5-15.

FIGURE 5-15   The bees take off together

Alice provides the **forAllInOrder** and **forAllTogether** statements to simplify the task of processing all of the values in the list data structure. In addition to these *statements*, Alice provides *messages* that you can send to a list variable to modify it or its items. More precisely, if you drag a list variable into the *editing area* and drop it anywhere a *statement* can appear, Alice generates the menu shown in Figure 5-16.

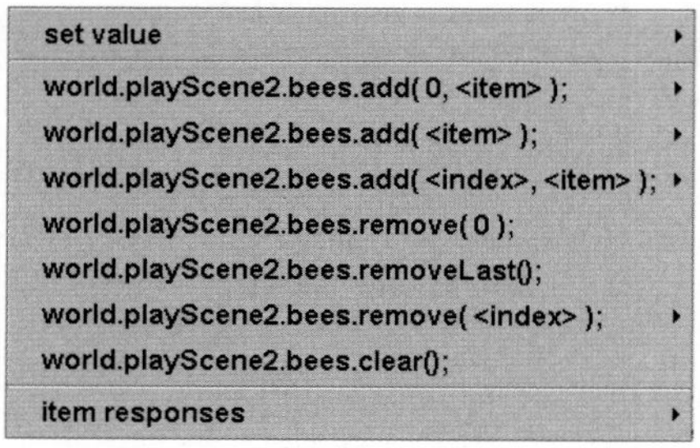

set value	▶
world.playScene2.bees.add(0, <item>);	▶
world.playScene2.bees.add(<item>);	▶
world.playScene2.bees.add(<index>, <item>);	▶
world.playScene2.bees.remove(0);	
world.playScene2.bees.removeLast();	
world.playScene2.bees.remove(<index>);	▶
world.playScene2.bees.clear();	
item responses	▶

FIGURE 5-16   The list methods menu

The three sections in this menu let you:

- Set the value of the list to another list (the **set value** choice)
- Send a message to the list (the middle portion of the menu)
- Send a message to any of the items in the list (the **item responses** choice)

Because the middle portion of the menu is unique to lists, we will examine it next.

List **Methods**. The messages you can send to a list include those shown in Figure 5-17.

Alice List Method	Behavior
`aList.add(0, val);`	Create a new item containing **val** at **aList**'s beginning
`aList.add(i, val);`	Insert a new item containing **val** at position **i** in **aList** (the item at position **i** shifts to position **i+1**, and so on)
`aList.add(val);`	Create a new item containing **val** at **aList**'s end
`aList.remove(0);`	Remove the first item from **aList**
`aList.remove(i);`	Remove the item at position **i** from **aList** (the item at position **i+1** moves to position **i**, and so on)
`aList.removeLast();`	Remove the last item from **aList**
`aList.clear();`	Remove all items from **aList**

FIGURE 5-17   List methods

Figure 5-6 showed how to initially define a list with a group of values. However, there are situations in which a program needs to modify the contents of a list *as it is running*. For example, once the bees are in the air, we might want to have the queen take off too, and add her to the **bees** list. The messages in Figure 5-17 allow a program to modify a list by adding and/or removing items.

Each item in a list has a **position**, or **index**, by which it can be accessed. The index of the first item is always zero, the index of the second item is always one, and so on. To illustrate, Figure 5-18 shows **bees** again, but this time showing the index of each list item.

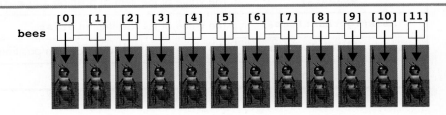

FIGURE 5-18   The list of 12 bees with index values

In the list messages **add(i, val)** and **remove(i)**, the value of **i** is the position or index at which the value will be added or removed. To illustrate, suppose we have the following list:

```
List aList = 2, 8, 4;
```

Suppose we then perform the following statements:

```
aList.remove(1);    // remove the item at index 1 (the 8)
aList.add(0, 1);    // insert 1 at the beginning
aList.add(2, 3);    // insert 3 at index 2
aList.add(5);       // append 5
```

As a result, the contents of **aList** will be **1, 2, 3, 4, 5**.

List Functions

Alice also provides function messages that we can send to a list to get information from it, as shown in Figure 5-19.

List Function	Return Value
aList.size()	The number of items in **aList**
aList.firstIndexOf(val)	The position of the first item containing **val** in **aList** (or -1 if **val** is not present in **aList**)
aList.lastIndexOf(val)	The position of the last item containing **val** in **aList** (or -1 if **val** is not present in **aList**)
aList[0]	The value of the first item in **aList**

FIGURE 5-19   List functions

continued

List Function	Return Value
aList[i]	The value of the item at position **i** in **aList**
aList.getLastItem()	The value of the last item in **aList**
aList.getRandomItem()	The value of an item at a random position in **aList**

FIGURE 5-19   List functions *(continued)*

To use these functions, you must drag a list definition into the *editing area* and drop it onto a *placeholder whose type is the function's return type*. For example, the top three functions — **size()**, **indexOf()**, and **lastIndexOf()** — each return a **Number**, so if you drop a list onto a **Number** placeholder, Alice will display a menu whose choices are these messages, as shown in the *left-hand* menu in Figure 5-20.

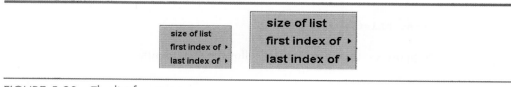

FIGURE 5-20   The list functions menus

However, if you drop a list onto a placeholder whose type is the type of item in the list (for example, **Object**), Alice will display the *right-hand* menu in Figure 5-20, from which you can choose one of the bottom four functions of Figure 5-19.

5.1.3   List Example 2: Buying Tickets

Suppose Scene 3 of a story has a line of people waiting for something (for example, to buy tickets to a film). After the first person has been served, she turns and walk away. The remaining people in the line then move forward, so that the person who was second is the new first person in line.

We might begin by building the scene shown in Figure 5-21.

FIGURE 5-21   People waiting in a line

Alice's list data structure makes it fairly easy to animate such a scene. The basic idea is to represent the line of people with a list containing each of the people in the scene. Then we can use the list methods and functions to move them around, using an algorithm like this:

```
1  personList = isis, randomGuy2, skaterGirl, skaterGuy, cleo;
2  while personList is not empty {
3      Set firstPerson to the first item in personList
4      Have firstPerson say "Two tickets please", and then "Thank you"
5      Have firstPerson turn left
6      Have firstPerson move off-screen
7      Remove the first item from personList
8      Advance the line, moving each person in personList forward
9  }
```

To determine whether a list is empty, we can compare its **size()** to zero. To get the first item in the list, we can use the **[0]** function. To "advance the line" we can either use a **forAllTogether** statement or a **forAllInOrder** statement. To remove the first item from the list, we can use the **remove(0)** method.

Figure 5-22 presents an Alice version of this algorithm, using a **forAllInOrder** statement to "advance the line."

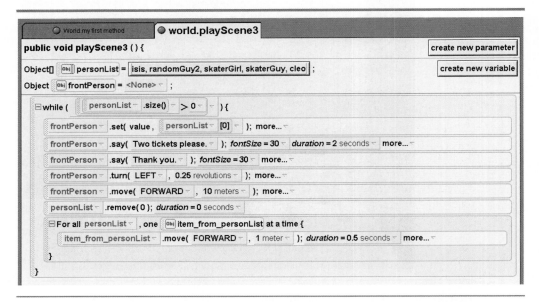

FIGURE 5-22   Animating a line of people

Figure 5-23 shows three screen shots of this scene, all taken during the first pass through the **while** statement in **playScene3()**.

FIGURE 5-23   Screen captures from **playScene3()**

To see how the people in line are moving, compare their positions against the background in each screen capture. For example, **cleo** is in front of the rounded window in the leftmost capture; in the rightmost capture, she and the others have moved forward.

The list is one of the two data structures available in Alice. The other is called the array, and we examine it next.

5.2   The Array Structure

Alice's second data structure is called the **array**. Like an Alice list, an array can store a group of values, each of which can be accessed through its position or index. However, unlike the list, the array is a *fixed-sized data structure*, meaning it cannot grow or shrink as your program runs. You can still change the values of the items in an array, but once your program begins running, its *capacity* (the maximum number of values it can store) cannot change. An array is thus a somewhat less flexible data structure than a list.

Why would anyone want to use an array instead of a list? There are two answers:

1. In Alice and most other programming languages, it takes less of a computer's memory to store a group of items in an array than it does to store the same group of items in a list. Put differently, if you have a group of items to store and the size of the group never changes, it is more *memory-efficient* to store the group in an array instead of a list.

2. In most other programming languages, items in a list cannot be accessed via index values. Instead, only the first and last item in the list can be accessed. The exact reason is beyond the scope of our discussion, but accessing an arbitrary item from a list is *much* more time-consuming than accessing an arbitrary item from an array, so most languages don't let you do it. So, if the solution to a problem requires a program to access arbitrary values from a group, then it's better to store the group in an array instead of a list. Put differently, to access an arbitrary group item, an array is more *time-efficient* than a list.

To see the Alice array in action, let's see an example.

5.2.1   Array Example 1: The Ants Go Marching

Suppose a user story has an ant marching along, singing the song "The Ants Go Marching." The lyrics to the song are as follows:

The ants go marching one-by-one *Hurrah! Hurrah!* *The ants go marching one-by-one* *Hurrah! Hurrah!* *The ants go marching one-by-one,* *the little one stopped to suck his thumb,* *and they all went marching* *down to the ground* *to get out of the rain* *BOOM! BOOM! BOOM!*	*The ants go marching two-by-two* *Hurrah! Hurrah!* *The ants go marching two-by-two* *Hurrah! Hurrah!* *The ants go marching two-by-two,* *the little one stopped to tie his shoe,* *and they all went marching* *down to the ground* *to get out of the rain* *BOOM! BOOM! BOOM!*
... *The ants go marching three-by-three,* *the little one stopped to climb a tree,* *...*	*...* *The ants go marching four-by-four,* *the little one stopped to shut the door,* *...*

.	...
..	...
The ants go marching five-by-five	*The ants go marching six-by-six*
The little one stopped to take a dive,	*The little one stopped to pick up sticks,*
...	*...*

...	...
The ants go marching seven-by-seven	*The ants go marching eight-by-eight*
The little one stopped to pray to heaven,	*The little one stopped to shut the gate,*
...	*...*

The ants go marching nine-by-nine	*The ants go marching ten-by-ten*
Hurrah! Hurrah!	*Hurrah! Hurrah!*
The ants go marching nine-by-nine	*The ants go marching ten-by-ten*
Hurrah! Hurrah!	*Hurrah! Hurrah!*
The ants go marching nine-by-nine,	*The ants go marching ten-by-ten,*
the little one stopped to check the time,	*the little one stopped to say, 'THE END',*
and they all went marching	*and they all went marching*
down to the ground	*down to the ground*
to get out of the rain	*to get out of the rain*
BOOM! BOOM! BOOM!	*BOOM! BOOM! BOOM!*

One way to build this story would be to send the ant 10 **say()** messages per verse times 10 verses = 100 **say()** messages. But many of the song's lines are exactly the same from verse to verse, so this approach would result in lots of wasteful, replicated effort.

Another way would be to recognize that this is basically a *counting problem*: the song is counting from 1 to 10. So perhaps we could use a **for** statement to count through the verses, and put statements within the **for** statement to make the ant sing a verse? This is good thinking; the difficulty is that each verse differs from the others in *two* ways:

- the number being sung (*one, two, ..., nine, ten*); and
- what the little ant does (*suck his thumb, tie his shoe, ..., check the time, say "THE END"*).

One solution is to make two indexed groups, one for each way the verses differ, as shown in Figure 5-24.

Group 1	
Index	**Numbers**
0	one
1	two
2	three
3	four

Group 2	
Index	**What the little ant does**
0	suck his thumb
1	tie his shoe
2	climb a tree
3	shut the door

FIGURE 5-24   Groups of strings

continued

Group 1	
Index	**Numbers**
4	five
5	six
6	seven
7	eight
8	nine
9	ten

Group 2	
Index	**What the little ant does**
4	take a dive
5	pick up sticks
6	pray to heaven
7	shut the gate
8	check the time
9	say 'THE END'

FIGURE 5-24   Groups of strings *(continued)*

If we defined two data structures (one for each group), then the **for** statement could count from 0 to 9, and on repetition *i*, retrieve the value associated with index *i* from each data structure.

Because the number of verses in the song is fixed, it makes sense to use array data structures to store the two groups. Defining an array variable is similar to defining a list variable, which we saw in Figures 5-5 and 5-6. The only difference is that we must specify that we want an **Array** variable instead of a **List** variable, as shown in Figure 5-25.

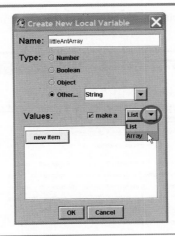

FIGURE 5-25   Creating an **Array** variable

Once we have created the array variable, we can fill it with values in exactly the same way as we would a list (see Figure 5-6).

Given the ability to define arrays, we can build this algorithm to solve the problem:

```
 1  Define numberArray = one, two, three, four, five, six, seven, eight,
    nine, ten;
 2  Define littleAntArray = suck his thumb, tie his shoe, climb a tree,
    shut the door, take a dive, pick up sticks, pray to heaven, shut the
    gate, check the time, say 'THE END',
 3  for each index 0 through 9 {
 4      repeatedLine = "The ants go marching " + numberArray[index] + "-by-"
 5      + numberArray[index];
 6      ant.say(repeatedLine);
 7      ant.say("Hurrah! Hurrah!");
 8      ant.say(repeatedLine);
 9      ant.say("Hurrah! Hurrah!");
10      ant.say(repeatedLine);
11      ant.say("The little one stopped to " + littleAntArray[index]);
12      ant.say("and they all went marching");
13      ant.say("down to the ground");
14      ant.say("to get out of the rain.");
15      ant.say("BOOM! BOOM! BOOM!);
16  }
```

Using this algorithm, we can build the program, as shown in Figure 5-26.

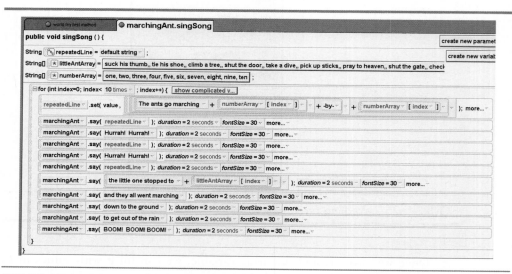

FIGURE 5-26   Singing "The Ants Go Marching"

When performed, this method (using just 12 statements and three variables) causes the **marchingAnt** to "sing" the entire 10-verse, 100-line song!

If we add a method that makes the ant march, and then have the ant sing the song as it marches, the result will appear something like what is shown in Figure 5-27.

FIGURE 5-27   The singing ant in action

5.2.2   Array Operations

Like lists, arrays are **indexed variables**, meaning their items can be accessed using an index value. For example, we could have written the "bees" program in Figure 5-12 using an array instead of a list. If we had done so, we could have drawn the **bees** group as shown in Figure 5-28:

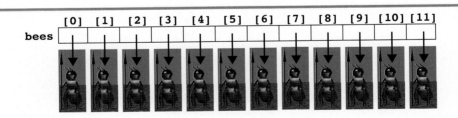

FIGURE 5-28   An array of 12 bees

We saw in Section 5.1.2 that Alice provides a variety of predefined operations that can be used with list variables. By contrast, there are only a few operations for array variables. These are listed in Figure 5-29.

Alice Array Operation	Behavior
`anArray[i] = val;`	Change the value at position *i* in `anArray` to `val`
`val.set(value, anArray[i]);`	Retrieve the value at position *i* in `anArray`
`anArray.length`	Retrieve the number of values in `anArray`

FIGURE 5-29   Array operations

The notation `anArray[i]` is called the **subscript operation**. As shown in Figure 5-29, there are two versions of the subscript operation. The first one is sometimes called the *write version*, because it changes (that is, writes) the value of item *i* of the array. The second one is sometimes called the *read version*, because it retrieves (that is, reads) the value of item *i* of the array.

If an array variable is dropped where a *statement* can appear, Alice displays a menu from which you can select the write version of the subscript operation. If an array variable is dropped onto a *placeholder* variable or value, Alice displays a menu from which you can select either the array's `length` attribute or the read version of the subscript operation.[2]

At the time of this writing, the Alice `forAllInOrder` and `forAllTogether` statements can only be used on a list, not on an array. Until this changes, if you want to process each of the values in an array, you must use a `for` statement like this:

```
for (int index = 0; index < anArray.length; index++) {
        // do something with anArray[index]
}
```

To illustrate, Figure 5-30 presents an alternative version of Figure 5-12 using an array.

---

2.   When this was written, Alice was very inconsistent in displaying these menus, for both arrays and lists. Hopefully, these problems will be fixed by the time you read this!

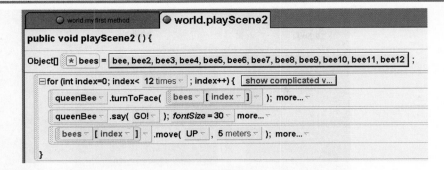

FIGURE 5-30   The bees take off using an array

This method produces exactly the same behavior as that of Figure 5-12. However, note that because we cannot use a **forAllTogether** statement on an array, we cannot use an array to produce the simultaneous behavior shown in Figure 5-14 and Figure 5-15.

5.2.3 Array Example 2: Random Access

Suppose we want to build the following simple story:

> **Scene: A castle has two magical doors. The left door tells the right door a random knock-knock joke.**

If the left door told the right door the same joke every time, then this story would quickly become boring and the user would not want to play the story more than twice. However, if each time the scene is played, the left door tells a *random* (that is, potentially different) knock-knock joke, we make the scene more interesting and worth revisiting.

We can begin by positioning the **camera** and **castle** as shown in Figure 5-31.

FIGURE 5-31   The castle doors

Our next problem is to figure out how to make the doors tell a knock-knock joke. Let's look at several jokes, to see what is the same and what is different about each one:

Joke 1	Joke 2	Joke 3
L: Knock-knock	L: Knock-knock	L: Knock-knock
R: Who's there?	R: Who's there?	R: Who's there?
L: Boo.	L: Who.	L: Little old lady.
R: Boo who?	R: Who who?	R: Little old lady who?
L: Don't cry, it's just a joke.	L: Is there an owl in here?	L: I didn't know you could yodel!

Comparing these (lame) jokes, we see that knock-knock jokes have the following structure:

L: Knock-knock
R: Who's there?
L: *name*
R: *name who?*
L: *punchline*

where *name* and *punchline* are the parts that vary from joke to joke.

If we make *name* and *punchline* array variables, then we can store multiple jokes in them. For example, to store the three jokes above, we would define *name* and *punchline* as follows:

```
String [] name = {"Boo", "Who", "Little old lady" };
String [] punchline = {"Don't cry, it's just a joke.",
                       "Is there an owl in here?",
                       "I didn't know you could yodel!"};
```

Such definitions create parallel data structures in which **punchline[0]** corresponds to **name[0]**, **punchline[1]** corresponds to **name[1]**, and so on. We can visualize them as shown in Figure 5-32.

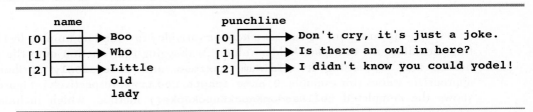

FIGURE 5-32   The **name** and **punchline** arrays

Once we have the parts of the jokes stored in arrays, we can tell the joke at index *i* as follows:

L: Knock-knock

R: Who's there?

L: *name[i]*

R: *name[i]* who?

L: *punchline[i]*

That is, if *i* has the value 0, then this will tell the "Boo who" joke; if *i* has the value 1, then it will tell the "Who who" joke, and so on.

Generating Random Numbers

To tell a random joke from the array, we need to generate a **random number** for the index *i*. That is we need to set *i* to a value that is randomly selected from the range of possible index values for the array. Fortunately, Alice makes this fairly easy by providing a **world** function named **Random.nextDouble()**, as shown in Figure 5-33.

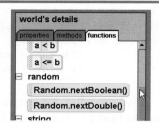

FIGURE 5-33   The world function `Random.nextDouble()`

Using this function, we can set a **Number** variable *i* to a random number by (1) setting the value of i to a placeholder value, (2) dragging the function onto the placeholder, and (3) setting its **minimum**, **maximum**, and **integerOnly** attributes to appropriate values (for example, **0**, **name.length**, and **true**, respectively). Figure 5-34 shows the completed **tellRandomKnockKnockJoke()** method, which includes the jokes above, plus two others.

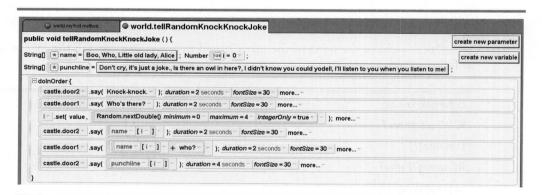

FIGURE 5-34   The `tellRandomKnockKnockJoke()` method

Each time this method is performed, it tells a knock-knock joke selected at random from the **name** and **punchline** arrays. By randomly generating the value of **i**, and then using that same value as the index for both **name[i]** and **punchline[i]**, we ensure that the name and punchline for a given joke match one another.

Random Details

The **Random.nextDouble()** function has two quirks to keep in mind:

- If you wish to generate an *integer* (that is, a whole number without decimal places like -1, 0, 1, or 1234), be sure to set the **integerOnly** attribute to **true**, or else the function will produce a *real* number (that is, a number with decimal places like -1.25, 0.05, 98.7654, etc.).

- In Figure 5-34, the arrays contain 4 items, indexed 0, 1, 2, and 3. To generate a random index value from the group {0, 1, 2, 3}, we specified a minimum value of 0, but a maximum value of 4. In general, if we want to generate a random number from the range **a** through **b**, then we should specify **a** as the minimum value and **b+1** as the maximum value. Put differently, whatever minimum value we specify is *included* in the range of randomly generated values, but whatever maximum value we specify is *excluded* from the range of randomly generated values.

Recall that in Figure 5-19, we saw that one of the messages we can send to an Alice list is the **getRandomItem()** function. In situations where we just need to retrieve one random item from a data structure, a list and this function provide an easy way to solve the problem.

However, we cannot use a list and the **getRandomItem()** function to solve the random knock-knock joke problem (at least not as easily). Do you see why not? The issue is that the problem has *two* data structures: one containing the names and one containing the corresponding punchlines. If we were to store the names and punchlines in two lists and then send each list the **getRandomItem()** function, the randomly selected punchline would be unlikely to correspond to the randomly selected name.[3]

5.3   Alice Tip: Using the `partNamed()` Function

Suppose that Scene 1 of a story begins as follows:

> Scene: The court of the fairy queen is crowded with fairy-courtiers talking amongst themselves. One of the fairies announces, "Her majesty, the Queen!" The fairy queen enters her court, and all the courtiers turn toward her. As she moves along the promenade leading to her throne, each courtier in succession turns to her and bows. Upon reaching her throne, the queen turns and says "Please rise." As one, the courtiers turn toward her and rise from their bows.

Looking over the nouns in the story, we might begin building this scene by creating a "fairy court" in a woodland setting, with a promenade leading to a throne, and a crowd of fairies flanking each side of the promenade. Figure 5-35 shows one possible realization of this scene using various fairy, forest, and other classes from the Alice Web Gallery.

---

3.   We could replace the two arrays in Figure 5-34 with two lists. Because Alice lists support the subscript operation, we could randomly generate an index *i* and then access the item at position *i* in each list. However, because the data structures' sizes remain fixed as the program runs, using an array is preferable.

FIGURE 5-35   The court of the fairy queen

We also chose class **OliveWaterblossom** as the fairy queen, added her to the world, and positioned her behind the camera (13 meters from the throne) to set up her entry to the court.

With the scene set, we are ready to think about generating the behavior required by the user story. We might break the actions down into the following sequence of steps:

1. One of the fairies announces, "Her majesty, the Queen!"

2. As the queen enters the court, each courtier simultaneously turns to face the camera.

3. Do together:

    a. Move the queen 13 meters forward (down the promenade, toward her throne).
    b. Make the queen's wings flap.
    c. As she passes each courtier, have him or her turn toward the queen and bow.

4. The queen turns 1/2 revolution (so that she is facing her courtiers).

5. The queen says "Please rise."

6. Together each courtier turns toward the queen and rises from his or her bow.

Together, these steps make up an algorithm we can use for the **playScene1()** method.

Defining The Method

What is the best way to implement this algorithm? Steps 1 and 5 require all courtiers to take a simultaneous action, and Step 2c requires each courtier to take an action one at a time. One way to elicit these simultaneous and one-at-a-time actions is to place the courtiers into a list data structure. Given such a list, we can use the **forAllTogether** statement to make all courtiers do the same thing simultaneously in Steps 1 and 5, and we can use the **forAllInOrder** statement to make them all do the same thing one at a time in Step 2c.

With this approach, we can revise the algorithm as follows:

1. Let **courtierList** be a list of all the courtier fairies.

2. The courtier nearest the throne announces the queen.

3. For all items in **courtierList** together:
    Each item in **courtierList** turns to face the camera.

4. Do together:

    a. The queen moves 13 meters forward (down the promenade, toward her throne).
    b. The queen's wings flap.
    c. For each item in **courtierList**, one at a time:
       The item in **courtierList** turns toward the queen and bows.

5. The queen turns 1/2 revolution.

6. The queen says "Please rise."

7. For all items in **courtierList** together:
    Each item in **courtierList** turns toward the queen and rises from his/her bow.

Most of these steps are straightforward to program in Alice. However, there are two subtle points to keep in mind as we do so.

Defining The List

One subtle part is that when we define the **courtierList** variable as a list of **Object** and then add fairies to it, the order of the fairies in the list is significant. That is, because we are using the **forAllInOrder** statement in Step 3c and this statement goes through the items in the list from first to last, we must be careful to add the fairies to the list so that those closest to the camera are earlier in the list and those who are farthest from the camera are later in the list. Otherwise, the fairies will not turn toward the queen and bow to her as she moves past them. Figure 5-36 presents a fragment of this list from the **playScene1()** method.

Object☐ 〖abc〗 courtierList = | shadeAniseed, petalBeamweb, sprightlyReedsmoke, mabHazelnut, meadSeafeather, lichenZenspider, leafFlameglimmer, h

FIGURE 5-36   Defining the courtier list

Making A Fairy Bow

The second subtle part is generating the bowing and rising behaviors for the courtiers. It is easy to make an individual fairy-courtier bow and rise, by "opening" the individual in the *object tree*, selecting their **upperBody** component, and then sending this component the **turn()** message, as shown in Figure 5-37.

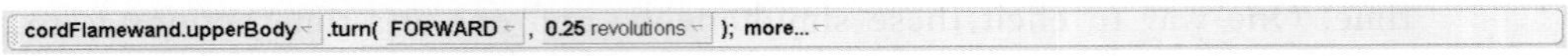

| cordFlamewand.upperBody ⌄ | .turn(FORWARD ⌄ | , 0.25 revolutions ⌄ |); more... ⌄ |

FIGURE 5-37   Making an individual courtier bow

The difficulty arises when we seek to use this approach with an item from the list within a **forAllInOrder** or **forAllTogether** statement. Although each item in the list is a fairy that has an **upperBody** component, we defined the **courtierList** variable as a list of **Object**s. Because not all Alice **Object**s have **upperBody** components (for example, buildings, fish, trees, etc.), Alice will not let us access the **upperBody** component of an item from the list. So we *can* make each courtier turn and face the queen by programming:

```
for all courtierList, one item_from_courtierList at a time:
    item_from_courtierList.turnToFace(oliveWaterblossom);
```

But we *cannot* make each courtier bow to the queen by programming:

```
for all courtierList, one item_from_courtierList at a time:
    item_from_courtierList.upperBody.turn(FORWARD, 0.25); // NO!
```

Because the lists are lists of **Object**s, we can only send a list item a message (or select a component) that is common to all **Object**s.

For this situation, every Alice object provides a function message called **partNamed(component)** that can be sent to that object to retrieve its part named **component**. In our situation, we know that every fairy in the list contains a component named **upperBody**, so we can send each fairy the **partNamed(upperBody)** message to retrieve its **upperBody** part, and then send that part the **turn()** message to make the fairy bow.

To use the **partNamed()** function, we begin with the statement shown in Figure 5-37, using the courtier's **upperBody** component as a placeholder. We then drag the courtier's **partNamed()** function onto the placeholder, yielding the statement shown in Figure 5-38.

| cordFlamewand ⌄ | .partNamed(⌄) ⌄ | .turn(FORWARD ⌄ | , 0.25 revolutions ⌄ |); more... ⌄ |

FIGURE 5-38   Using the **partNamed()** function

If we click the list arrow for **partNamed()**'s argument, and choose **other...** from the menu that appears, Alice displays a dialog box where we can type the name of the part we wish to access (**upperBody** in this case). When we do this, we get the statement shown in Figure 5-39.

cordFlamewand .partNamed(upperBody) .turn(FORWARD , 0.25 revolutions); more...

FIGURE 5-39   The `partNamed()` function

In the statement in Figure 5-39, **cordFlamewand** is a placeholder that we need to replace with an item from the list. To do so, we can drag and drop this statement into a **forAllInOrder** (or **forAllTogether**) statement, specify the **courtierList** as the **forAllInOrder** statement's list variable, and then drag the loop's **item_from_courtierList** variable onto the placeholder to replace it. The resulting statement is shown in Figure 5-40.

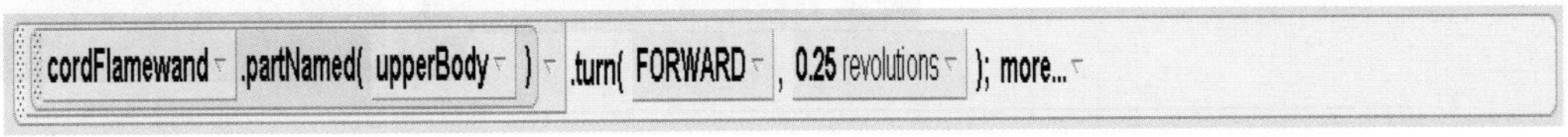

cordFlamewand .partNamed(upperBody) .turn(FORWARD , 0.25 revolutions); more...

FIGURE 5-40   Replacing the placeholder with a list item

Using this same approach, we can make the courtiers rise at the end of the scene. Figure 5-41 shows the completed **playScene1()** method.

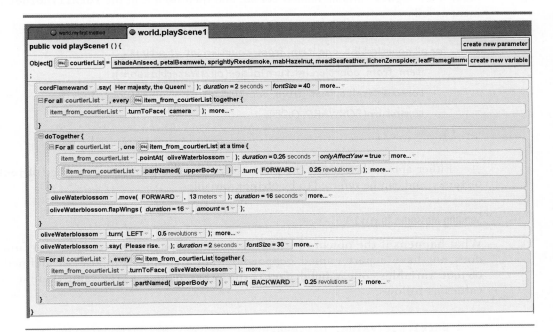

FIGURE 5-41   The `playScene1()` method (final version)

When we run the program, we get the desired behavior. Figure 5-42 presents three screen captures: one partway through the **forAllInOrder** statement, one after all have bowed and the queen says "Please rise.", and one at the end of the scene.

FIGURE 5-42   Screen captures from `playScene1()`

Components Are Objects

The **partNamed()** function thus provides a means of retrieving a component of an object. The components of an object are themselves objects, so in **playScene1()**, we could have defined an **Object** variable named **torso**, and then used it in the **forAllInOrder** statement as follows:

```
for all courtierList, one item_from_courtierList at a time {
    item_from_courtierList.turnToFace(oliveWaterblossom);
    torso.set(value, item_from_courtierList.partNamed(upperBody));
    torso.turn(FORWARD, 0.25);
}
```

Either approach is okay. The point is that the components of an Alice **Object** are **Object**s, and can be referred to by **Object** variables.

Sending Messages to `null`

What happens if the object to which we send the **partNamed(component)** function does not have a part named **component**? For example, suppose we defined two **Object** variables, one named **part1**, the other named **part2**, and then set their values as follows:

```
part1.set(value, OliveWaterblossom.partNamed(upperBody));
part2.set(value, OliveWaterblossom.partNamed(xyz));
```

Because **OliveWaterblossom** does not have a component named **xyz**, the **partNamed()** function returns a special "zero" value named **null**, that denotes the absence of an **Object**. This value **null** is stored in variable **part2**, instead of a reference to a component. We can envision these two variables as shown in Figure 5-43.

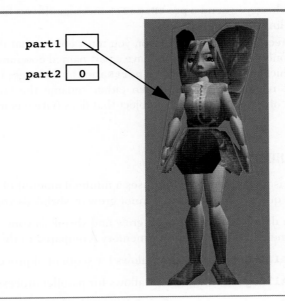

part1
part2   0

FIGURE 5-43   Variables with non-**null** and **null** values

Where **part1** refers to the queen from the waist up, **part2** refers to *nothing*. If the program then erroneously tries to send a message to **part2**:

```
part2.turn(FORWARD, 0.25);
```

Alice will generate an error message:

```
Alice has detected a problem with your world:
subject must not be null.
```

Alice will display this error any time a message is sent via a variable whose value is **null**, which Alice usually displays as **<None>**. This error may appear for a variety of reasons, including the following:

- You deleted an object from your world to which your program was sending a message.
- You deleted a variable from a method or world through which a message was being sent.
- You misspelled the name of the component in the **partNamed()** function.
- You sent the **partNamed(component)** function to an object that does not have a part named **component**.

To correct the first two kinds of errors (which are by far the most common), look through your program's methods for statements in which a message is sent to **<None>**. When you find such a statement, either replace **<None>** with a valid object or delete/disable the statement.

To correct the second kind of error, check the spelling of the component in each statement where you send a **partNamed()** message. If you find one that is incorrect, correct its spelling.

To correct the third kind of error, you must ensure that the **partNamed(component)** function is only sent to objects that have a part named **component**. Check the parts of each object to which you are sending the **partNamed()** message. If you find one that does not have a part named **component**, then either rename the component in that object, or replace that object with a different object that does have a component named **component**.

5.4   Chapter Summary

❏ An array is a data structure that uses a minimal amount of your computer's memory to store a sequence of items, but cannot grow or shrink as your program runs.

❏ A list is a data structure that can grow and shrink as your program runs, at the cost of using some additional computer memory (compared to the array).

❏ The **forAllInOrder** statement allows for sequential processing of the items in a list.

❏ The **forAllTogether** statement allows for parallel processing of the items in a list.

❏ The **Random.nextDouble()** function provides a way to generate random numbers.

❏ The **partNamed(component)** function lets us retrieve a part of an object (usually so that we can send it a message).

❏ The **null** value is a special "zero" value used to indicate the *absence* of an object. In the *editing area*, Alice usually displays **<None>** to represent the **null** value.

5.4.1   Key Terms

array	iterate
data structure	list
forAllInOrder statement	**null**
forAllTogether statement	**partNamed()** function
index	position
item	random number

Programming Projects

5.1 Using the **Cheerleader** class from the Alice Gallery, build a world containing 5–6 cheerleaders who lead a cheer at a sporting event. Your cheer can be either funny or serious, and it can either be a cheer unique to your school or a standard cheer (for example, "The Wave").

5.2 *This Old Man* is a silly song with the lyrics below. Create an Alice program containing a character who sings this song, using as few statements as possible.

This old man, he played one. He played knick-knack on my drum, with a knick-knack paddy-wack give a dog a bone. This old man came rolling home.	This old man, he played two. He played knick-knack on my shoe, with a knick-knack paddy-wack give a dog a bone. This old man came rolling home.
This old man, he played three. He played knick-knack on my knee, ...	This old man, he played four. He played knick-knack on my door, ...
This old man, he played five. He played knick-knack on my hive, ...	This old man, he played six. He played knick-knack on my sticks, ...
This old man, he played seven. He played knick-knack up in heaven, ...	This old man, he played eight. He played knick-knack on my gate, ...
This old man, he played nine. He played knick-knack on my spine, with a knick-knack paddy-wack give a dog a bone. This old man came rolling home.	This old man, he played ten. He played knick-knack once again, with a knick-knack paddy-wack give a dog a bone. This old man came rolling home.

5.3 Create a city scene featuring a parade. Store the paraders (that is, vehicles, people, etc.) in a data structure and use it to coordinate their movements. Make your parade as festive as possible.

5.4 Build a world containing a person who can calculate the average, minimum, and maximum of a group of numbers in his or her head. Use a **NumberDialog** to get the numbers from the user. Have your person and each **NumberDialog** tell the user to enter a special value (for example, -999) after the last value in the sequence has been entered. Store the group of numbers in a data structure, and write three new world functions — **average()**, **minimum()**, and **maximum()** — that take a data structure as their argument and return the average, minimum, and maximum value in the structure, respectively. When all the numbers have been entered, have your person "say" the group's average, minimum, and maximum values.

5.5 Create a scene in which a group of Rockettes do a dance number (for example, the Can-Can). Store the Rockettes in a data structure, and use **forAllInOrder** and/or **forAllTogether** statements to coordinate the movements of their dance routine.

5.6 Create a "springtime" scene that runs for a minute or so, starting with an empty field but ending with the field covered with flowers. The flowers should "grow" out of the ground as your scene plays. Make your program as short as possible by storing the flowers in a data structure.

5.7 Proceed as in Problem 5.6, but use random-number generation to make the flowers appear in a different order or pattern every time your program is run.

5.8 Create a scene in which two people are talking near a not-very-busy intersection, which uses four stop signs to control the traffic. Build the intersection using buildings and roads. Define two data structures: one containing a group of vehicles, and one containing the four directions a vehicle can move through the intersection (for example, north, south, east, and west). As your characters talk, use random numbers to select a vehicle and its direction.

5.9 Choose an old pop song that has several unique arm or body motions and whose lyrics are available on the Internet (for example, *YMCA* by the Village People, *Walk Like An Egyptian* by the Bangles, etc.). Using Alice, create a "music video" for the song, in which several people sing the song and use their arms or bodies to make the motions. Make your video as creative as possible, but try to avoid writing the same statements more than once. If you have access to a *legal* digital copy of the song, use the **playSound()** message to play it during your video.

5.10 Create a scene containing a group of similar creatures from the Alice gallery (for example, a herd of horses, a school of fish, a pack of wolves, etc.). Store your group in a data structure, and write a method that makes the group exhibit *flocking behavior*, in which the behavior of one member of the group causes the rest of the group to behave in a similar fashion. (Hint: designate one member of the group as the leader, and make the leader the first item in the data structure.)

Chapter 6
Events

It's not the events of our lives that shape us, but our beliefs as to what those events mean.

ANTHONY ROBBINS

*Often do the spirits
Of great events stride on before the events,
And in to-day already walks to-morrow*

SAMUEL TAYLOR COLERIDGE

To understand reality is not the same as to know about outward events. It is to perceive the essential nature of things. The best-informed man is not necessarily the wisest. Indeed there is a danger that precisely in the multiplicity of his knowledge he will lose sight of what is essential. But on the other hand, knowledge of an apparently trivial detail quite often makes it possible to see into the depth of things. And so the wise man will seek to acquire the best possible knowledge about events, but always without becoming dependent upon this knowledge. To recognize the significant in the factual is wisdom.

DIETRICH BONHOEFFER

In the event of a water landing, I have been designed to act as a flotation device.

DATA (BRENT SPINER), IN *STAR TREK: INSURRECTION*

Objectives

Upon completion of this chapter, you will be able to:

❏ Create new events in Alice

❏ Create handler methods for Alice events

❏ Use events to build interactive stories

Most of the programs we have written so far have been scenes from stories that, once the user clicks Alice's **Play** button, simply proceed from beginning to end. For some of our **interactive programs**, the user must enter a number or a string, but entering such values via the keyboard has been all that we have required of the user in terms of interaction with the program.

When a user clicks Alice's **Play** button for a program, it *triggers* a change in the program — usually creating a flow that begins at the first statement in **world.my_first_method()**. An action by the user (or the program) that causes a change in the program is called an **event**. For example, clicking Alice's **Play** button triggers a **When the world starts** event.

Alice supports a variety of events, including those listed in Figure 6-1.[1]

Alice Event	Triggered By	Triggered When
`When the world starts`	the user	the user clicks Alice's **Play** button
`*While the world is running`		the world is running
`When a key is typed`	the user	the user releases a keyboard key
`*While a key is pressed`		the user holds down a keyboard key
`When the mouse is clicked on something`	the user	the user clicks the left mouse button while pointing at an object
`*While the mouse is pressed on something`		the user holds down the left mouse button while pointing at an object
`While something is true`	the program	a condition remains true
`*When something becomes true`		a condition becomes true
`When a variable changes`	the program	a variable changes its value
`Let the mouse move <objects>`	the user	the user moves the mouse
`Let the arrow keys move <subject>`	the user	the user presses one of the arrow keys
`Let the mouse move the camera`	the user	the user moves the mouse
`Let the mouse orient the camera`	the user	the user moves the mouse

FIGURE 6-1   Alice events

1.   An event marked with an asterisk (*) is accessible by (1) creating the event above it in Figure 6-1, (2) right-clicking on that event, and then (3) choosing **change to ...** from the menu that appears.

There are two steps to making a program respond when an event occurs:

1. Choose (or define) a method providing the behavior to occur in response to the event.

2. Tell Alice to invoke that method whenever the event occurs.

Invoking a method in response to an event is called **handling the event**, and a method that is invoked in response to an event is often called an **event handler**. A program that solves a problem or tells a story mainly through events and handlers is called an **event-driven program**.

In the rest of this chapter, we will see how to build event-driven programs. While we will not cover all Alice events, we will provide a representative introduction to what they can do.

6.1   Handling Mouse Clicks: The Magical Doors

To let us see how an event-driven world differs from those we have built before, let us revise the scene-story from Section 5.2.3 as follows:

> Scene: A castle has two magical doors. When the user clicks on the right door, it opens; but when the user clicks on the left door, it tells the right door a random knock-knock joke.

Because some of the behavior is the same as in the world we built in Section 5.2.3, we will begin with that world. As before, the initial shot is as shown in Figure 6-2.

FIGURE 6-2   The castle doors

We will deal with each door separately. However, before we begin, we should prevent the left door from telling jokes when we run the world. To do so, we delete the `tellRandomKnockKnockJoke()` message from `my_first_method()`.[2]

6.1.1   The Right Door

You may recall from the Alice tutorials that handling mouse clicks is easy in Alice. To do so, we follow two steps:

1. If the event should trigger behavior that requires more than one message, we define a method that produces that behavior. This method will be the handler.

2. We create a new event in the *events area* that invokes the handler — either the method we defined in Step 1, or the single message that produces the required behavior.

To illustrate, the behavior to make the right door open can be elicited with a single message, `turn()`, so we need not create a new method. Instead, we proceed to Step 2 by clicking the **create new event** button and choosing **When the mouse is clicked on something** from the menu that appears, as shown in Figure 6-3.

FIGURE 6-3   Creating a new mouse event

When we select this choice, Alice creates a new event in the *events area*, as shown below.

FIGURE 6-4   A new mouse event

---

2.   Alternatively, we could achieve the same effect by deleting **When the world starts do world.my_first_method()** from the *events area*.

To satisfy the user story, we need this event to be triggered by clicking on the right door (**castle.door1**), rather than **anything**. To make this happen, we click the list arrow next to **anything** and select **castle->door1**, modifying the event as shown in Figure 6-5.

When ☐ is clicked on castle.door1 ▾ , do Nothing ▾

FIGURE 6-5   A mouse event for the right door

The object from which an event originates — **castle.door1** in this case — is called the **event source**.

To handle this event, we can replace **Nothing** with the message **castle. door1.turn(LEFT, 0.25);** by opening up the **castle** in the *object tree*, selecting **door1**, and then from the *methods* pane of the *details area*, dragging the **turn()** message to the *events area* and dropping it on **Nothing**. Figure 6-6 shows the resulting event.

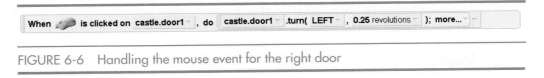

When ☐ is clicked on castle.door1 ▾ , do castle.door1 ▾ .turn(LEFT ▾ , 0.25 revolutions ▾); more... ▾ ▾

FIGURE 6-6   Handling the mouse event for the right door

Congratulations — you have just handled your first event! When we click Alice's **Play** button, nothing happens until the user clicks the right door, at which point it swings open.

6.1.2   The Left Door

Dealing with the left door is nearly as easy as the right door, but only because we already have a method that makes the left door tell a random knock-knock joke (see Figure 5-33). That is, if we had not already written **world.tellRandomKnockKnockJoke()**, we would have to write a handler method for this event, as described in Step 1 above.

Since we already have a method to serve as a handler, we can proceed to Step 2 of the event steps. To do so, we use the same approach we saw in Figure 6-3 through Figure 6-6, but specifying **castle.door2** as the source of this event, and dragging-and-dropping **world.tellRandomKnockKnockJoke()** as its handler. This is shown in Figure 6-7.

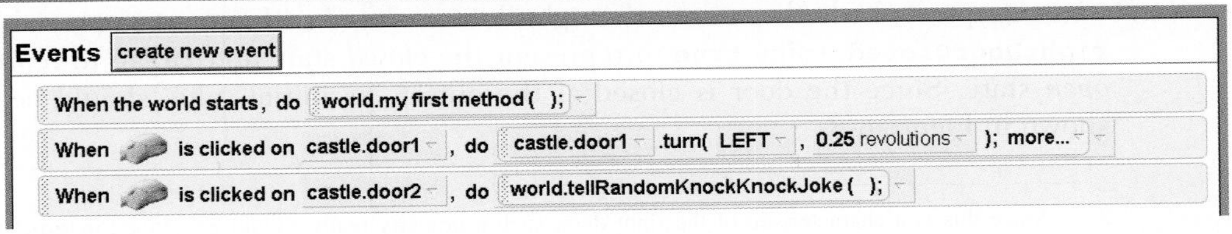

Events create new event

When the world starts, do world.my first method ( ); ▾

When ☐ is clicked on castle.door1 ▾ , do castle.door1 ▾ .turn(LEFT ▾ , 0.25 revolutions ▾); more... ▾ ▾

When ☐ is clicked on castle.door2 ▾ , do world.tellRandomKnockKnockJoke ( ); ▾

FIGURE 6-7   Handling the mouse event for the left door

That's it! Now, when we click Alice's **Play** button, clicking on the left door produces a random knock-knock joke, while clicking on the right door causes that door to open.

Note that, unlike past worlds we have built, **world.my_first_method()** does nothing in this new world. Instead, all of the interesting behavior lies in the handler methods, which are triggered by the event of the user clicking the mouse.

6.1.3   The Right Door Revisited

If we test the world thoroughly, we find that the right door opens correctly *the first time* we click on it. However if we subsequently click on the right door again, it turns left *again* (precisely what we told it to do). The mistake lies in the *logic* we used in defining how that door should behave. Such mistakes are called **logic errors**. A better response to a mouse click on the right door would be to open the door if it is closed and to close the door if it is open.

It is important to see that it is okay to revise the user story when testing reveals a weakness. Just as a filmmaker may rewrite a scene the night before it is shot, a programmer may have to rewrite a part of the user story to improve the overall program.

Generating the new behavior requires more than one message, so we will write a handler method and invoke it in place of the **turn()** message shown in Figure 6-6.

Design

To design this method, we can revise the right door part of the user story as follows:

> **When the user clicks on the right door, if it is closed, it opens; otherwise, it closes.**

Notice that the revised story contains the magic word *if*. This strongly suggests that the method will need an **if** statement.

Programming: Storing the Door's State

One way to produce this new behavior is to add a new property to the castle, to indicate whether or not its right door is closed.[3] To do so, we select **castle** in the *object tree*, click the *properties* tab in the *details area*, and then click the **create new variable** button, as we saw back in Section 3.3.

The right door is in one of two states: either it is *closed* or it is *open*. This means that we can represent whether or not the right door is closed with a **Boolean** variable named **rightDoorClosed**, using **true** to represent the *closed* state and **false** to represent the *open* state. Since the door is closed at the outset, its initial value should be **true**, as shown in Figure 6-8.

---

3.   Since this is a characteristic of the right door, such a property really should be defined in **castle.door1**. Unfortunately, Alice only lets you add properties, methods, and questions to an object at the "top" level of the *object tree*, so the best available place to store this property is **castle**.

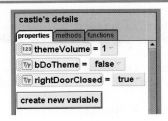

FIGURE 6-8   Storing the state of the castle's right door

When the user clicks on the right door, the handler method for that event can use an **if** statement to determine which way to **turn()** it (**LEFT** or **RIGHT**), and then update the value of **rightDoorClosed** from **true** to **false** (or vice versa) to reflect the door's changed state.

Programming: Defining the Handler

We create a handler method the same way as any other method: by choosing the *methods* tab in the *details area*, clicking the **create new method** button, naming the method, and then defining its behavior. As usual, if a handler method affects the behavior of a single object, it should be defined within that object; otherwise it should be stored in the **world**. Figure 6-9 shows the **castle.openOrCloseRightDoor()** method.

```
○ world.my first method    ● castle.openOrCloseRightDoor

public void openOrCloseRightDoor () {                                  create new parameter
                                                                      create new variable

  doInOrder {
    if ( castle.rightDoorClosed ) {
      castle.door1 .turn( LEFT , 0.25 revolutions ); more...
    } else {
      castle.door1 .turn( RIGHT , 0.25 revolutions ); more...
    }
    castle.rightDoorClosed .set( value , ! castle.rightDoorClosed ); more...
  }
}
```

FIGURE 6-9   Handling clicks on the castle's right door

The last statement in Figure 6-9 uses the logical *not* operator (**!**) we saw in Section 4.1.4 to invert the value of **rightDoorClosed** from **true** to **false** when opening the door, and from **false** to **true** when closing the door.

The approach shown in Figure 6-9 can be generalized into a standard pattern for situations in which an object can be in one of two states (for example, *open-closed*, *in-out*, *on-off*, etc.) to switch the object from one state to the other. We can generalize the pattern for such **two-state behavior** as follows:

```
if (booleanStateVariable) {
    // do what is needed to change the object
    // from the first state to the second state
} else {
    // do what is needed to change the object
    // from the second state to the first state
}
booleanVariable = !booleanVariable. // update the state variable
```

Programming: Handling the Event

Given the **openOrCloseRightDoor()** handler method shown in Figure 6-9, we can finish the program by specifying that it be the handler for the **When the mouse is clicked on castle.door1** event, by dragging the new method and dropping it on top of the previous handler (the **castle.door1.turn()** message). Figure 6-10 shows the resulting *events area*.

Events create new event

When the world starts, do world.my first method ( );

When [hand] is clicked on castle.door1 , do castle.openOrCloseRightDoor ( );

When [hand] is clicked on castle.door2 , do world.tellRandomKnockKnockJoke ( );

FIGURE 6-10   The (revised) *events area*

Now, a click on the closed right door opens it, and a click on the open right door closes it.

6.1.4   Event Handling Is Simultaneous

One tricky thing about events is that two events can occur almost simultaneously, requiring their handlers to run at the same time. For example, in the "castle doors" program we wrote in this section, a user could click on the left door and then click on the right door, before the left door finishes the joke. Figure 6-11 shows two screen captures under these circumstances.

FIGURE 6-11   Handling simultaneous events

As shown in Figure 6-11, Alice handles such simultaneous events quite well. The first (left) screen capture shows the left door beginning its knock-knock joke while the right door is opening. The handlers for the left and right doors thus run simultaneously. When the right door's handler finishes, the left door's handler keeps running, as seen in the second screen capture.

Handlers running simultaneously usually work well, but if two running handlers both modify the same property of an object, a conflict may arise. For example, to tell a knock-knock joke, the left door's handler sends both doors **say()** messages. If the right door's handler also sent either door a **say()** message, then the simultaneous performance of both handlers would interfere with the joke and create a conflict. To avoid such conflicts, avoid designing programs in which two different events simultaneously modify the same property of the same object.

6.1.5   Categorizing Events

In this section, we have seen how to handle a **mouse event** — an event that is triggered when the user moves the mouse or clicks a mouse button. A **keyboard event** is triggered when the user presses a keyboard key. Because they are initiated by a user action, mouse and keyboard events are both known as **user events**. By contrast, a **program event** is triggered when the world starts running, or the program changes the value of a variable or condition.

6.2   Handling Key Presses: A Helicopter Flight Simulator

Now that we have seen how mouse click events can be handled, let's look at keyboard events.

6.2.1   The Problem

> Scene: Catastrophe! The mayor's cat is lost, bringing your city's government to a halt. As the city's only helicopter pilot, you have been asked to help find the mayor's cat. You find yourself in the cockpit of a running helicopter at an airport outside the city. Fly the helicopter and find the mayor's cat.

6.2.2   Design

We can build the scene using the classes from the Alice Gallery (see below), but let's first spend a few minutes thinking what the user must do: how he or she will fly the helicopter.

Flying a helicopter is complicated: the user needs to be able to make the helicopter move *up*, *down*, *forward*, *backward*, and turn *left* or *right*. It would be difficult to elicit all six of these behaviors using a mouse, so we will instead use keyboard keys for each of them. After a bit of thought, we might decide to operate the helicopter as follows:

> To make the helicopter ascend (take off), use the 'a' key. To descend (land), use the 'd' key. When the helicopter is in the air, use the up and down arrow keys to move it forward and backward. Similarly, when the helicopter is in the air, use the left and right arrow keys to turn it left and right.

These keys are chosen for their:

- **Mnemonic values**: 'a' is the first letter in *ascend*, and 'd' is the first letter in *descend*, making these keys easy to remember. Likewise, the up, down, left, and right arrow keys point in the directions we want the helicopter to move, making their meanings easy to remember.
- **Convenient positions**: 'a' and 'd' are near one another on most keyboards, allowing the user to easily control the helicopter's elevation with two fingers of one hand. Likewise, the four arrow keys are usually grouped together, allowing the user to easily control the helicopter's forward, backward, left, and right motion with the fingers on the other hand.

It is important to consider *human factors* when building interactive stories. If the story requires complex behaviors, make the controls for your user as convenient and easy to use as possible. Making programs easy to use is an important aspect of programming known as **usability**.

6.2.3   Programming in Alice

To construct the scene, we can build an Alice world containing an airport, a city terrain, an assortment of buildings, a helicopter, and a (Cheshire) cat. After arranging the buildings to resemble a small city, we place the cat somewhere within the city (exactly where is for you to find out), position the helicopter at the airport, and then position the camera to be peering out the front of the helicopter. We then set the **camera**'s **vehicle** property to be the **helicopter**, so that any message that moves the **helicopter** will also move the **camera**.

Making the Helicopter's Propellor Spin

The helicopter's engine is running when the story begins, so its propellor should be spinning when the world starts. The **Helicopter** class has a method named **heli blade()** that continuously spins its **propellor** and **rotor**. By using this method as the handler for Alice's default **When the world starts** event (see Figure 6-12), the helicopter's propellor begins spinning as soon as we press Alice's **Play** button.

FIGURE 6-12   Making the helicopter's propellor spin

Making the Helicopter Ascend

A helicopter must be in the air before it can go forward or backward, turn left or right, or descend. As a result, it makes sense to define the **helicopter.ascend()** method first, while keeping those other operations in mind.

Our other five operations must to be able to determine if the helicopter is in the air. (If it is not, those operations should do nothing.) To store this information, we can create a **Boolean** property for the **helicopter** named **inTheAir**, initially **false**, as shown in Figure 6-13.

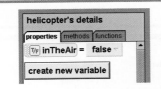

FIGURE 6-13   The **helicopter.inTheAir** property

With this property in place, we can define the **ascend()** method as shown in Figure 6-14.

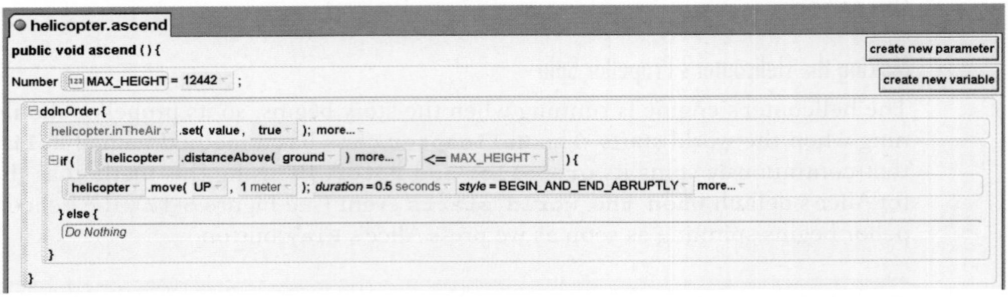

FIGURE 6-14   The `ascend()` method

Since helicopters cannot fly infinitely high, we first define a constant named **MAX_HEIGHT** and set its value to the maximum altitude a helicopter has attained (according to the Internet, 12,442 meters). The body of the method then sets **helicopter.inTheAir** to **true**, and moves the helicopter up 1 meter if it has not already attained the maximum altitude. To smooth the animation, we set the **move()** message's *style* attribute to **BEGIN_AND_END_ABRUPTLY**. To make it move upwards at a reasonable rate, we set its *duration* attribute to **0.5** seconds, which effectively makes the helicopter ascend at 2 meters per second.

With the **ascend()** method defined, our next task is to associate it with the **'a'** keyboard event. To do so, we click the **create new event** button in the *events area*, and select **When a key is typed**, as shown in Figure 6-15.

FIGURE 6-15   Creating a new keyboard event

Alice then generates the **When a key is typed** event shown in Figure 6-16.

When any key ~ | **is typed, do** Nothing ~

FIGURE 6-16   The when a key is typed event

If we use this event to make the 'a' key trigger the **ascend()** method, then each press of the 'a' key will move the helicopter up 1 meter. Put differently, to climb just 100 meters, the user would have to press the 'a' key 100 times, which is no fun for the user!

A better approach is to use the **While a key is pressed** event from Figure 6-1. As indicated there, we can convert a **When a key is typed** event to a **While a key is pressed** event by right-clicking on the **When a key is typed** event, and then selecting **change to -> While a key is pressed** from the menu, as shown in Figure 6-17.

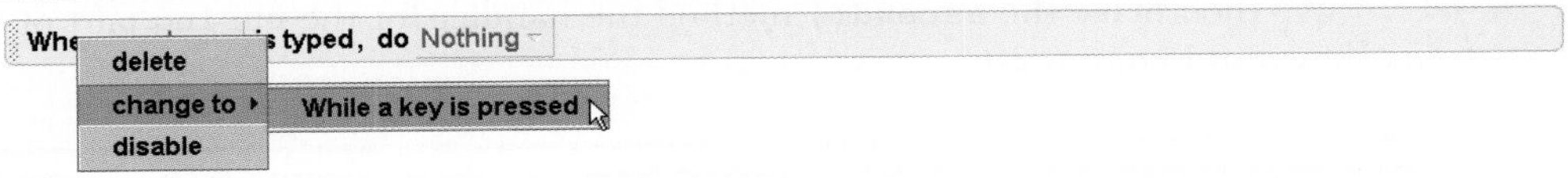

Whe[...] [...] s typed, do Nothing ~
- delete
- change to ▸   While a key is pressed
- disable

FIGURE 6-17   Changing When a key is typed into While a key is pressed

Selecting this choice causes Alice to replace the **When a key is typed** event with a **While a key is pressed** event, as shown in Figure 6-18.

While any key ~ | **is pressed**
   Begin: <None> ~
   During: <None> ~
     End: <None> ~

FIGURE 6-18   The While a key is pressed event

As seen in Figure 6-18, this event allows *three* different handlers to respond to one key event:

- **Begin**: a handler here is performed *once*, when the key is first pressed.
- **During**: a handler here is performed *continuously*, as long as the key remains down.
- **End**: a handler here is performed *once*, when the key is released.

For the problem at hand, we will only need one of these parts: the **During** part.

To specify that we want the 'a' key to trigger this event, we click the list arrow next to **any key** and choose **letters->A** from the menu that appears, as shown in Figure 6-19.

While any key is pressed
Space
Enter
Up
Down
Left
Right
letters
numbers
• any key
A
B
C
D
create new parameter

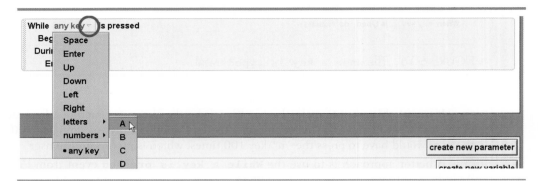

FIGURE 6-19 Making `'a'` trigger an event

We then make the **`ascend()`** method the handler for the **`During`** part of this event, as shown in Figure 6-20.

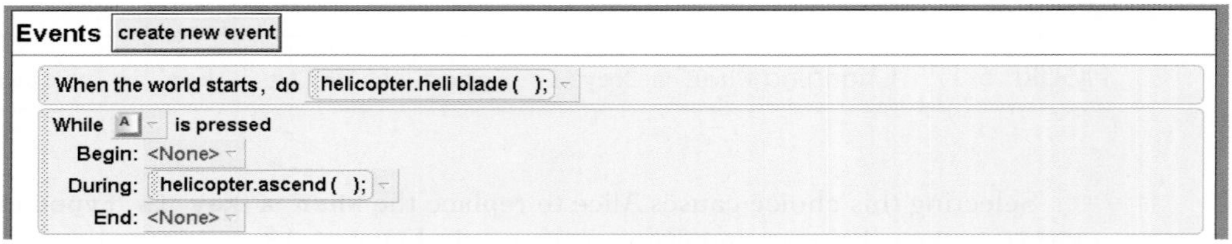

Events
create new event
When the world starts, do helicopter.heli blade ( );
While A is pressed
Begin: <None>
During: helicopter.ascend ( );
End: <None>

FIGURE 6-20 Associating `'a'` with **`helicopter.ascend()`**

With this event defined, holding down the `'a'` key will make the **`helicopter`** ascend smoothly into the air, and set **`helicopter.inTheAir`** to **`true`**.

Making the Helicopter Descend

To make the helicopter descend, we write a **`descend()`** method to serve as a handler for the `'d'` keyboard event. If we think through its behavior, it has two things to accomplish:

1. If the **`helicopter`** is above the ground, the **`helicopter`** should move down 1 meter.
2. Otherwise, the **`helicopter.inTheAir`** property should be set to **`false`**.

Figure 6-21 presents a definition for **descend()** that achieves both of these goals.

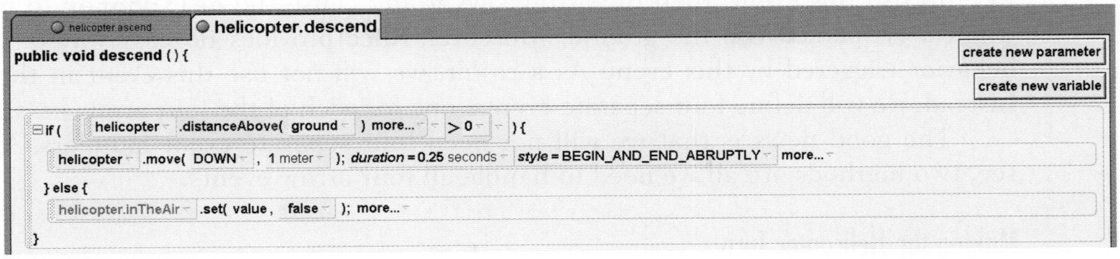

FIGURE 6-21   The `descend()` method

Our method first checks to see if the helicopter is above the ground. If not, it sets the **inTheAir** property to **false**. Since the **ascend()** and **descend()** methods control the helicopter's vertical movement, they are responsible for changing the value of **inTheAir** when necessary. No other methods should modify this property (though they will read its value).

If the helicopter is above the ground, our method moves it down 1 meter. As in **ascend()**, we set the *style* of the **move()** method to **BEGIN_AND_END_ABRUPTLY** to smooth the animation. Unlike **ascend()**, we set its *duration* to **0.25** seconds, so that the helicopter descends at a rate of 4 meters per second (to simulate the effect of gravity on its descent).

We can associate the **descend()** method with the **'d'** event using the same approach we used for **'a'** in Figure 6-15 through Figure 6-19. The result is the event shown in Figure 6-22.

FIGURE 6-22   Associating `'d'` with `helicopter.descend()`

With this event in place, we can now use **'d'** key to land the helicopter!

The Arrow Keys

As we saw in Figure 6-1, Alice provides a **Let arrow keys move <subject>** event. You might be tempted to use this event to control the **helicopter** in the program, by creating an event like that shown in Figure 6-23.

FIGURE 6-23   Control using the arrow keys?

This kind of an event works great in many situations, and it would be nice if it worked in ours. The problem for us is that a helicopter should *not* move unless it is in the air. If we were to use this event, then the arrow keys *would* cause the **helicopter** to move, even when it is "parked" on the ground! Moreover, Alice provides no easy way to modify the behavior triggered by this event. As a result, we will not use this event in the program. Instead, we will define four separate events: one for each of the four arrow keys.

The good news is that we will not need four separate event handlers. As we shall see, two methods are all we need to handle all four arrow events.

Making the Helicopter Turn

To make the helicopter turn left or right, we could define two separate methods like we did for ascending and descending. However, these methods would be nearly identical, differing only in the direction we want the helicopter to turn. Instead of defining separate methods, we will use a single method, and pass an argument (**LEFT** or **RIGHT**) to specify the direction we want the helicopter to turn. The basic logic is as shown in Figure 6-24.

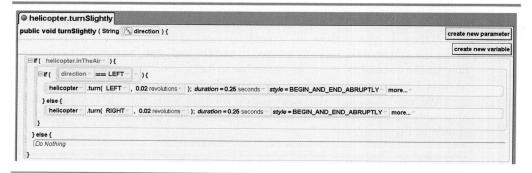

FIGURE 6-24   The `turnSlightly()` method

We named the method **turnSlightly()**, to keep it distinct from the existing **turn()** method, and because it only turns the **helicopter** a small, fixed amount (**0.02** revolutions).

With this definition to serve as a handler, we can associate it with the left and right arrow keys using the approach shown in Figure 6-15 through Figure 6-19, but passing **Left** as an argument to the handler for the left arrow key event, and **Right** as an argument to the handler for the right arrow key event. Doing so produces the two events shown in Figure 6-25.

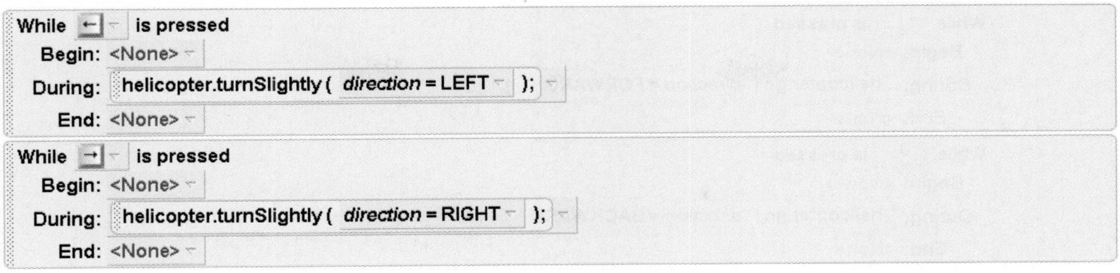

FIGURE 6-25   The left and right arrow events

Using these events, we can turn the helicopter left or right, but only when it is in the air.

Moving the Helicopter Forward or Backward

Our final operations are to move the helicopter forward or backward in response to the up and down arrow keys. As with turning the helicopter, we can do both of these in a single method, by passing **FORWARD** or **BACKWARD** as an argument to specify which direction to go. As in **turnSlightly()**, this method must only let the helicopter move if it is in the air. Figure 6-26 presents a definition for this method, which we have named **go()**.

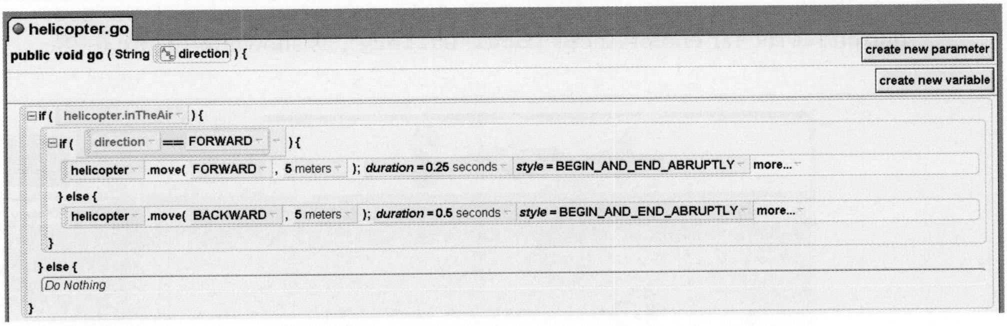

FIGURE 6-26   The go() method

To make the helicopter move forward twice as fast as it goes backward, we use a *distance* of **5** meters for each, but a *duration* of **0.25** seconds for forward and **0.5** seconds for backward. In each case, we use the **BEGIN_AND_END_ABRUPTLY style** to smooth the animation.

With a handler in place, all we have to do is associate it with the appropriate up and down arrow key events, using the same approach we have seen before, as shown in Figure 6-27.

```
While ↑ - is pressed
  Begin: <None> -
 During: helicopter.go ( direction = FORWARD - ); -
   End: <None> -
While ↓ - is pressed
  Begin: <None> -
 During: helicopter.go ( direction = BACKWARD - ); -
   End: <None> -
```

FIGURE 6-27   The up and down arrow events

At this point, our program is operational, provided there is someone there to explain to users what they are supposed to do. In the next section, we will see how to add instructions.

6.3   Alice Tip: Using 3D Text

In the last section, we built a working helicopter flight simulator. However, for a program with such a complex user interface (the user must use both hands and operate six keys), it is a good idea to present some operating instructions when the program begins.

To do so, we return to Alice's **Add Objects** screen, and click the **Create 3D Text** button (at the far end of Alice's **Local Gallery**), as shown in Figure 6-28.

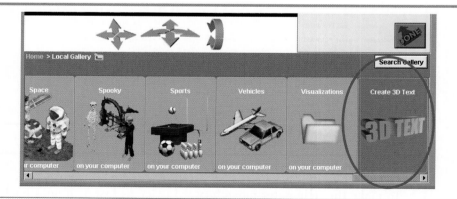

FIGURE 6-28   The create 3D text button

When this button is clicked, Alice displays the **Add 3D Text** dialog box shown in Figure 6-29.

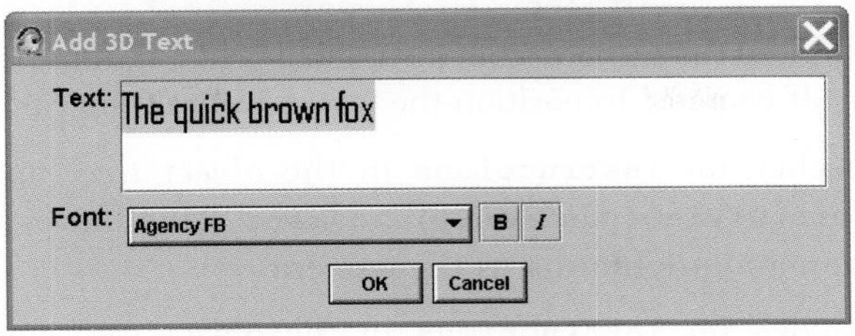

FIGURE 6-29   The `Add 3D Text` dialog box

Using this dialog box, we can replace **The quick brown fox** with any textual information we want to appear in our world, such as:

- *instructions* for the user
- an *opening title* for the story
- *closing credits* for the story

and so on. We can specify that the text be displayed in a particular font using the **Font** drop-down box, and make the text bold or italic using the **B** and **I** buttons.

To make the instructions for the helicopter, we can type the text shown in Figure 6-30.

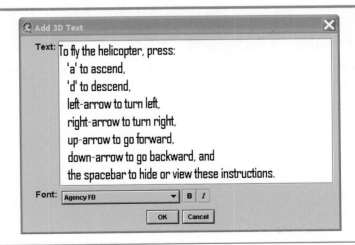

FIGURE 6-30   Instructions for the flight simultor

When we click the **OK** button, Alice inserts a three-dimensional version of these instructions into the world, and names it **To fly the helicopter**. To discuss it more conveniently, we will right-click on it and rename it **instructions**.

6.3.1   Repositioning Text that Is Off-Camera

If we have moved the camera from its original position, Alice will add new 3D text at a position that is off-camera. To position the text in front of the camera, we can use these steps:

1.   Right-click on **instructions** in the *object tree*, and then choose **methods->setPointOfView(<asSeenBy)->camera**. This moves the text to be in the same position and orientation as the camera.

2.   Right-click on **instructions** in the *object tree*, and then choose **methods->move(<direction>,<amount>)->FORWARD->10 meters**. This moves the text forward so that we can see it. However since its point of view is like that of the camera, its front is facing away from us, making it backwards to our view.

3.   Right-click on **instructions** in the *object tree*, and then choose **methods->turn(<direction>,<amount>)->LEFT->1/2 revolution**. This spins the text 180 degrees, making it readable to us.

From here, we can use the controls at the upper right of the **Add Objects** window to resize and reposition the text as necessary to make the **instructions** fit the screen.

We will make the instructions appear or disappear whenever the user presses the spacebar. One way to make this occur is to make the **instructions** *move with the camera*, so that the spacebar event handler just has to make them visible to make them appear, or invisible to make them disappear.[4] To make them move with the camera, we set the **instructions.vehicle** property to **camera** in the *details area*. At the same time, we set the **instructions.color** property to **yellow**, to (in theory) make them show up well.

6.3.2   Adding a Background

Unfortunately, when we view the results of our work, the **instructions** are nearly impossible to read, as can be seen in Figure 6-31.

---

4.   This approach is simple because the camera moves with the helicopter which flies throughout the world. For text that should only appear once (like titles or credits), it makes more sense to build a dedicated scene for displaying the text, and then moving the camera to and from that scene when necessary.

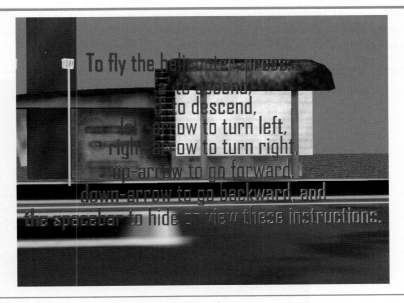

FIGURE 6-31   Instructions that are hard to read

To improve their visibility we can add a *background* behind the **instructions**. To make such a background, we can add an object from the **Shapes** folder in Alice's **Local Gallery**, as shown in Figure 6-32.

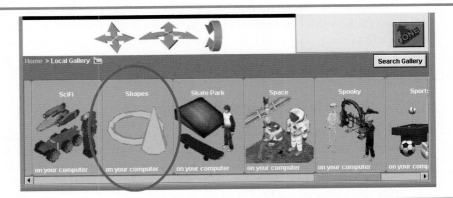

FIGURE 6-32   Alice's **shapes** folder

There, we find a **Square** class that (since our view is rectangular) we can use as a background for the **instructions**. If we drag and drop it into the world, we can use the controls at the upper right of the **Add Objects** window to resize the **square** to fill the screen, and reposition the **square** so that it is behind the **instructions**. (Or reposition the **instructions** to be in front of the **square**.) When we are finished, we can increase the contrast by setting the **square.color** property to **black**, and using right-click->**methods** to make the **light** turn to face these instructions.[5] The result is the easier-to-read screen shown in Figure 6-33.

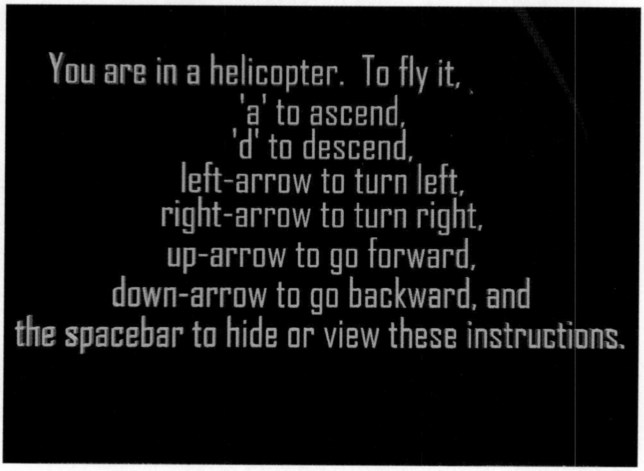

You are in a helicopter. To fly it,
'a' to ascend,
'd' to descend,
left-arrow to turn left,
right-arrow to turn right,
up-arrow to go forward,
down-arrow to go backward, and
the spacebar to hide or view these instructions.

FIGURE 6-33   Instructions that are easy to read

Since we want the background to move with the **instructions**, we set the **square.vehicle** property to be **instructions**.

This approach can be used to create any kind of on-screen text we want to appear in the story, such as titles or credits. Once we have one 3D text object in the right position, we can add others to the world, and move them to the same position by using right-click->**methods**->*objectName*.**setPointOfView(<asSeenBy>)** to move new text to the position and orientation of the existing 3D text.

6.3.3 Making Text Appear or Disappear

We are almost done! Our next task is to write an event handler that makes the **instructions** and **square** (the instructions' background) disappear when they are visible, and appear when they are invisible, so that the user can make them appear or disappear using the spacebar.

This is another example of the two-state behavior we saw back in Figure 6-9. However, **instructions** and **square** already have an **isShowing** property that indicates whether or not they are visible, so we need not define any new properties. Instead, we can just toggle **instructions.isShowing** and **square.isShowing** to elicit the desired behavior, as shown in the **toggleInstructionVisibility()** method in Figure 6-34.

---

5.   If we leave the light as it is, some portions of the 3D text may be darker than others, if the text is in the shadows. By making the light face the instructions, we illuminate the text uniformly, eliminating such shadows.

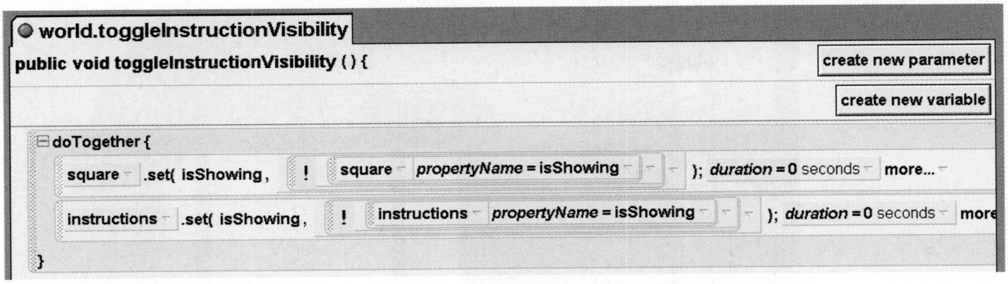

FIGURE 6-34   Toggling the visibility of `instructions` and `square`

When this method is performed, it uses the ! (NOT) operator to invert the **square** and **instruction** objects' **isShowing** properties. That is, if **isShowing** were **true** for each object *before* the method was performed, **isShowing** is **false** for each of them *after* the method finishes. Conversely, if **isShowing** was **false** for each of them *before* the method runs, **isShowing** is **true** for each *after* the method finishes.

To finish the program, we must make this method the handler for spacebar events. To do so, we can use the **When a key is typed** event shown in Figure 6-16, replace **any** with **Space**, and then drag the **world.toggleInstructionVisibility()** method onto **Nothing** to make it the event's handler. The result is the event shown in Figure 6-35.

FIGURE 6-35   Associating `space` with `world.toggleInstructionVisibility()`

Now, when the program begins running, the **instructions** appear as shown in Figure 6-33. When the user is ready and presses the spacebar, the instructions and background disappear, revealing the scene behind them. The scene that appears depends on the position and orientation of the **camera**. Figure 6-36 shows the scene.

FIGURE 6-36   After the user presses the spacebar

The black object visible in the upper-right corner of Figure 6-36 is the helicopter's rotor blade.

At this point, we have a version of the program that is sufficient for testing with users. For additional enhancements (for example, adding a title, closing, and so on), see the Programming Problems at the end of the chapter.

> If 3D text objects or backgrounds are to be fixed in place in front of the camera, they should be the last objects you add to a world or scene. The reason is that they will usually lie between the camera and any objects you subsequently place in the world; if you try to click on these latter objects, the 3D text or background will intercept your click.

6.4   Alice Tip: Scene Transitional Effects for the Camera

In Section 2.4, we saw how to use **Dummies** to mark camera positions, and how to use the **setPointOfView()** message to change the position of the **camera** to that of a dummy. This approach provides a convenient way to shift the camera from its position at the end of a given scene to a new position at the beginning of the next scene.

Instead of instantaneously jumping from the end of one scene to the beginning of the next scene (a transition called a *cut*), filmmakers often use special camera effects like *fades* or *wipes* to smooth the transition between scenes. Such **transition effects** can make the transition between scenes seem less abrupt and jarring to the viewer, or be used to convey a sense of time elapsing between the scenes.

Alice does not provide any built-in transitional effects. However, it does provide us with raw building blocks that we can use to create our own. With a little time and effort, we can build credible transitional effects. In this section, we will see how to do so.

6.4.1 Setup for Special Effects

Before we see how to create the effects themselves, we need to do a bit of setup work. The basic idea is to add four black shutters or "flaps" outside of the camera's viewport, that we can manipulate to create the effects. These shutters should be positioned at the top-left-right-bottom positions outside of the camera's viewing area, as shown in Figure 6-37.

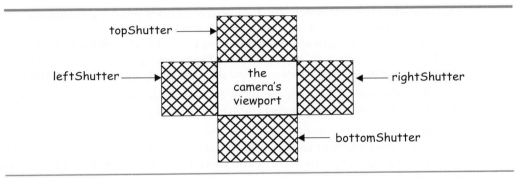

FIGURE 6-37 Surrounding the camera with four shutters

To create such shutters in Alice, we add four **square** objects to a world; change the **color** property of each **square** to **black**; change the **vehicle** property of each **square** to the **camera**; rename them **topShutter**, **leftShutter**, **rightShutter**, and **bottomShutter**; and position them as shown in Figure 6-38.

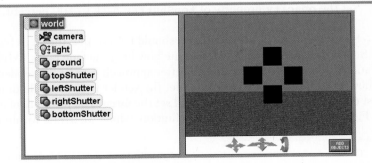

FIGURE 6-38 Using four squares for shutters

Moving each square to a position outside of the camera's viewing area is tricky, because we cannot easily drag them to the right position. Instead, we can position a square at the center of the screen, and then drag it towards the camera until it completely fills the viewing area. We can then use right-click->`methods`->*`objectName`*.`move(<direction>,<amount>)` with the appropriate arguments to move the square just outside the viewing area, using trial-and-error to find the right distance. (For us, this distance was about 0.08 meters.[6])

With shutters in place, we can perform a variety of special effects by writing methods that move the shutters. We perform such effects using *complementary pairs* of methods, in which one method "undoes" the actions of the other.

6.4.2   The Fade Effect

Our first effect is a *fade* effect, which causes the entire screen to gradually darken until it is completely black, and then lightens, exposing a new scene. To achieve this effect, we write two complementary methods: **fadeToBlack()** and **fadeFromBlack()**. We can perform the fade-to-black effect by setting the **topShutter**'s opacity to zero percent, moving it down to cover the camera's viewport, and then setting its opacity back to 100 percent.

With the screen dark, we can move the camera to its position at the beginning of a new scene without the user seeing the scenery flash by.

With the camera in place for the new scene, we can perform a fade-from-black effect by setting **topShutter**'s opacity to zero percent, moving it up to its original position, and setting its opacity back to 100 percent, so that the **topShutter** is exactly as it was at the beginning of the fade-to-black effect.

Fade to Black

Using the **topShutter**, we can achieve the fade-to-black effect as follows:

1. Set the **opacity** property of **topShutter** to 0 percent, so that it is invisible.

2. Move **topShutter** down so that it is in front of the camera's viewing area.

3. Set the **opacity** property of **topShutter** back to 100 percent, making it visible.

For Steps 1 and 2, the **duration** should be 0 so that the steps happen instantaneously. For Step 3, the **duration** will determine how long the fade takes. While we could make this duration last a fixed length of time, a better approach is to let the sender of this message specify how long the fade should take. To let the sender pass this fade time as an argument, we must define a parameter to store it, and set the **duration** attribute of Step 3 to that parameter. Figure 6-39 shows the resulting definition, which we define within **camera**.

---

6.   To move the **leftShutter** left and the **rightShutter** right, we had to turn each 180 degrees, as the way they were facing caused the LEFT and RIGHT directions to move them the opposite way.

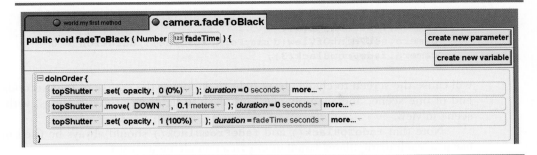

FIGURE 6-39 The `fadeToBlack()` method

With this method, the message **`camera.fadeToBlack(5);`** will cause the screen to darken over the course of five seconds. You may have to adjust the distance you move **`topShutter`**, depending on its placement and size with respect to the camera.

Fade From Black

The fade-from-black method has to "undo" everything the fade-to-black method did, in the reverse order, so as to leave the **`topShutter`** in its original position:

1. Set the **`opacity`** property of **`topShutter`** to 0 percent.

2. Move **`topShutter`** up so that it is out of the camera's viewing area.

3. Set the **`opacity`** property of **`topShutter`** to 100 percent.

As before, we should allow the sender to specify the effect's *time*. In this method, it controls the **`duration`** of Step 1, while Steps 2 and 3 occur instantaneously, as shown in Figure 6-40.

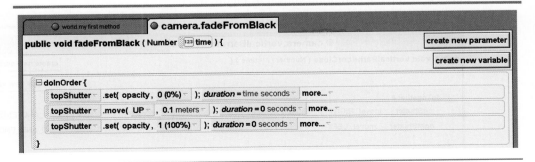

FIGURE 6-40 The `fadeFromBlack()` method

With these two methods, the messages:

```
camera.fadeToBlack(4);
camera.setPointOfView(dummyForNextScene); duration = 0
camera.fadeFromBlack(3);
```

will cause the screen to change from light to dark over the course of four seconds at the end of one scene, and then change from dark to light over three seconds, with a new scene in view.

Note that **fadeToBlack()** and **fadeFromBlack()** should always be used in pairs, because each manipulates **topShutter** in a complementary way.

6.4.3   The Barndoor Edge Wipe Effect

Edge wipe effects are transitions in which one or more edges move across the screen to hide the end of one scene and expose the beginning of the next scene. One kind of edge wipe transition is the *barndoor wipe*, in which the shutters move like the doors of a barn, sliding closed at the end of a scene and then opening on a new scene. Two common barndoor edge wipes are:

- *vertical*, in which the "doors" close and open from the sides of the screen.

- *horizontal*, in which the "doors" close and open from the top and bottom of the screen.

In this section, we will show how to use the shutters to achieve the vertical effect. The horizontal effect is similar and is left for the exercises.

Vertical Barndoor Effects

We can perform a *vertical barndoor close* effect by simultaneously moving the left and right shutters towards one another. As before, the best approach is to let the sender of the message pass the effect's *time* as an argument, and then use that argument's parameter as the **duration** value for each shutter's movement. We define this method within **camera**, using the definition shown in Figure 6-41.

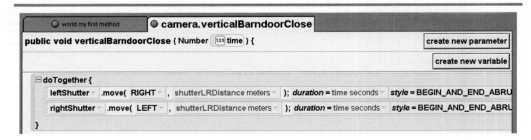

FIGURE 6-41   The **verticalBarndoorClose()** method

To simplify changing the distance the left and right shutters must move, we defined a **camera** property named **shutterLRDistance**, which we then used to control the shutter movements.

The complementary effect — the *vertical barndoor open* effect — can be achieved by simultaneously moving the left and right shutters apart, as shown in Figure 6-42.

```
○ world.my first method      ● camera.verticalBarndoorOpen

public void verticalBarndoorOpen ( Number [123] time ) {          create new parameter

                                                                  create new variable

⊟ doTogether {
    leftShutter⁻ .move( LEFT⁻ , shutterLRDistance meters⁻ ); duration = time seconds⁻ style = BEGIN_AND_END_ABRUP
    rightShutter⁻ .move( RIGHT⁻ , shutterLRDistance meters⁻ ); duration = time seconds⁻ style = BEGIN_AND_END_ABR
}
```

FIGURE 6-42 The `verticalBarndoorOpen()` method

Using these two methods, a programmer can send messages like this:

```
camera.verticalBarndoorClose(4);
camera.setPointOfView(dummyForNextScene); duration = 0
camera.verticalBarndoorOpen(3);
```

to "close the door" over the course of four seconds, shift the camera to the next scene, and then "open the door" over three seconds. Because they act as complementary operations, these methods should be used in pairs, or the shutters will not be in place for subsquent transitions.

The *horizontal barndoor edge wipe* is similar, but involves moving the top and bottom shutters instead of the left and right shutters. Building this effect is left as an exercise.

6.4.4 The Box Iris Wipe Effect

Our last effect is a different wipe effect called an *iris wipe*, in which the screen is darkened except for an area called the *iris* that shrinks (the iris is closing) at the end of a scene, and expands (the iris is opening) to expose a new scene. This effect is usually used to center the viewer's attention on something in the scene, which is encircled by the iris as it closes.

We can define a "box iris close" effect using the shutters, by simultaneously moving all four shutters towards the center of the camera's viewport. As in the preceding effect methods, we let the sender of the message specify the *time* the effect should take. For added flexibility, we also let the sender specify what *percentage* the iris should close, as shown in Figure 6-43.

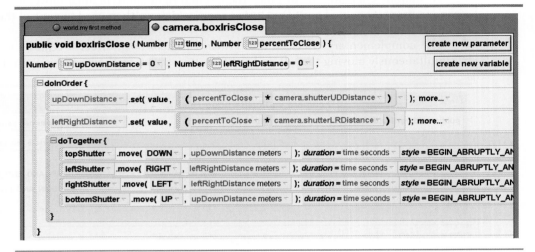

FIGURE 6-43   The `boxIrisClose()` method

We first compute how far to close each shutter, by multiplying the parameter **percentToClose** by each shutter's close distance. We then simultaneously move each shutter that distance using the value of parameter **time** as the *duration*. As shown in Figure 6-44, when this method runs, the shutters outline a shrinking box that contains roughly **percentToClose** of the screen area.

FIGURE 6-44   The box iris effect (closing)

The complementary **boxIrisOpen()** method is similar, as shown in Figure 6-45.

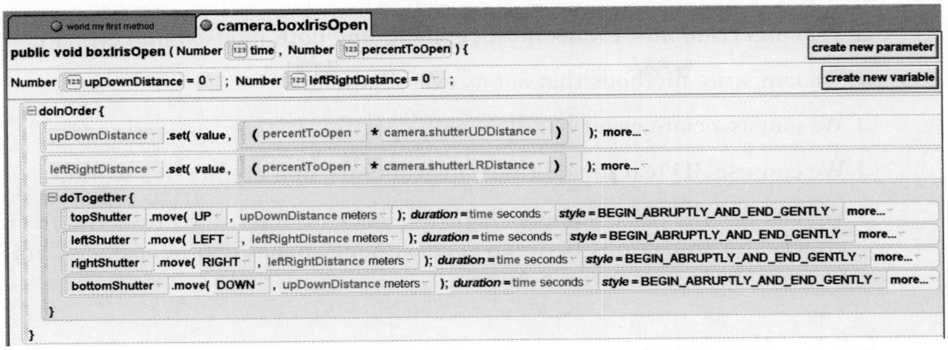

FIGURE 6-45 The `boxIrisOpen()` method

With these methods, we can now create interesting transitions:

```
camera.boxIrisClose(3, 0.75);
// do something interesting inside the iris
camera.boxIrisClose(2, 0.25);
// move camera to the next scene
camera.boxIrisOpen(5, 100);
```

6.4.5 Reusing Transition Effects

If you search on the Internet for terms like *transition*, *effect*, *fade*, and *wipe*, you can find many other transition effects that can be defined using techniques like those we presented in this section. (To define them, you may need to add more shapes to the camera.) We hope that this section has provided you with an introduction into how such effects can be created. However, once we have defined a nice group of transition effects, how do we reuse them in different programs?

Unfortunately, the **save object as...** technique presented in Section 2.3 will not save properties that are objects, so with the **camera**'s shutters being **Square**s, we cannot rename, save, and import the modified **camera** into a different world and have its shutters come with it, even if we were to make the four shutters properties of the **camera**.[7]

Instead, we define all of these transitions in a "template world" we call **TransitionEffects** that contains nothing but the **camera**, the **light**, the **ground**, and the **square**s we use for the transitions. For any story in which we want transitions, we open this **TransitionEffects** world as the starting world for the story, and then use **File-> Save world as...** to save it using a name appropriate for that story. Of course, this means that we must plan ahead and know in advance that we will be using transitions in the story. This is one more reason to spend time carefully designing your program before you start programming.

---

7. This was true when this book was written. It may not be true by the time you read this. Check and see!

6.5   Chapter Summary

❏ We can create new events in Alice, including both mouse and keyboard events.

❏ We can write methods that act as event handlers.

❏ We can associate event handlers with specific events.

❏ We can use 3D text to add titles, instructions, and credits to a world.

❏ We can use the Alice **square** shape as a background for 3D text, and to create "special effects" for transitions between scenes. Alice shapes can be used as "building blocks" to build other structures in Alice.

6.5.1   Key Terms

event	logic error
event-driven program	mouse event
event handler	program event
event source	transition effect
handling an event	two-state behavior
interactive program	usability
keyboard event	user event

Programming Projects

6.1 Choose one of the robots from the Alice Gallery, and provide events and handlers so that the user can control the robot using the keyboard. For example, use the arrow keys to make the robot go forward, backward, left, or right; use other keys to control the robot's arms (or other appendages). Build a world in which the user must navigate the robot through obstacles.

6.2 Using the **dragon.flapWings();** method we wrote in Section 2.2.1, build a short story in which a dragon flies from place to place in search of adventure, landing periodically to eat, talk, and anything else required by your story. Make **dragon.flapWings()** the handler of a **While something is true** event, so that the dragon automatically flaps its wings whenever it is above the ground.

6.3 Build a world containing a puzzle the user must solve. Place characters in the world who can provide hints to the puzzle's solution when the user clicks on them. Let the user navigate through the world using the arrow keys.

6.4 Add the following enhancements to the helicopter flight simulator program we built in Sections 6.2 and 6.3 (in increasing order of difficulty):

a. Add a "title" screen that names the program, and describes the problem to be solved.

b. Add a "congratulations" screen that appears when the user finds and clicks on the cat.

    c. Modify the program so that when the helicopter descends over the roof of any of the buildings, it lands on the roof instead of passing right through it.

    d. Modify the program so that if the helicopter collides with anything in the world as it moves forward, backward, left, or right, the helicopter "crashes" and the world displays a "better luck next time" screen.

6.5 Build methods to perform the following transition effects:

    a. Build a method **fadeTo(someColor, fadeTime);** that lets the sender specify the color to which the screen should fade, and **fadeFrom(fadeTime)** that complements **fadeTo()**. Then revise the **fadeToBlack()** and **fadeFromBlack()** methods so that they use **fadeTo()** and **fadeFrom()**.

    b. Build a method **barWipeCover(direction, time);** that, at the end of a scene, moves a single shutter from one of the edges to cover the screen; and a method **barWipeUncover(direction, time);** that complements **barWipeCover()**. The direction argument should be either **LEFT**, **RIGHT**, **UP**, or **DOWN**.

    c. In a *diagonal wipe*, a shutter crosses the screen from one corner to the opposite corner. Write complementary methods that perform the two parts of a diagonal wipe.

    d. A *bowtie wipe* is like a barndoor wipe, but the shutters coming from the sides are wedges that form a bow-tie when they first touch one another. Write complementary methods that perform the two parts of a bowtie wipe.

    e. A *rotating octagonal iris wipe* is an iris wipe in which the iris is a rotating octagon rather than a rectangle. Write complementary methods that perform the two parts of a rotating octagonal iris wipe.

6.6 Choose a popular game like chess, checkers, mancala, master mind, etc. Create a board and pieces for the game. Add event handlers that allow the user to move the pieces interactively.

6.7 Using the **Carrier** and **FighterPlane** classes from Alice's Web Gallery, create a carrier-jet simulation, in which the user must fly the **fighterPlane**, taking off from and landing on the **carrier**.

6.8 Using the **WhackAMoleBooth** class from the Alice Gallery **Amusement Park** folder, program a whack-a-mole game in which the **mole** pops its head out of a random hole in the booth for a short, random length of time before ducking down again, and the user tries to bop the mole with the **bopper**. Play a sound each time the user successfully bops the mole.

6.9 Proceed as in Problem 6.8, but make your program a continuously running series of games. Limit each game to some fixed length of time (for example, 60 seconds). Have the user enter his or her name at the beginning of a game. Your program should keep track of how many times the user bops the mole during the game, and when the time expires, display (a) that number as the user's score for this game, and (b) the top five scores since the program began running. Play a special sound if the user beats the highest score (becoming the new top score).

6.10 Design and build your own original, interactive computer game.

Appendix A
Alice Standard Methods and Functions

A.1 Alice Standard Methods

Alice *methods* are messages that we can send to an object commanding it to do something. The object then responds with a behavior (hopefully the one we intended). The following table provides a complete list of Alice's standard methods, which are the commands to which all Alice objects will respond.

Method	Behavior Produced
obj.move(*dir*, *dist*);	*obj* moves *dist* meters in direction *dir* = **UP**, **DOWN**, **LEFT**, **RIGHT**, **FORWARD**, or **BACKWARD**
obj.turn(*dir*, *revs*);	*obj* turns *revs* revolutions in direction **LEFT**, **RIGHT**, **FORWARD**, or **BACKWARD** (that is, about its UD- or LR-axis)
obj.roll(*dir*, *revs*);	*obj* rotates *revs* revolutions in direction **LEFT** or **RIGHT** (that is, about its FB-axis)
obj.resize(*howMuch*);	*obj*'s size changes by a factor of *howMuch*
obj.say(*message*);	*obj* says *message* (via a cartoon balloon)
obj.think(*thought*);	*obj* thinks *thought* (via a cartoon balloon)
obj.playSound(*soundFile*);	*obj* plays the audio file *soundFile*
obj.moveTo(*obj2*);	*obj*'s *position* becomes that of *obj2* (*obj*'s *orientation* remains unchanged)
obj.moveToward(*obj2*, *dist*);	*obj* moves *dist* meters toward the position of *obj2*

continued

Method	Behavior Produced
obj.moveAwayFrom(*obj2*,*dist*);	*obj* moves away from *obj2*, *dist* meters from its current position
obj.orientTo(*obj2*);	*obj*'s *orientation* becomes that of *obj2* (*obj*'s *position* remains unchanged)
obj.turnToFace(*obj2*);	*obj* rotates about its UD-axis until it is facing *obj2*
obj.pointAt(*obj2*);	*obj* rotates so that its FB-axis points at *obj2*'s center
obj.setPointOfView(*obj2*);	*obj*'s *position* and *orientation* change to that of *obj2*
obj.setPose(*pose*);	*obj* assumes the pose specified by *pose*
obj.standUp();	*obj* rotates so that its UD-axis is vertical
obj.moveAtSpeed(*dir*,*mps*);	*obj* moves direction **UP**, **DOWN**, **LEFT**, **RIGHT**, **FORWARD**, or **BACKWARD** at *mps* meters/sec (for **duration** secs)[1]
obj.turnAtSpeed(*dir*,*rps*);	*obj* turns direction **LEFT**, **RIGHT**, **FORWARD**, or **BACKWARD** at *rps* revolutions/sec (for **duration** secs)
obj.rollAtSpeed(*dir*,*rps*);	*obj* rolls direction **LEFT** or **RIGHT** at *rps* revolutions/sec (for **duration** secs)
obj.constrainToPointAt(*obj2*);	*obj* points at *obj2* for the duration of this message

---

1. To make *obj* accelerate: use *obj*.moveAtSpeed(*dir*,*speed*), make *speed* a variable, and use a **doTogether** block to simultaneously perform the **moveAtSpeed()** method while changing the value of *speed*.

A.2   Alice Standard Object Functions

Alice *functions* are messages we can send to an object to ask it a question. The object responds by producing a *result* — the answer to our question. The following table provides a complete list of Alice's standard functions — the questions that all Alice objects will answer:

Function	Result Produced
`obj.isCloseTo(dist,obj2)`	**true**, if *obj* is within *dist* meters of *obj2*; **false**, otherwise
`obj.isFarFrom(dist,obj2)`	**true**, if *obj* is at least *dist* meters away from *obj2*; **false**, otherwise
`obj.distanceTo(obj2)`	the distance between *obj* and *obj2*'s centers
`obj.distanceToTheLeftOf(obj2)`	the distance from the left side of *obj2*'s bounding box to *obj*'s bounding box (negative if *obj* is not left of *obj2*)
`obj.distanceToTheRightOf(obj2)`	the distance from the right side of *obj2*'s bounding box to *obj*'s bounding box (negative if *obj* is not right of *obj2*)
`obj.distanceAbove(obj2)`	the distance from the top of *obj2*'s bounding box to *obj*'s bounding box (negative if *obj* is not above *obj2*)
`obj.distanceBelow(obj2)`	the distance from the bottom of *obj2*'s bounding box to *obj*'s bounding box (negative if *obj* is not below *obj2*)
`obj.distanceInFrontOf(obj2)`	the distance from the front of *obj2*'s bounding box to *obj*'s bounding box (negative if *obj* is not in front of *obj2*)
`obj.distanceBehind(obj2)`	the distance from the back of *obj2*'s bounding box to *obj*'s bounding box (negative if *obj* is not in back of *obj2*)
`obj.getWidth()`	the width (LR-axis length) of *obj*'s bounding box
`obj.getHeight()`	the height (UD-axis length) of *obj*'s bounding box
`obj.getDepth()`	the depth (FB-axis length) of *obj*'s bounding box
`obj.isSmallerThan(obj2)`	**true**, if *obj2*'s volume exceeds that of *obj*; **false**, otherwise

continued

Function	Result Produced
`obj.isLargerThan(obj2)`	**true**, if *obj*'s volume exceeds that of *obj2*; **false**, otherwise
`obj.isNarrowerThan(obj2)`	**true**, if *obj2*'s width exceeds that of *obj*; **false**, otherwise
`obj.isWiderThan(obj2)`	**true**, if *obj*'s width exceeds that of *obj2*; **false**, otherwise
`obj.isShorterThan(obj2)`	**true**, if *obj2*'s height exceeds that of *obj*; **false**, otherwise
`obj.isTallerThan(obj2)`	**true**, if *obj*'s height exceeds that of *obj2*; **false**, otherwise
`obj.isToTheLeftOf(obj2)`	**true**, if *obj*'s position is left of *obj2*'s left edge; **false**, otherwise
`obj.isToTheRightOf(obj2)`	**true**, if *obj*'s position is right of *obj2*'s right edge; **false**, otherwise
`obj.isAbove(obj2)`	**true**, if *obj*'s position is above *obj2*'s top edge; **false**, otherwise
`obj.isBelow(obj2)`	**true**, if *obj*'s position is below *obj2*'s bottom edge; **false**, otherwise
`obj.isInFrontOf(obj2)`	**true**, if *obj*'s position is before *obj2*'s front edge; **false**, otherwise
`obj.isBehind(obj2)`	**true**, if *obj*'s position is in back of *obj2*'s rear edge; **false**, otherwise
`obj.getPointOfView()`	the point of view (*position + orientation*) of *obj*
`obj.getPosition()`	the *position* (with respect to the world's axes) of *obj*
`obj.getQuaternion()`	the *orientation* (with respect to the world's axes) of *obj*
`obj.getCurrentPose()`	the current **Pose** (*position + orientation* of subparts) of *obj*
`obj.partNamed(piece)`	the subpart of *obj* named **piece**

A.3   Alice World Functions

Alice *world functions* are implementations of commonly needed computations. The following table provides a complete list of Alice's world functions.

Function	Result Produced
`!a`	**true**, if *a* is **false**; **false**, otherwise
`(a && b)`	**true**, if *a* and *b* are both **true**; **false**, if *a* or *b* is **false**
`(a || b)`	**true**, if either *a* or *b* are **true**; **false**, if neither *a* nor *b* is **true**
`a == b`	**true**, if *a* and *b* have the same value; **false**, otherwise
`a != b`	**true**, if *a* and *b* have different values; **false**, otherwise
`a < b`	**true**, if *a*'s value is less than *b*'s value; **false**, otherwise
`a > b`	**true**, if *a*'s value is greater than *b*'s value; **false**, otherwise
`a <= b`	**true**, if *a*'s value is less than or equal to *b*'s value; **false**, otherwise
`a >= b`	**true**, if *a*'s value is greater than or equal to *b*'s value; **false**, otherwise
`Random.nextBoolean()`	a pseudo-randomly chosen **true** or **false** value
`Random.nextDouble()`	a pseudo-randomly chosen number
`a + b`	the string consisting of *a* followed by *b* (concatenation)
`what.toString()`	the string representation of *what* (string conversion)
`NumberDialog(question)`	a number entered by the user in response to *question*

continued

Function	Result Produced
`BooleanDialog(question)`	**true** if the user responds to **question** by clicking the dialog box's **Yes** button; **false** otherwise.
`StringDialog(question)`	a string entered by the user in response to **question**
`mouse.getDistanceFromLeftEdge()`	the number of pixels the mouse is from the left edge of the window (corresponds to x of an [x,y] coordinate)
`mouse.getDistanceFromTopEdge()`	the number of pixels the mouse is from the top edge of the window (corresponds to y of an [x,y] coordinate)
`getTimeElapsedSinceWorldStart()`	the number of "ticks" since the world began running
`getYear()`	a number representing the current year
`getMonthOfYear()`	a number representing the current month (Jan-0, Feb-1, etc.)
`getDayOfYear()`	a number representing the current day of the year
`getDayOfMonth()`	a number representing the current day of the month
`getDayOfWeek()`	a number representing the current day of the week (Sun-1, etc.)
`getDayOfWeekInMonth()`	a number for how many times the current day of the week has occurred in the current month
`isAM()`	**true** if the current time is between midnight and noon; **false**, otherwise
`isPM()`	**true** if the current time is between noon and midnight; **false**, otherwise
`getHourOfAMOrPM`	the hour value of the current time, 12-hour format
`getHourOfDay`	the hour value of the current time, 24-hour format
`getMinuteOfHour`	the minute value of the current time

continued

Function	Result Produced
`getSecondOfMinute`	the second value of the current time
`Math.min(a, b)`	the minimum of *a* and *b*
`Math.max(a, b)`	the maximum of *a* and *b*
`Math.abs(a)`	the absolute value of *a*
`Math.sqrt(a)`	the square root of *a*
`Math.floor(a)`	the largest integer smaller than *a*
`Math.ceiling(a)`	the smallest integer larger than *a*
`Math.sin(a)`	the sine of *a*
`Math.cos(a)`	the cosine of *a*
`Math.tan(a)`	the tangent of *a*
`Math.asin(a)`	the angle whose sine is *a*
`Math.acos(a)`	the angle whose cosine is *a*
`Math.atan(a)`	the angle whose tangent is *a*
`Math.atan2(x, y)`	the polar coordinate angle associated with Cartesian coordinate (*x*, *y*)
`Math.pow(a, b)`	*a* raised to the power *b* (a^b)
`Math.natural log of(a)`	the number x such that $e^x == a$; e being Euler's number
`Math.exp(a)`	Euler's number *e* raised to the power *a* (e^a)
`Math.IEEERemainder(a, b)`	the remainder of *a/b* using integer division
`Math.round(a)`	the integer whose value is closest to *a*
`Math.toDegrees(r)`	the angle in degrees corresponding to radians *r*
`Math.toRadians(d)`	the angle in radians corresponding to degrees *d*
`superSquareRoot(a, b)`	the bth root of *a*
`getVector(right, up, forward)`	an x-y-z vector [x==`right`, y== `up`, z==`forward`]

Appendix B
Recursion

Hundreds of years before there were computers, programming languages, or loop statements, mathematicians were defining functions, many of which required repetitive behavior. One way to provide such behavior without using a loop is to have a function or method *invoke itself*, causing its statements to repeat. Such a method (or function) is called **recursive**. To illustrate, suppose we were to define a method for Alice's **camera** named **repeatRoll()** as follows:

```
void camera.repeatRoll() {
    camera.roll(LEFT, 1);
    camera.repeatRoll();
}
```

When invoked, this method will make the **camera** roll left one revolution, and then it will invoke itself. That second invocation will make the **camera** roll left one revolution, and then it will call itself. That third invocation will make the **camera** roll left one revolution, and then it will call itself, and so on. Thus, the result is an "infinite" repetition, or **infinite recursion**.[1]

To avoid infinite repetition, recursive methods and functions typically have (1) a **Number** parameter, (2) an **if** statement that only performs the recursion if the parameter's value exceeds some lower bound, and (3) a recursive call within the **if** statement that passes a value smaller than the parameter as an argument. The net effect is that the function or method counts downward toward the lower bound, typically 0 or 1. To illustrate, we might revise the preceding **repeatRoll()** method as follows:

```
void camera.repeatRoll(Number count) {    // the parameter count
    if (count > 0) {                       // if statement guards
        camera.roll(LEFT, 1);                 the recursive call
        camera.repeatRoll(count - 1);
    }
}
```

---

1. Since each recursive call consumes additional memory, the looping behavior will eventually end — when the program runs out of memory. However, we will become tired of the **camera** rolling long before that occurs!

When invoked with a numeric argument **n**, this version of the function will roll the **camera** **n** times and then stop. For example, if we send the message **camera.repeatRoll(3);**

1. This starts **repeatRoll(3)**, in which parameter **count == 3**.

2. The method checks the condition **count > 0**.

3. Since the condition is true, the method (a) rolls the **camera** left 1 revolution, and (b) sends the message **camera.repeatRoll(2);**.

4. This starts **repeatRoll(2)**, a new version in which parameter **count == 2**.

5. The method checks the condition **count > 0**.

6. Since the condition is true, the method (a) rolls the **camera** left 1 revolution, and (b) sends the message **camera.repeatRoll(1);**.

7. This starts **repeatRoll(1)**, a new version in which parameter **count == 1**.

8. The method checks the condition **count > 0**.

9. Since the condition is true, the method (a) rolls the **camera** left 1 revolution, and (b) sends the message **camera.repeatRoll(0);**.

10. This starts **repeatRoll(0)**, a new version in which parameter **count == 0**.

11. The method checks the condition **count > 0**.

12. Since the condition is false, the method terminates; flow returns to the sender of **repeatRoll(0)** — **repeatRoll(1)** — the version where **count == 1**.

13. The version in which **count == 1** terminates; flow returns to the sender of **repeatRoll(1)** — **repeatRoll(2)** — the version in which **count == 2**.

14. The version in which **count == 2** terminates; flow returns to the sender of **repeatRoll(2)** — **repeatRoll(3)** — the version in which **count == 3**.

15. The version in which **count == 3** terminates; flow returns to the sender of **repeatRoll(3)**.

Steps 1 through 11, in which the repeated messages are counting downward toward the lower bound, are sometimes called the **winding phase** of the recursion. Steps 12 through 15, in which the chain of recursive messages terminate, are sometimes called the **unwinding phase** of the recursion.

Recursion thus provides an alternative way to achieve repetitive behavior. When the recursive message is the last behavior-producing statement in the method, as follows:

```
void camera.repeatRoll(Number count) {
   if (count > 0) {
      camera.roll(LEFT, 1);
      camera.repeatRoll(count - 1);   // the last statement
   }
}
```

it is called **tail recursion**, because the recursive message occurs at the end or "tail" of the method. Any function defined using tail recursion can be defined using a loop, and vice versa. But in Section B.2, we will see that one recursion method can produce behavior that would require multiple loops.

B.1 Tail Recursion

Suppose that at the end of Scene 1 of a story, the main character goes to sleep at 11 p.m., and the **camera** zooms in to a closeup of the clock in his or her bedroom. Shot 1 of Scene 2 begins with that same clock, showing the time to be 11 p.m. Suppose that our story calls for the clock's hands to spin, indicating that time is "flying ahead." When the hands reach 3 a.m., a fairy appears and works some sort of mischief on the sleeping main character. (Exactly what mischief the fairy works is left up to you.)

To build the scene, we can go to the Alice Gallery, add a **bedroom** from the **Environments** folder, add a **Dresser** from the **Furniture** folder, add a **mantleClock** from the **Objects** folder, and add **OliveWaterblossom** from the **People** folder as our fairy. To set the scene, we can manually advance the clock's hands to 11 p.m. (using right-click**->methods->mantleClock.roll()** messages), make **OliveWaterblossom** smaller, position her next to the clock, set her **opacity** to zero, and then position the **camera** appropriately. Our scene thus starts as shown in Figure B-1.

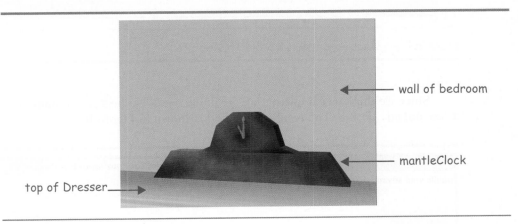

wall of bedroom

mantleClock

top of Dresser

FIGURE B-1   Beginning of Scene 2

To follow the story, we need a way to make the clock's hands spin forward to 3 a.m. Since this is a counting problem, we could use a **for** loop; but for variety, let's use tail recursion. The basic algorithm is as follows:

```
Algorithm: advance-the-clock's-hands hours hours
Given: hours, the number of hours to spin the clock's hands forward
1 If hours > 0:
   a   Spin the hour and minute hands forward one hour
   b   advance-the-clock's-hands hours-1
```

Building a **mantleClock.advanceHands()** method this way is straightforward. However, when we perform the recursion by dragging and dropping the **mantleClock.advanceHands()** method into the same method, Alice warns us that we're sending a recursive message, as shown in Figure B-2.

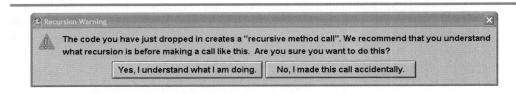

FIGURE B-2   Alice's recursion warning dialog box

Since we think we know what we are doing, we click the **Yes, I understand what I am doing.** button. The resulting method is shown in Figure B-3.

FIGURE B-3   An **advanceHands()** method

When invoked with a positive **hours** value, this method spins the clock's hands forward one hour, and then invokes itself recursively with **hours-1** as an argument. The method thus "counts down" recursively from whatever **hours** value it receives initially, until it is invoked with an **hours** value of 0, at which point the recursion terminates.

We can use this method to build the **playScene2Shot1()** method, as shown in Figure B-4.

○ world.my first method	● **world.playScene2Shot1**	○ mantleClock.advanceHands

public void playScene2Shot1 ( ) {

doInOrder {
    mantleClock.advanceHands (*hours* = 4);
    OliveWaterblossom .set(opacity , 1 (100%)); more...
    OliveWaterblossom .say(I'm feeling mischievous...); *duration* = 2 seconds *fontSize* = 30 more...
    // The fairy does something magical...
}

FIGURE B-4   The **playScene2Shot1()** method

When performed, the scene begins with the setup shown in Figure B-1. The **advanceHands(4)** message then spins the clock's hands forward four hours, after which **OliveWaterblossom** appears and says she's feeling mischievous, as shown in Figure B-5.

FIGURE B-5   The end of Shot 1 of Scene 2

If you compare the definition of the **advanceHands()** method with the **repeatRoll()** method we described earlier, you'll see that both follow the same basic pattern:

Simplified Pattern for Tail Recursion:

```
void tailRecursiveMethod ( Number count ) {
  if ( count > LOWER_BOUND ) {
     produceBehaviorOnce();
     tailRecursiveMethod( count-1 );
  }
}
```

where:

produceBehaviorOnce() *produces the behavior to be repeated.*

A method that follows this pattern will produce results equivalent to those produced by the following nonrecursive pattern:

```
void nonRecursiveMethod( Number count ) {
  for ( int i = count; i > 0; count-- ) {
     produceBehaviorOnce();
  }
}
```

Tail recursion provides an alternative way to solve counting problems and other problems in which solutions require repetition. In the next section, we will see that useful work can be done *following* the recursive call.

B.2   General Recursion

Suppose that Scene 3 of our story begins the same way as Scene 2: with a closeup of the clock in the main character's bedroom showing 11 p.m., the next night. In this scene, our story calls for time to fly ahead eight hours to 7 a.m., once again indicated by the clock's spinning hands. Then **OliveWaterblossom** appears, once again intent on mischief. In this scene, her mischief is to reverse time everywhere except for the main character, so that upon waking up after eight hours of sleep — fully rested — it will be 11 p.m. again! To indicate that time is flowing in reverse, we must spin the clock's hands backward eight hours.

We could accomplish this by using our **advanceHands()** method to spin the clock's hands forward eight hours, and then writing a **reverseHands()** method to make the hands spin backward eight hours, using either tail recursion or a **for** loop. Instead, let's see how recursion lets us perform both of these steps in one method.

The key idea is to use recursion's winding phase to spin the hands forward (as before), and then to use the unwinding phase to make the hands spin backward. In between the two phases — when we have reached our lower bound — **OliveWaterblossom** can work her magic.

```
Algorithm: wind-and-unwind-the-clock's-hands hours hours
Given: hours, the number of hours to spin the clock's hands forward

 1  If hours > 0:
    a    Spin the hour and minute hands forward one hour
    b    wind-and-unwind-the-clock's-hands hours-1
    c    Spin the hour and minute hands backward one hour

 2  Else:
    a    OliveWaterblossom appears
    b    OliveWaterblossom works her magic
```

Understanding how this works can be difficult the first time you see it. One way to understand it is to see that Step 1c does the exact opposite of Step 1a. That is, during the winding phase, Step 1a spins the clock's hands forward one hour; then Step 1b sends the recursive message, preventing flow from reaching Step 1c (for the time being). When the lower bound is reached, the **if** statement's condition is false, so **OliveWaterblossom** works her magic. And since no recursive message is sent, the repetition halts. The recursion then starts to unwind, with flow returning to Step 1c in each message, which "undoes" the effects of Step 1a. Figure B-6 gives a numbered visualization of what happens when **hours** has the value 8. The steps that are performed within each message at a given point are highlighted.

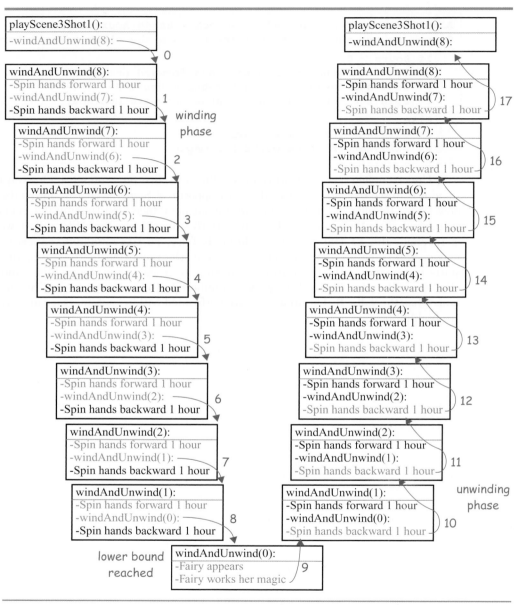

FIGURE B-6   Recursive winding and unwinding

We can define this method in Alice, as shown in Figure B-7.

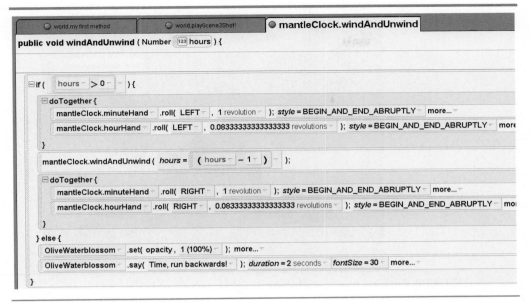

FIGURE B-7   The `windAndUnwind()` method

Given such a method, **playScene3Shot1()** is quite simple, as shown in Figure B-8.

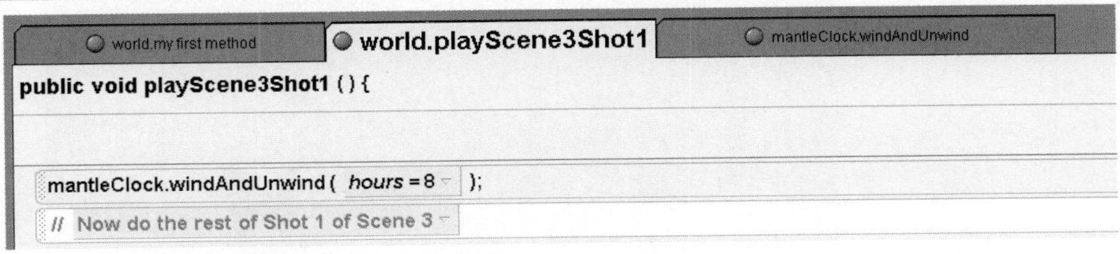

FIGURE B-8   The `windAndUnwind()` method

When performed, the method starts out with the scene shown in Figure B-1. Once again, we see "time fly" as the hands wind forward, but this time they advance eight hours. Our fairy then appears and says her line, as shown in Figure B-9.

FIGURE B-9   Time has flown forward eight hours

The hands then spin backward, returning to their original positions, as shown in Figure B-10.

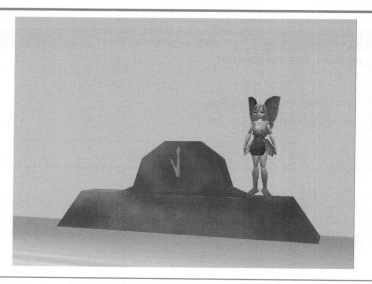

FIGURE B-10   Time has flown backward eight hours

It is thus possible to do work during both the winding and the unwinding phases of a chain of recursive messages. Any statements that we want to be performed during the winding phase must be positioned before the recursive call, and any statements that we want to be performed during the unwinding phase must be positioned after the recursive call.

The following pattern can be used to design many recursive methods:

Simplified Pattern for Recursion:

```
void recursiveMethod ( Number count ) {
   if ( count > LOWER_BOUND ) {
      windingPhaseBehavior();
      recursiveMethod( count-1 );
      unwindingPhaseBehavior();
   } else {
      betweenPhasesBehavior();
   }
}
```

B.3   Recursion and Design

Now that we have seen some examples of recursive methods, how does one go about designing such methods?

Recall that recursive methods usually have a **Number** parameter. Designing a recursive method generally involves two steps: (1) identifying the **trivial case** — how to solve the problem when the value of this parameter makes the problem trivial to solve; and (2) identifying the **nontrivial case** — how to use recursion to solve the problem for all of the other cases. Once we have done so, we can plug these cases into this template:

```
someType recursiveMethod(Number count) {
    if (count indicates that this is a nontrivial case) {
        solve the problem recursively, reducing count
    } else { // it's the trivial case
        solve the trivial version of the problem
    }
}
```

To illustrate, let's apply this approach to one of the functions mathematicians defined recursively long before there were computers.

Pretend for a moment that you are an elementary school student, and your teacher just caught you misbehaving during math class. As a "punishment," your teacher makes you stay in at each recess until you have calculated 10! (10 factorial), 20! (20 factorial), and 30! (30 factorial). Even with a calculator, this will take a long time because the factorial function *n!* is defined as shown in Figure B-11.

$$n! = 1 \times 2 \times \ldots \times (n-1) \times n$$

FIGURE B-11   *n!*, in open-form notation

That is, 1! == 1; 2! == 2; 3! == 6, 4! == 24, 5! == 120, and so on. 0! is also defined to equal 1, and the function is not defined for negative values of *n*.

While we could solve this problem by hand, doing so would be long and tedious, and we would lose lots of recess time. Instead, let's write an Alice program to solve it!

To do so, we can begin as we did in Section 3.5.2, and build a scene containing a character (**Roommate**, in this case) who can do factorials "in her head," positioned within an Alice **School** environment, as shown in Figure B-12.

FIGURE B-12   Setting the scene to compute *n!*

With such a scene in place, we just have to (1) write a **factorial()** function, (2) get **n** from the user, (3) invoke and save the answer of **factorial(n)**, and (4) display the answer.

Let's begin by writing the **factorial()** function. If we examine the description given in Figure B-11, it should be evident that this is a counting problem, and so we could solve it using a **for** loop. However, let's instead see how the mathematicians would have solved it back in the days before there were **for** loops.

B.3.1   The Trivial Case

We start by identifying the trivial case. What is a version of the problem that is trivial to solve? Since 0! == 1 and 1! == 1, we actually have two trivial cases: when n == 0, and when n == 1. In either case, our function needs to return the value 1.

B.3.2   The Nontrivial Cases

To solve the nontrivial cases, we look for a way to solve the general *n!* problem, assuming that we can solve a smaller but similar problem (for example, *(n-1)!*). If we compare the two:

$$n! = 1 \times 2 \times \ldots \times (n-1) \times n$$

$$(n-1)! = 1 \times 2 \times \ldots \times (n-1)$$

it should be evident that we can rewrite the equation in Figure B-11 by performing a substitution, as shown in Figure B-13.

$$n! = (n-1)! \times n$$

FIGURE B-13   *n!*, in recursive, closed-form notation

B.3.3   Solving the Problem

The trivial and nontrivial cases can be combined into a complete solution to the problem, as shown in Figure B-14.

$$n! = \begin{cases} (n-1)! \times n, \text{ if n} > 1 \\ 1, \text{ if n} == 0 \text{ OR n} == 1 \\ \text{undefined, otherwise} \end{cases}$$

FIGURE B-14   Recursive algorithm for *n!*

The equation given in Figure B-14 can serve as an algorithm for us to define our `factorial()` function in Alice, as shown in Figure B-15.

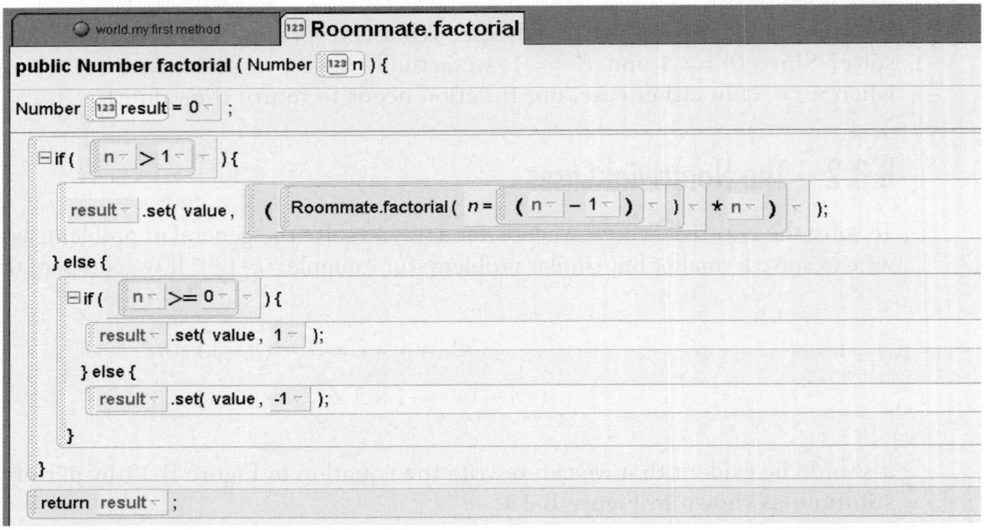

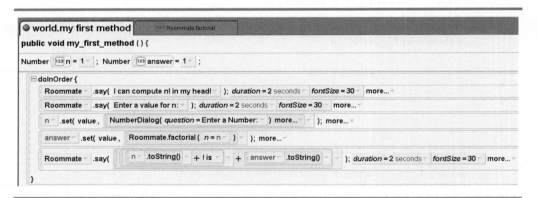

FIGURE B-15   The `factorial()` function in Alice

Note that because *n!* is undefined when **n** is negative, and *n!* never returns **−1** under normal circumstances, we have our function return **−1** when **n** is negative.

With this function defined, we can now finish our program, as shown in Figure B-16.

FIGURE B-16   The `factorial()` program in Alice

When run, the program has us enter a value for **n**, and then displays **n!**. After testing our function on easily verified values (such as 0, 1, 2, 3, 4, and 5), we can solve the problems our teacher assigned. Figure B-17 shows the result when we use the program to compute 10!.

FIGURE B-17   The `factorial()` program in Alice

It's recess time!

B.4   A Final Recursive Method

As a final example, consider the following user story.

Scene 1, Shot 1: zeus, socrates, aliceLiddell, plato, euripides, and the whiteRabbit are all waiting to practice basketball. The coach says, "Okay, everyone line up by height!" The players line up, tallest to shortest.

Scene 1, Shot 2: The coach says, "No, line up the other way — shortest to tallest!" The players reverse their order.

Scene 1, Shot 1 is mainly to get things set up, so we will leave it as an exercise. What we want to do is is to build Scene 1, Shot 2, especially the part in which the players reverse their order.

It is fairly easy to get our scene to the point shown in Figure B-18.

FIGURE B-18   Scene 1, Shot 2 (beginning)

But how can we make our players reverse their order?

Since we have a group of players, and their number is fixed, one idea is to store them in an array, tallest to smallest, as shown in Figure B-19.

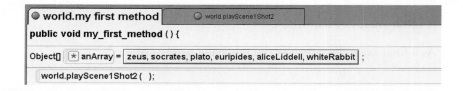

FIGURE B-19   Scene 1, Shot 2 (beginning)

The first array element is the tallest player, the second array element is the second tallest player, and so on. We can visualize **anArray** as shown in Figure B-20.

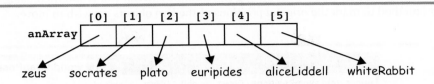

FIGURE B-20   Visualizing `anArray`

With the players in order within the data structure, we can transform our problem into this one:

Reverse the positions of the players in anArray.

One way to accomplish this is to (1) make the first and last players in the array swap positions within our world, as shown in Figure B-21, and then (2) reverse the remaining players in the array (that is, ignoring the **whiteRabbit** and **zeus**) the same way — a recursive solution!

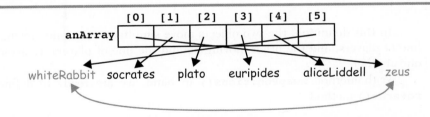

FIGURE B-21   The tallest and smallest players swap positions

To do so, we would need a method named **reverse()**, to which we can pass the array containing our players, plus the indices of the players that are to swap positions:

```
reverse(anArray, 0, 5);
```

Our method requires three parameters: an **Object** array, a **Number** to store the first index, and a **Number** to store the second index:

```
void reverse(Object [] arr, Number index1, Number index2) {
}
```

To get two objects to swap positions, we can write a method named **swapPositions()**, and then pass it the two objects whose positions we want to swap. Figure B-22 shows one way to do this, which is by adding two dummies to our world and then using them within our method to mark the original positions of the two objects we wish to move.

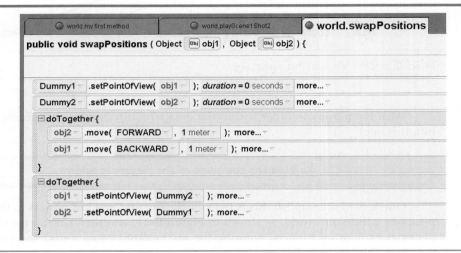

FIGURE B-22   Exchanging two objects' positions

In this definition, the two objects move simultaneously, one moving in front of the line of players, and the other moving behind the line of players, to avoid colliding with one another.

With method **swapPositions()** in hand, we are ready to define the recursive **reverse()** method.

B.4.1   The Trivial Case

As we have seen, the first step in defining a recursive method is to find a case where the problem is trivial to solve. Since our **reverse()** method has this form:

```
void reverse(Object [] arr, Number index1, Number index2) {
}
```

any trivial cases must be identified using the **Number** parameters, **index1** and **index2**.

At this point, it is helpful to generalize from the specific problem at hand to the more general problem of reversing the positions of objects stored in an arbitrary array **arr**, where **index1** contains the index of the array's first element, and **index2** contains the index of the array's last element. Thinking this way, there are two cases in which the problem of reversing the positions of the items in **arr** is trivial to solve:

1. If there is just one object in **arr**, then the object is already in its final position, so we should do nothing. There is one object in the array when **index1 == index2**.

2. If there are zero objects in **arr**, then there are no objects to move, so we should do nothing. There are zero items in the array when **index1 > index2**.

Since we do the same thing (nothing) in each of our trivial cases, the condition **index1 >= index2** will identify both of our trivial cases. Conversely, the condition **index1 < index2** can be used to identify our nontrivial cases.

B.4.2 The Nontrivial Cases

We have hinted at how the nontrivial cases can be solved. Since **index1** is the index of the first (tallest) object in the array, and **index2** is the index of the smallest object in the array, we:

1. Swap the positions of the objects in **arr[index1]** and **arr[index2]**.

2. Reverse the rest of the objects (ignoring the ones we just swapped) recursively.

The trick is to figure out how to do Step 2. Drawing a diagram is often helpful, as shown in Figure B-23:

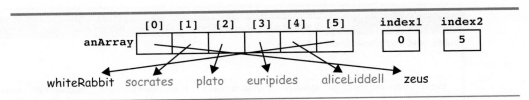

FIGURE B-23 Visualizing the recursive step

This allows us to clearly see the sub-array of objects that Step 2 must reverse; it begins at index 1 and ends at 4. However, to correctly solve the problem, we must express the arguments in Step 2 in terms of changes to our method's parameters, **index1** and **index2**. Expressed this way, the sub-array to be processed by Step 2 begins at index **index1+1**, and ends at **index2-1**. That is, we can solve the nontrivial cases of the problem as follows:

1. Swap the positions of the objects in **arr[index1]** and **arr[index2]**.

2. Recursively invoke **reverse(arr, index1+1, index2-1)**.

That's it! Figure B-24 presents a definition of **reverse()** that uses this approach.

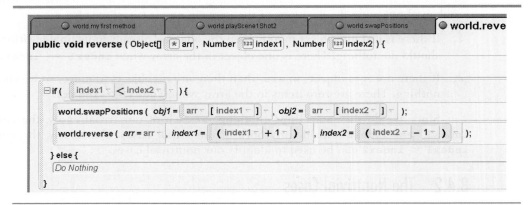

FIGURE B-24   The recursive `reverse()` method

Note that our **reverse()** method does not change the order of the objects within the array. It merely uses the array as a table from which it can identify the tallest and shortest players, the next tallest and next shortest players, and so on.

Given this definition, we can finish **playScene2Shot2()**, as shown in Figure B-25.

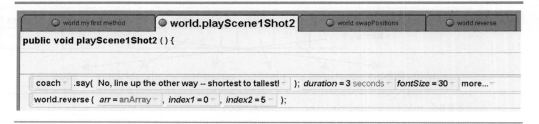

FIGURE B-25   The recursive `reverse()` method

Figure B-26 presents some screen captures taken as **playScene1Shot2()** runs. Compare them to the initial setting shown in Figure B-18 to see the progression of changes.

FIGURE B-26   Screen captures of Scene 1, Shot 2

Figure B-27 provides a conceptual view of what happens as **reverse()** runs.

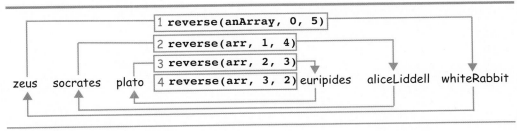

FIGURE B-27   Conceptualizing `reverse()`

The fourth message, **reverse(arr, 3, 2)**, invokes the trivial case, halting the recursion.

Recursion is a powerful programming technique that can be used to solve any problem that can be decomposed into one or more "smaller" problems that are solved in the same way.

Index

Symbols

++ (increment) operator 124
== (equality) operator 115

Numerics

3D objects
    orientation 59–62
    position 57–59
3D text 193–199

A

ADD OBJECTS button 12
Alice
    downloading 3
    installation 3
    Statements 18
Alice Gallery 12
animal parameter 83
arguments
    recursion 220
arrays 144, 157
    indexed variables 161
    integers, generating 167
    marching ants example 157–161
    random access example 163–167
    read version 162
    subscript operations 162
    write version 162
arrow keys, keyboard events and 191
asSeenBy attribute 127, 139
attributes 91
    asSeenBy 127, 139
    duration 127
    methods 18
    objects, retrieiving 95–98
axis 58

B

background 196–198
bees example 145–150
Boolean functions 109–110
Boolean operators 111–112, 139
Boolean type 108
Boolean variables 110
borders
    green 15
    red 15
bounding boxes 14
    functions 26
buttons
    ADD OBJECTS 12
    capture pose 89
    create new event 180
    create new function 99
    create new method 32
    create new variable 110, 146
    drop dummy at camera 51
    Play 10
    Redo 10
    Undo 10, 22
buying tickets example 154–156

C

camera object 10
    dummies and 50
    editing area and 16
    setPointOfView( ) message and 54–57
capture pose button 89
classes, objects and 13
clipboard 45–46
    editing area and 45
    statements and 46
code, reusing 45–49
comments, methods 40
computeHypotenuse( ) method 75
concatenating strings 79

conditions in if statements 115–117
control structures 108
controls
    doInOrder 15
    doTogether 19
    editing area 11
counting loop, for statement 123–125
create new event button 180
create new function button 99
create new method button 32
create new variable button 110, 146

D

data structures 144
debugging 16–17
declaring variables 78
defining variables 67
depth, objects 24
design
    recursion and 229–233
details area 25–27
    functions tab 96
    methods pane 15
    panes 11
    subparts 14
distanceInFrontOf( ) function 71
distanceTo( ) function 71
doInOrder control 15
doTogether control 19
downloading Alice 3
dragging methods 15
dragon flapping wings example 38–42
drop dummy at camera button 51
dummies 50–54
dummy objects 52
duration attribute 127

E

Edit menu 10
editing area 11
    camera and 16
    clipboard and 45
    controls 11
equality (==) operator 115
errors, logic errors 182
event handling 184, 184–185
events 178
    creating 180
    handlers, defining 183
    keyboard 185, 186–193
    logic errors 182
    mouse clicks 179–185
    program events 185

events area 11
examples
    bees 145–150
    buying tickets 154–156
    dragon flapping wings 38–42
    jumping fish 85–88
    Old MacDonald's farm 81–85
    storing computed values 67–75
    storing user-entered values 75–80
    toy soldier marching 42–44
expressions menu 72

F

Fibonacci series 135
fibonacci( ) function 136–139
File menu 10
fixed-sized data structure (see arrays)
flapWings( ) message 38
flow 5
flow control
    for statement 121–125
    functions and 134–139
    pausing 118
    selective 112–114
    statements 108
    while statement 127–134
flow diagram 108
for statement 108, 121–123, 139
    counting loop 123–125
    nested 126
    while statements and 131
fullName variable 97
functions 26
    attributes, retrieving 95–98
    Boolean 109–110
    distanceInFrontOf( ) 71
    distanceTo( ) 71
    fibonacci( ) 136–139
    flow control and 134–139
    lastIndexOf( ) 154
    lists 153–154
    Math.sqrt( ) 78
    NumberDialog( ) 77
    parameters and 99–102
    partNamed( ) 167–174
    size( ) 154
    standard 213–215
    wait( ) 139
    world 215–218
functions pane 11, 25–27
functions tab 14
    details area 96

G

general recursion 224–229
green borders 15
ground object 10

H

heBuilder 25
height, objects 24
Help menu 10

I

if statement 108, 114–115
    conditions 115–117
if statements 139
increment (++) operator 124
indexed variables, arrays 161
indexOf( ) function 154
infinte recursion 219
installing Alice 3
integers, generating 167
isShowing property 22
iteration 150

J

jumping fish example 85–88

K

keyboard events 185, 186–193

L

lastIndexOf( ) function 154
light object 10
list menu 148
lists 144
    bees example 145–150
    buying tickets example 154–156
    defining 169
    entries 148
    functions 153–154
    iterations 150
    methods 152
    operations 150–154
    variables, defining 146
local variables 67
logic errors 182
loops
    for statement 123–125

iterations 150
nested 125–127

M

make a List checkbox 146
marchRight( ) method 43
Math.sqrt( ) function 78
menus
    Edit 10
    expressions 72
    File 10
    Help 10
    Tools 10
messages 14, 21
    attributes 18
    flapWings( ) 38
    move( ) 43
    resize( ) 24
    roll( ) 40
    say( ) 17
    sending 15–16
    set( ) 23
    statements and 32
    turn( ) 43
method variables 67, 67–80
methods 15, 211–213
    comments 40
    computeHypotenuse( ) 75
    defining 169
    dragging 15
    lists 152
    marchRight( ) 43
    move( ) 59
    names 33
    object methods 38–44
    pane 25
    pointAt( ) 15
    scenes 32–36
    shots 36–38
    singVerse( ) 82
methods pane 11, 15, 24
methods tab 14
mnemonic values, keyboard events and 186
more... 18
mouse clicks 179–185
move( ) message 43
move( ) method 59

N

naming
    methods 33
    objects 13
nested for statements 126
nested loops 125–127

noise parameter 83
nontrivial case, recursion 229, 231, 237
nouns 5, 21
NumberDialog( ) function 77

O

object methods 38–44
object tree 10
  properties 21
object variables 67, 89
objects 21
  adding 12–14
  attributes 91
      retrieving 95–98
  bounding box, functions 26
  bounding boxes 14
  classes and 13
  color 91
  depth 24
  dummy 52
  height 24
  naming 13
  opacity 91
  orientation 59–62
  position
      3D 57–59
      quad view 27–28
  renaming 13
  subparts 14–15
  vehicle 91
  width 24
Old MacDonald's farm example 81–85
operators
  Boolean 111–112, 139
  equality (==) 115
  increment (++) 124
  relational 110–111
orientation of objects, 3D 59–62
  pitch 60
  point of view 62
  roll 61
  yaw 60

P

panes
  details area 11
  functions 25–27
  methods 24, 25
  properties 21

parameters 67, 80–88
  animal 83
  functions 99–102
  noise 83
  values
      validation 118–120
partNamed( ) function 167–174
pausing program flow 118
pitch, orientation 60
Play button 10
point of view, orientation 62
pointAt( ) method 15
positioning objects
  3D 57–59
  axis 58
print( ) statement 34
pristine 9
program design 4–5
program events 185
program style 11–12
properties
  modifying from within program 22
  vehicle 92–95
properties pane 11, 21
properties tab 14
property variables 67, 89–92

Q

quad view 27–28

R

read version, arrays 162
recursion
  arguments
      numeric 220
  design and 229–233
  general 224–229
  infinite recursion 219
  introduction 219
  nontrivial 237
  nontrivial case 229, 231
  tail recursion 220, 221–224
  trivial case 229, 231, 236
  unwinding phase 220
  winding phase 220
red borders 15
Redo button 10
relational operators 110–111
renaming objects 13

repetition, for statement and 121–123
resize( ) message 24
return statements 97
reusing code 45–49
    objects in different worlds 46
roll( ) message 40
roll, orientation 61

S

say( ) message 17
scenes
    methods 32–36
    transitions 200–207
            barndoor wipe effect 203
            box iris effect 205
            edge wipe effect 203
            fade effect 201
            reusing transitions 206
            special effects 200
scrolling through statements 36
selective flow control 112–114
sending messages 15–16
set( ) message 23
setPointOfView( ) message
    camera control and 54–57
    dummies and 50
sheBuilder 25
shots, methods for 36–38
singVerse( ) method 82
size( ) function 154
software design 21
software engineering 21
software implementation and testing 21
spirals, Fibonacci series and 135
standard functions 213–215
state, storing 182
statements 18
    clipboard and 46
    flow control 108
    for 108, 121–123, 139
            nested 126
    if 108, 114–115, 139
            conditions 115–117
    messages and 32
    print( ) 34
    return 97
    scrolling through 36
    wait( ) 117
    while 108, 127–134, 139
storing computed values 67–75
storing user-entered values 75–80
storyboard sketches 6–8, 21
string operations 78
strings, concatenating 79
subparts, objects 14–15
    details area 14
subscript operations, arrays 162

T

tail recursion 220, 221–224
targets, pointAt( ) method 16
templates 8
testing 16–17, 21
text
    3D 193–199
    hiding/unhiding 198–199
    off-camera, repositioning 195
Tools menu 10
toy soldier marching example 42–44
transition diagrams 8
transitions between scenes 200–207
    barndoor wipe effect 203
    box iris effect 205
    edge wipe effect 203
    fade effect 201
    reusing transitions 206
    special effects 200
trivial case, recursion 229, 231, 236
turn( ) message 43
tutorials 3–4
types, Boolean 108

U

Undo button 10, 22
unwinding phase, recursion 220
user stories 5–6, 21

V

validation 118–120
values
    computed, storing 67–75
    sequences 144
    user-entered, storing 75–80
values, validation 118–120
variables
    Boolean 110
    data structures 144
    declaring 78
    defining 67
    fullName 97
    initial value 69
    lists, defining 146
    local variables 67
    method variables 67, 67–80
    object variables 67, 89
    parameters 67
    property variables 67, 89–92
vehicle property 92–95
verbs 5

W

wait( ) function 139
wait( ) statement 117
welcome window 8
while statement 108, 127–134, 139
    for statements and 131
width, objects 24
winding phase, recursion 220

wizards 89
world functions 215–218
write version, arrays 162

Y

yaw, orientation 60